Greek Mind/Jewish Soul

The Wisconsin Project on American Writers

Frank Lentricchia, General Editor

Greek Mind/Jewish Soul

The Conflicted Art of Cynthia Ozick

Victor Strandberg

The University of Wisconsin Press

The University of Wisconsin Press
114 North Murray Street
Madison, Wisconsin 53715

3 Henrietta Street
London WC2E 8LU, England

Library of Congress Cataloging-in-Publication Data
Strandberg, Victor H.
    Greek mind/Jewish soul : the conflicted art of Cynthia Ozick /
Victor Strandberg.
    228 p.   cm.—(The Wisconsin project on American writers)
    Includes bibliographical references (p. 195) and index.
    ISBN 0-299-14260-4 (cl.)   ISBN 0-299-14264-7 (pb.)
    1. Ozick, Cynthia—Criticism and interpretation. 2. Judaism in literature.
    3. Jews in literature. I. Title.
    PS3565.Z5Z87   1994
    813'.54—dc20   94-589

To Arne, Bill, and John
for auld lang syne.
"These grains of life will stay forever."
—Cynthia Ozick

Contents

Preface

About ten years ago, I received a surprise invitation from William Scheick to write a long essay on Cynthia Ozick for a Special Issue of his journal, *Texas Studies in Literature and Language,* which was to be devoted to three neglected women writers (Ozick, Shirley Hazzard, and Anne Redmon). Not knowing Ozick's work, I looked at her only available books (*The Pagan Rabbi* and *Bloodshed*), judged them to be first-rate, and accepted the invitation. The resulting essay, which was published in the Summer 1983 issue of *TSLL,* has been assimilated into this book-length study with such changes as I thought appropriate.

Some greatly favorable responses to that original essay, described by several scholars as seminal and indispensable, encouraged me to undertake this longer study, which was occasioned by Ms. Ozick's extensive burst of creativity since 1983. In addition to the three novels and two volumes of essays she has published since then, her oeuvre includes more novellas, stories, interviews, letters, reviews, and essays, along with some personal correspondence between us in which she most graciously agreed to answer such questions as I might care to put into writing. Throughout this book, Ms. Ozick's willingness to conduct a long-term, written "interview" through this exchange of letters has made an important contribution, for which I am most grateful.

Because serious scholarship has focused on Ozick for barely a decade—most of it in the last half decade—two primordial tasks of criticism remain in progress: to define the author's intellectual moorings, and—with them in view—to render an interpretive reading of her books. In its effort to perform those tasks, this book divides into three major sections. Chapter 1 is an account of the intellectual ambience of the writer as revealed in essays, interviews, letters, and a variety of incidental writings. Chapter 2 is an interpretive reading of the fiction (and some poetry) that attempts to analyze its interplay of themes, characters, and narrative devices. Chapter 3, entitled "Judgment," begins with an overall review of Ozick scholarship and ends with my personal evaluation of her achievement. The purpose of the whole enterprise can be simply stated: I shall consider the book a success if it substantially facilitates my reader's grasp of the artist's writings.

Other books about Cynthia Ozick have been, will be, and should be written, giving differing interpretations and approaches to her work. Some of those books have focused or will focus more meaningfully on the specifically Jewish character of her work than I, a Gentile, can aspire to do. Others will espouse the kind of postmodern theory in which I have taken little interest, subjecting her work to the psycholinguistic processes of deconstruction, for example, or putting primary emphasis on social abstractions that I have treated as secondary—class, race, gender, homophobia, late capitalism, imperialism (involving the Palestinian question), Marxism, the new historicism, and similar issues. Whatever approach other critics may choose, I hope we shall all hold in common a respect for clear, largely jargon-free language so as to make both our own work and Ms. Ozick's more intelligible to the sophisticated readers from all backgrounds whom, in my judgment, we should aim to serve. This book, in any case, was written out of that intention.

My strong thanks go to Frank Lentricchia, whose professional encouragement was indispensable to the making of this book. And I am deeply grateful to Susan Tarcov for her superb editorial work on the manuscript.

Author's Note

For simplicity's sake, I shall refer to Cynthia Ozick's books within my main text in the following fashion:

(TR) *Trust*. New York: New American Library, 1966.
(PR) *The Pagan Rabbi and Other Stories*. New York: Knopf, 1971.
(BL) *Bloodshed and Three Novellas*. New York: Knopf, 1976.
(LE) *Levitation: Five Fictions*. New York: Knopf, 1982.
(AA) *Art & Ardor*. New York: Knopf, 1983.
(CG) *The Cannibal Galaxy*. New York: Knopf, 1983.
(MS) *The Messiah of Stockholm*. New York: Knopf, 1987.
(MM) *Metaphor & Memory*. New York: Knopf, 1989.
(SH) *The Shawl* ("The Shawl" and "Rosa"). New York: Knopf, 1990.

For additional economy of style, I have identified Ms. Ozick's letters to me in my main text in this manner: (Ltr 4/15/87).

I also refer in my main text to three frequently cited interviews by citing the name of the interviewer in this manner:

(Kauvar 385) refers to page 385 of an interview conducted by Elaine M. Kauvar in *Contemporary Literature* 26, no. 4 (Winter 1985).

(Scheick) refers to an interview conducted by William J. Scheick and Catherine Rainwater in *Texas Studies in Literature and Language* 25, no. 2 (Summer 1983).

(Teicholz) refers to an interview conducted by Tim Teicholz in "The Art of Fiction" Series (XCV) of the *Paris Review* 29 (Spring 1987).

Greek Mind/Jewish Soul

The Matrix of Art

Despite her frequent invocation of D. H. Lawrence's warning, "Trust the tale, not the teller," Cynthia Ozick's own practice of criticism has made generous use of biography to analyze writings by two Eliots, T. S. and George, along with favorite writers such as Virginia Woolf, Edith Wharton, and Henry James. Her primary reason for disavowing the New Criticism was "its pretense that the poem was a finished, sealed unit, as if nothing outside the text could ever have mattered in the making of the poem" (AA 179); and what was most untenable about that pretense was precisely its disregard for the author: "The history, psychology, even the opinions, of a writer were declared irrelevant to the work and its word" (AA 163). To the extent that Ozick has portrayed her life and thought in interviews, essays, and letters, any attempt to understand her art should likewise begin with the figure behind the typewriter.[1] In this opening chapter, we shall trace out some personal, cultural, and aesthetic concerns that pervade the life and art of Cynthia Ozick. In general, it will best enhance our understanding to unwind these threads in chronological sequence.

Beginnings

Irresistible evidence attests the importance of the early years. "I am what I was," says the eighty-year-old Wallace Fowlie in his book of reminiscences entitled *Memory*. "For better or worse, we are what we learned as children," is Joan Didion's way of putting it. Concerning her earliest impressions, Cynthia Ozick declared that "these grains of life will stay forever." In "Spells, Wishes, Goldfish, Old School Hurts," a *New York Times* essay, she described some of those grains in vivid detail, allowing her readers to see in hindsight the materials of art coming into formation.[2]

In this short piece about her childhood Ozick illuminates a showcase of future artistic motifs. Here the career-long tension in her work between Jewish and Gentile cultures—between Pan and Moses, Hellenism and Hebraism, Magic and the Law—traces back to her earliest memories. The dominant Jewish heritage was linked in her memory with her father's "beautiful Hebrew paragraphs, his Talmudist's rationalism," his study "in Yiddish [of] all of Sholem Aleichem and Peretz," and the letters she wrote in childhood Yiddish to a grandmother in Moscow who knew no English. She simultaneously developed an avid taste for Gentile literature, however, beginning with "the secret bliss of the Violet Fairy Book." The "shivery unearthly feelings that a child gets from myths, Norse tales, fairy books," as she later recalled them, suggest a warning that Reynolds Price raised about such reading. "I think when scholars are trying to find out what influences writers, they invariably go wrong because they leave out childhood reading," he says, which "is obviously the most influential of all in forming the fantasy life and impressing the unconscious."[3] Although Ozick moved on to the standard classics—Cervantes, Swift, Dickens, Twain, Charlotte Brontë, Louisa May Alcott, and Lewis Carroll—she proved Price correct by her lifelong interest in pagan gods, dryads, golems, and other versions of magic and fantasy.

A subtler but deeply ingrained motif of Ozick's early years was the imminence of poverty. At the time she was too young to care that "the lion-eyed landlady has raised, threefold, in the middle of that Depression that I have never heard of, the Park View Pharmacy's devouring rent," but she was old enough to take in a permanent image of what it all meant to her parents:

> My mother, not yet 40, wears bandages on her ankles, covering oozing varicose veins: back and forth she strides, dashes, runs, climbing cellar stairs or ladders; she toils behind drug counters and fountain counters. Like my father, she is on her feet until one in the morning, the Park View's closing hour. (AA 301)

A scene like this, reinforcing Ozick's recognition in childhood of "the heavy power of a quarter," bears an ancestral relationship to a number of motifs in the artist's fictions. From her earliest work, *Trust,* we may cite the corruptive power of Allegra's wealth, for example, as contrasted with the healthy vigor of the moneyless Purses and the final apotheosis of the penniless Tilbeck. The same spirit recurs, undiminished, in her late work, such as *The Shawl,* which vibrates with authorial contempt for the class consciousness it portrays among European and American Jews. According to Arthur Hertzberg's *The Jews in America,* this mode of class identity characterizes the larger Jewish community. "American Jewish history is also the story of . . . the Jewish poor of Europe," he writes, pointing out that in the year of maximum immigration (1906, the year Ozick's mother came to America), the two hundred thousand Jews who passed into the United States included only fifty who declared themselves professionals.[4] Ozick thus experienced a shock of recognition in her belated reading of Dreiser's *Sister Carrie,* whose "cramped flats and teeming streets," she wrote in 1986, "are the fabric of our grandparents' world; we know it with the kind of intimacy we cannot bring to Hawthorne's Puritans or James's high-caste international visitors."[5]

One other implication of this scene in the Park View Pharmacy should be noted before we leave it: Cynthia Ozick never uses her parents as models in her fiction. Her father figures in *Trust*—William, Enoch, and Tilbeck—bear no resemblance to the long-suffering druggist in the *Times* sketch, nor do father figures like Joseph Brill in *The Cannibal Galaxy* and the two fathers in "The Pagan Rabbi." The discrepancy is even more striking with Ozick's mother figures: neglectful or exploitative mothers like Allegra Vand in *Trust,* Hester Lilt in *The Messiah of Stockholm,* and Ruth Puttermesser (vis-à-vis her golem-child) contrast rather than compare with Ozick's own mother, whom she describes as "a great encourager on all fronts" from earliest childhood (Ltr 6/6/90). Nowhere in her writing does Ozick's filial attitude differ from that of her Yiddish/Hebrew dedication in *Levitation:* "Mama, Shiphra [her name], O my maminke [beautiful, precious mother]". The Hebrew verses in this dedication, from Psalms originally addressed to God, are a final index of filial feeling: Translation: "You uplifted my soul with strength" (Psalm 138.3). ". . . Every night I drench my bed, with my tears I soak my couch" (Psalm 6.7).[6]

Although no trace of Hemingway's filial spite may be found in Ozick's pages, something like Hemingway's primal wound does find expression, not relating to losses in love and war such as Ernest suffered but rather relating to the "Old School Hurts" of her essay's title. The depth of the wound can be gauged from her foreword to *Art & Ardor,* which defines this essay as having a topic of such compelling force as to make it unique among all her essays:

> I never meant to write essays. Only once have I ever written a piece of nonfiction on purpose and for its own sake, self-propelled. The desire came on me spontaneously, long ago, just after reading George Orwell's "Such, Such Were the Joys . . .," a memoir of Orwell's melancholy childhood in an English boarding school. . . . Though my own childhood was as far from an English boarding school as can be imagined, the essay's theme was Orwell's: school injustice and school humiliation. (AA ix–x)

The essay that she published, "We Ignoble Savages" (in the *Evergreen Review* of November-December 1959), is a long, bitter memoir of "the lusterless octet of those years between 1933 and 1941," or age five to thirteen. To the essay's catalogues of harms inflicted by the teaching staff Ozick later added deeds perpetrated by fellow students. Primary among these hurts is the ostracism imposed upon the Jewish child by the majority culture. Although New York is, in Ozick's own words, "a city of Jews" (BL 49), she was the only Jewish child among her classmates in Public School 71—a status that could not help but affect any small child profoundly:

> My classmates were Irish, Scottish, German, Swedish, (some) Italian, and pretty evenly divided between Catholics and Protestants (no, I guess the Catholics had the edge). I was the only Jewish kid. . . . There were two Catholic churches; I was terrified of them both, and was obliged to pass one or the other on the way to school; so, with shaking knees, I used to race past on the opposite side of the street. . . . (Ltr 6/6/90)

Her first encounter with the Protestant heritage proved more frustrating than scary, foreshadowing a sometimes embittered lifelong struggle to valorize her own heritage against the annihilating ignorance of the majority culture:

> I met my first WASP when a new girl named Jane Jones [a pseudonym] moved in—she was from a mysterious place called "the midwest." It was second grade, and I recall in full detail our opening get-acquainted conversation. Jane Jones, starting off with the standard question: "Cynthia, what are you?" (This always meant what is your religion.) Me: "I'm Jewish." "Yes, but are you Protestant or Catholic?" Me: "I'm Jewish." Jane Jones, getting exasperated . . .: "Well, I *know* that, you said it already. But are you Protestant or Catholic?" Me: "I'm *Jewish*." Jane Jones (now really exasperated): "O.K., O.K., you're Jewish. BUT ARE YOU PROTESTANT OR CATHOLIC? YOU HAVE TO BE ONE OR THE OTHER!" (Ltr 6/6/90)

In time, the comic innocence of this scene was to give way to something permanently harmful, an ongoing slander against the child's Jewish identity: "in P.S. 71 I am publicly shamed in Assembly because I am caught not singing Christmas carols; in P.S. 71 I am repeatedly accused of deicide" (AA 302). When, during her teens, these injuries were amplified unimaginably by news of the Holocaust, there was compelling reason, both personally and historically, why Ozick's work would later disclose a pervasive hatred of Western/Christian civilization (though the hatred cannot extirpate contrary feelings):

> My dispraise of Diaspora . . . is centered on a revulsion against the values—
> very plainly I mean the beliefs—of the surrounding culture itself: a revulsion
> against the Greek and Pagan modes, whether in the Christian or post-Christian
> vessels, or whether in their vessels of *Kulturgeschichte*. It is a revulsion against—
> I want to state it even more plainly—against what is called, strangely, Western
> Civilization. (AA 157)

Jew-baiting was not the only "old school hurt" for the future artist. Considering Ozick's voracious appetite for books in her childhood, only extraordinary obtuseness on the part of the school's teaching staff can explain their failure to recognize their brightest pupil. "I had no encouragement of any kind in elementary school," she recollects—"where, in fact, I believed I was stupid and wholly incapable, despite the fact that I excelled at reading, grammar, and spelling; these were simply not valued by most of my teachers" (Ltr 6/6/90). The memory was painful enough to bear repetition in another interview. "I'm still hurt by P.S. 71," Ozick said in 1989; "I had teachers who hurt me, who made me believe I was stupid and inferior" (Teicholz 182–83).

But though "the effect of childhood hurt continues to the grave," Ozick says, it has this useful side effect: "A writer is buffeted into being by school hurts—Orwell, Forster, Mann" (AA 304). Later, repeatedly, Ozick would say that retaliation for these early slights would be a serious motive for her fiction. In answering the query "What book made you decide to become a writer?" she answered that her stimulus was not a book; instead, "it was the hope of revenge against the book-hating, Jew-hating P.S. 71."[7] To an interviewer's opinion that "*The Cannibal Galaxy* had an edge of bitterness to it" (in its satire on American schooling), she explained:

> I've discussed "revenge" with other writers, and discovered I'm not alone in
> facing the Medusalike truth that one reason writers write . . . is out of revenge.
> Life hurts; certain ideas and experiences hurt; one wants to . . . replay the old
> bad scenes and get the *Treppenworte* said—the words one didn't have the
> strength or the ripeness to say when those words were necessary for one's
> dignity or survival. (Teicholz 183)

Although there were enough Old School Hurts to explain Ozick's strong penchant for irony and satire, some failures in her early life lay beyond the reach of irony's exorcism. As with so many other writers—one thinks of a particular favorite of hers, Emily Dickinson—Ozick's artistic inclinations produced a sense of alienation within more intimate circles than the schoolyard: "I am incognito. No one knows who I truly am. The teachers in P.S. 71 don't know. Rabbi Meskin, my *cheder* teacher, doesn't know. . . . My

brother doesn't care. My father doesn't notice" (AA 302). Among children
this sensibility may be commonplace enough to be almost universal. But
inasmuch as a similar lack of validation would extend for about twenty
years into her writing career, it is not surprising that Ozick's fiction features
a series of mute, burnt-out, or otherwise thwarted potential artists, including the nameless (identity-less) narrator of *Trust,* Edelshtein in "Envy; or,
Yiddish in America," and Lars Andemening in *The Messiah of Stockholm.*
"I've never fully recovered," Ozick said of those school years. "You never
really recover from early futility and worthlessness" (Kauvar 385).

Our final entry in the list of Old School Hurts relates to gender. As
precociously as the second grade, Ozick had assimilated Freud's embittering
insight about anatomy affecting destiny: "[Betty Taylor] was extremely
pretty and it was clear in the first hour [that we met] that she would become
hugely 'popular'" (Ltr 6/6/90). Predictably, this principle was to register
most crucially during the teenage period. During her first day of college, at
age seventeen, the atmosphere of sexual competition impinged with the
effect of a new kind of ostracism: "The engaged girls—how many of them
there seemed to be!—flash their rings. . . . There is no feminism and no
feminists: I am, I think, the only one. . . . When the Commons overflows,
the engaged girls cross the street to show their rings at the Chock Full
[restaurant]" (MM 116–17). As with the Jew-hating, book-hating P.S. 71,
this motif of Hymen triumphant was to engender a mood of defiance, most
notably in the withering contempt toward marriage displayed by a series of
Ozick personae such as the narrator of *Trust,* Una in "An Education," and
the protagonist in "The Doctor's Wife."

Ozick's first day at college produced other notable images of the artist in
transition. Carrying over from her past is the familiar skirmish with poverty: arriving at New York University with her lunch in a paper bag, she has
only ten cents in her purse, for subway fare home. So she cannot purchase
the magazine that has just aroused her neophyte's hunger—"*Partisan Review:*
the table of the gods" (MM 114). The deprivation, however, has fixed
Ozick's eye on something better than a magazine—"these bohemian streets
. . . the honeypot of poets." Here in Washington Square the artist's eye
captured a scene of urban lowlife vitality that was to recur in the garb of
fiction on Tilbeck's island in *Trust,* in Puttermesser's New York City, and in
Persky's Miami (in *The Shawl*). The cadence, the imagery, and the rush of
energy in the passage join with its proletarian sympathy to give us a sense of
the artist finding her calling:

> the benches of Washington Square are pimpled with this hell-tossed crew,
> these Mad Margarets and Cokey Joes, these volcanic coughers, shakers, groan-

ers, tremblers, droolers, blasphemers, these public urinators with vomitous breath and rusted teeth stumps, dead-eyed and self-abandoned, dragging their makeshift junkyard shoes, their buttonless layers of raggedy ratfur. The pretzel man with his toilet paper rolls [stripped and used as spindles for pretzels] conjures and spews them all—he is a loftier brother to these citizens of the lower pox, he is guardian of the garden of the jettisoned. They rattle along all the seams of Washington Square. They are the pickled city, the true and universal City-below-Cities, the wolfish vinegar-Babylon that dogs the spittled skirts of bohemia. The toilet paper rolls are the temple columns of this sacred grove. (MM 115–16)

That closing phrase—"temple columns of this sacred grove"—is a reminder of something that went very well in high school. From 1942 to 1946, Hunter College High School had grounded Ozick well in the classics, an education that would undergird her lifelong flirtation (in fiction only) with the pagan gods of antiquity. "In high school," she writes, "it was Latin class, the *Aeneid* in particular, that instigated the profoundest literary feelings—O *infelix Dido!*" (Ltr 6/6/90). Thus she could write, about her first day of college, that "until now, the fire of my vitals has been for the imperious tragedians of the *Aeneid*. . . . My adolescent phantoms are rowing in the ablative absolute with *pius* Aeneas" (MM 116, 119). At the university she continued to study Latin writers, including Pliny, Horace, Catullus, and Plautus, along with Edward Gibbon the classicist historian. Together with her concurrent grounding in Hebrew, this study of Latin literature led directly to Matthew Arnold's discourse on Hebraism and Hellenism. During her student years, she says, "at least for me, the world was dividing itself into an Arnoldian vision of Hellenism and Hebraism. When I read and read in Hebrew sources, I would dream the difference from the Greek; and vice versa" (Ltr 1/14/82).

In contrast with P.S. 71, Ozick's college years brought high distinction, as her omnivorous greed for books led to Phi Beta Kappa honors and an English honors thesis on Blake, Coleridge, Wordsworth, and Shelley. "I was saturated in the Romantic poets," she recalls, which made her "a zealous monist then, captivated by the fusion of soul and nature" (Ltr 6/6/90). Two eventual products of this episode were Ozick's startlingly original novella "The Pagan Rabbi," and her massive, unpublished first novel with title taken from Blake, *Mercy, Pity, Peace, and Love.* "I really *believed* in Mercy, Pity, Peace, and Love," she recalls, a penchant which made her "slow to 'get' social clues—especially about this thing called 'class'" (Ltr 7/13/90). We may infer that her belated awareness of class discrimination marks off that abortive first novel from her next work, the bitingly class-conscious *Trust.* (It is worth noting that the two titles taken together form a continuum—Mercy, Pity, Peace, and

Love; and Trust—but the latter term proves so untenable, in the novel *Trust,* as to subvert Blake's quartet of noble abstractions.)

In her personal life, Ozick's college years stamped one scar on her soul that would erupt into print nearly a half century later. In the 30 March 1992 *New Yorker,* Ozick finally addressed her troubled relationship with a class-mate who had died two decades before the essay was published and whose hairlessness found its way into her title, "Alfred Chester's Wig." Deliber-ately prodded by their English teacher, the two freshmen sharpened their weekly five-hundred-word character sketches like dueling weapons: "Chester and I were roped-off roosters, or a pair of dogs set against each other—pit bulls. . . . All this was Mr. Emerson's scheme" (82). But in the end their classroom rivalry both confirmed her calling as a writer and strengthened her friendship with Chester, as they toured bookstores and attended parties together.

What broke their friendship, after the vital intimacy of their college years, was a mutual administering of pain. Early on, he wounded her by having a brilliant career while she labored through a decade of oblivion, giving her all to a three-hundred-thousand-word novel that she in the end discarded. By chance, he turned out to be the expert reader who evaluated her first pub-lished story for a little magazine, a task he completed by sending her a contemptuous, patronizing letter of acceptance. She in turn inflicted a friend-ship-terminating wound during a transatlantic exchange of letters on "the nature of love" by insisting that his homosexuality was artificially induced, not his natural orientation. Implicitly, the artifice in the case was his physi-cal freakishness—a totally hairless body, "short and ovoid" and topped by a wig, that made him feel (she infers) "abnormal, monstrous, freakish . . . too horrifically ugly" (91). Thus inhibited from moving the female friendships of his youth toward Eros, she deduces, he found outlets elsewhere.[8] Chester's response—"a savage bellow," she calls it—was written in capital letters: "YOU KNOW NOTHING ABOUT LOVE!" (91–92). She was at work, at the time, on her Eros-driven first novel, *Trust.*

Ironically, it was Chester himself who gave Cynthia Ozick her first kiss, from which she "shrank back, and told him I could not think of him like that—he was my brother" (85). But if Eros lay dormant at this juncture, Apollo did not. She absorbed the image of Sacred Beauty, important for *Trust,* from Chester's entourage. His close friend Diana, for example—"one of the beauties, among the loveliest of all"—implied the pagan resonance of Sacred Beauty not only in her name but in her very physiognomy: "In after years, I happened on a replica of her face on the salvaged wall of an ancient Roman villa" (86). Chester himself, despite the stigma of his hairless condi-tion and homosexuality, contributed pagan-wise to the making of Tilbeck with his "breezy erotic spirit" reminiscent of "the goat-god Pan at play" (90). And at a party in Chester's honor, it seemed that Astarte herself reposed (her actual name is given out as Tatyana), emitting a "mustard glow" that would recur during the night of Tilbeck's apotheosis:

> In the middle of that carpet, a young woman lay in a mustard glow. . . . Her mustard-colored hair flowed out over the floor. Her mustard-colored New Look skirt was flung into folds around her. She was sprawled there like an indolent cat. . . . She had tigers' eyes, greenly chiaroscuro. . . . [It] was the majesty of pure sexuality. It was animal beauty. . . . Tatyana stretched her catlike flanks and laughed her mermaid's laughter. She was woman, cat, fish— silvery, slithery, mustard-colored. She spread her hair and whirled it. . . . With the holy power of their femaleness, her eyes traversed our faces. (87, 88)

Besides furnishing material for later manipulation into art, Ozick's relationship with Alfred Chester built confidence in other respects. "He was my conduit and guide," she says. "Without him, I would have been buried alive in Washington Square, consumed by timidity" (86). But behind her timidity was an avid thirst for general education, a subject of disdain for him, which in the end built a foundation for her art that would outlast his brilliant, mercurial talent. "I felt in myself stirrings of history, of idea," she writes; "I was infatuated with German and Latin, I exulted over the Reformation. I suppose that this enthusiasm meant I was more *serious* than Chester" (84).

In part because of her greater seriousness, by the time she published her first novel their careers displayed a sharply contrary profile, hers ascending steadily from oblivion toward a distinctive place among our most eminent Jewish-American writers, while his lapsed from high success into hapless ruination. Shortly before he was expelled from the MacDowell Writers' Colony because of obnoxious behavior, Chester wrote to friends saying, "I hate myself too. I can't stand it anymore not having any stable I . . . I don't know who I am" (94). A few years before his premature death at forty-two, Alfred Chester brought his search for identity to a Jewish conclusion, moving to Jerusalem where he composed his last significant work, "Letter from a Wandering Jew." From it, Ozick cites lines that speak as much for her and her lifework as for her old college mate: "does a Jew ever stop being a Jew? Especially one like me whose parents had fled the Russian pogroms for the subtler barbarisms of New York?" (96). Even if we disregard Ozick's personal involvement with this man, it is easy to see the grounds of her lifelong fascination. Had he not been a real person, he could have figured into any number of Ozick's stories as her quintessential fictional character. But of equal importance is Ozick's self-portrait as an artist in "Alfred Chester's Wig," a palimpsest that traces back to her ur-self in freshman English.

During these formative years, Ozick's most important discovery in fiction came about through blind serendipity: "I came, by chance, upon 'The Beast in the Jungle' at seventeen, knowing nothing about James; and that did it. That story was included in a science fiction anthology my brother brought home from the public library" (Ltr 6/6/90). Eventually this chance encounter would lead to a master's thesis, "Parable in the Later Novels of Henry James," and thereafter to a fictional oeuvre bearing strong traces throughout of the Jamesian imprint. The other writers that she favored she describes as "Everyone's List":

> When I think of the writers who have been most important to me, . . . the most prominently cherished have been James, Forster, Chekhov; and then Tolstoy, Conrad, George Eliot, Mann, Melville's "Bartleby the Scrivener." . . . Most readers have the same list, and I can't think of anything that distinguishes mine, except a kind of obsessiveness, a craze for reading the same thing over and over again. (I used to read Forster's *The Longest Journey* every year.) (Ltr 1/14/82)

Although, decades later, George Eliot would be assimilated into the Puttermesser stories, her singularity as the only female on the above list suggests a feebleness of feminist consciousness in this phase of Ozick's beginnings. It was a phase that would soon end.

Feminism

Cynthia Ozick's birthdate, 17 April 1928, fell in the decade when American women first exercised their voting franchise, and a dozen years before the economic necessities of World War II gave a new thrust to the movement for women's equality. In 1946, she gave the graduating address at her all-girls' school—"Hunter High (finishing school cum Latin prep)"—and then completed her undergraduate studies at Washington Square College (the liberal arts segment of NYU) without much sense of sexist bias affecting her academic life. Ironically, it was during graduate study at Columbia University, in 1951, that she first ran afoul of the problem. During her seminar with Lionel Trilling, "the Great Man presided awesomely" over a class that was all-male except for Ozick and one other female, an older woman "who talked like a motorcycle, fast and urgent. Everything she said was almost brilliant, only not actually on point, and frenetic with hostility."[9] Given the Crazy Lady's increasing aggressiveness, it was understandable that Trilling tried to overcome her by shutting his eyes or by "cutting her dead and lecturing right across the sound of her strong, strange voice." It came as a shock, however, when Ozick—at that time "bone-skinny, small, sallow and myopic, and so scared I could trigger diarrhea at one glance from the Great Man"—received her term paper back containing a rebuke to the Crazy Lady: "because we were a connected blur of Woman, the Famous Critic, master of ultimate distinctions, couldn't tell us apart. The Crazy Lady and I! . . . *He couldn't tell us apart!*" (CL 674–75).

Going out from academe into the real world merely confirmed Ozick's experience of sex bias. A brief fling at writing advertising copy produced the revelation that a male colleague with the same experience and work load as hers was earning half again as much money (AA 299). As she moved into her career as a writer, sexist put-downs—some of them authored by female literati—seemed ubiquitous in her profession. "For many years," she writes, "I had noticed that no book of poetry by a woman was ever reviewed without reference to the poet's sex. . . . In the two decades of my scrutiny, there were *no* exceptions whatever" (CL 676). The situation proved a stimulus to one of her most blatantly sarcastic works of fiction. "Determined to ridicule this convention," she says, "I wrote a tract, a piece of purely tendentious mockery, in the form of a short story. I called it 'Virility'" (CL 676). To the author's amazement, "in every review the salvo went unnoticed. Not one reviewer recognized that the story was a sly tract. Not one reviewer saw the smirk or the point" (CL 677). There was no avoiding the subtlety-be damned lesson: "Moral: In saying what is obvious, never choose cunning. Yelling works better."

Artistically, the most momentous result of Ozick's experience of sexism was a crucial deformation of her first and most ambitious novel, *Trust*. Although the novel, nearly seven years in gestation, was huge enough to have "contained everything—the whole world," Ozick confesses that "there was one element I had consciously left out . . . [because] I was considerably afraid of it. It was the question of the narrator's 'sensibility.'" The author's wry explanation of this deficiency warrants full-scale citation:

> Everything I was reading in reviews of other people's books made me fearful: I would have to be very, very cautious, I would have to drain my narrator of emotive value of any kind. I was afraid to be pegged as having written a "women's" novel, and nothing was more certain to lead to that than a point-of-view seemingly lodged in a woman; no one takes a woman's novel seriously. I was in terror, above all, of sentiment and feeling, those telltale taints. I kept the fury and the passion for other, safer characters.
>
> So what I left out of my narrator entirely, sweepingly, with exquisite consciousness of what I *was* leaving out, was any shred of "sensibility." I stripped her of everything, even a name. . . . My machine-narrator was there for efficiency only, for flexibility, for craftiness, for subtlety, but never, never, as a

"woman." I wiped the "woman" out of her. And I did it out of fear, out of vicarious vindictive critical imagination. (CL 682–83)

The reviews of *Trust* bore out Ozick's forebodings exactly. The *New York Times Book Review,* using a picture of a naked woman, spoke of the narrator's longing for "some easy feminine role," allowing a "coming to terms with the recalcitrant sexual elements in her life." *Time* magazine called Ozick "a housewife" (CL 682–83).

Three decades after its composition, Ozick's own pronouncements on *Trust* have been so contradictory as to raise a question after the title—which Ozick do we trust? With at least half her being Ozick can sometimes regard the book with passionate warmth and nostalgia: "I do know in my deepest sinew that I will never again write so well, that I will never again have that kind of high ambition or monastic patience or metaphysical nerve and fortitude. That belongs, I suppose, to the ambition, strength, and above all arrogance of youth" (Ltr 1/14/82). But this statement, made in 1982, seems qualified to the point of nullification by other statements made before and after. At length, in July 1991, she assigned to *Trust* the status of an unresolvable paradox:

> Sigh. About *Trust.* I suppose I hold both points of view at once.
>   . . . And at the same time what I told you remains true: the energy and meticulous language-love that went into that book drew on sources that were never again so abundant. In certain ways it is simply an immensely long poem. In terms of a young writer looking for recognition, it *was* a "towering mistake." It was obsessive—I was possessed by a passion almost absolutist, the passion for literature. . . . So yes: I do care more for *Trust* than for anything else; and it probably was a "towering mistake."
>   No wonder the word "ambivalence" had to be invented! (Ltr 7/20/91)

Bad as they were, the novelistic problems posed by being Jewish and female proved secondary to the deepest personal problem posed by *Trust,* the dilemma of Ozick's artistic identity. In her essay "The Lesson of the Master" (1982) and in several interviews, she has referred to the period of *Trust* as a colossal, irremediable waste of youth and talent, which should surely have gone into apprentice work instead of a fifteen-year obsession with writing a Great Jamesian Novel. "What happened was this," she says:

> in early young-womanhood I believed, with all the rigor and force and stunned ardor of religious belief, in the old Henry James, in his scepter and his authority. I believed that what *he* knew at sixty I was to encompass at twenty-two . . . to be, all at once, with no progression or evolution, the author of the equivalent of *The Ambassadors* or *The Wings of the Dove.* . . . For me, the Lesson of

the Master was a horror, a Jamesian tale of a life of mishap and mistake and misconceiving. . . . To be any sort of competent writer one must keep one's distance from the supreme artists. (AA 295–97)

Although she eventually recovered her admiration for Henry James, never again would Ozick assume the WASP persona of *Trust,* nor indeed any major persona outside her Jewish-American heritage. In effect, Ozick's concept of the artist changed during the seven years that she spent writing *Trust,* and the change subsequently settled into permanence. "After *Trust* I became a Jewish writer," she says; "'I began with an American novel,' I put it to myself, 'and I ended up with a Jewish one.'"[10] Nor, after *Trust,* would Ozick ever again permit fear of rejection to undercut her status as a woman writer. Moving freely among her male and female personae, Ozick has followed her imagination wherever it led, true to her conviction that the Muse has no gender.

Eventually a convergence between Ozick's two primary modes of victimization proved irresistible, as she drew the analogy between Jews losing their memory of injustice and women losing theirs: "A Jew reading of the aesthetic glories of European civilization without taking notice of his victimization during, say, the era of the building of the great cathedrals, is self-forgetful in the most dangerous way" (CL 677). Although she rejects as "foul, putrid, tainted, stinking" any analogy between the Holocaust and women's predicament, she warns against degrading woman's humanity in the same tones that she has applied elsewhere to the denial of Jewish humanity: "What happens is that the general culture, along with the object of its debasement, is also debased. If you laugh at women, you play Beethoven in vain" (CL 678).

Although Ozick likens—up to a point—the two modes of victimization, there are obvious incompatibilities in her status as both a feminist and an Orthodox Jew.[11] Like other religious traditions which have tried to keep their heritage pure over millennia—one thinks of the Roman Catholic Church and of Islam—Orthodox Judaism has maintained some undeniable practices of male supremacy. The size of the *minyan*—the assembly of Jews who can conduct synagogue worship—must include ten bar mitzvahed males; women don't count. During Orthodox worship, men only occupy the sanctuary, while women stay apart in a sort of gallery for spectators.[12] Some Orthodox congregations still maintain a ritual bath in which women are expected to ablute the inherent uncleanness of menstruation. The Orthodox tradition has included a prayer of thanksgiving for men only, in which they thank the Creator for not making them women.

Given its genesis in the millennium before Christ, it is not surprising that

Holy Writ—the Torah—likewise includes a disheartening measure of misogyny. Alongside the majesty of his call to righteousness, the Prophet Isaiah
ascribes to his God a disproportionate rage at the young women of his time:

> Moreover the Lord saith, "Because the daughters of Zion are haughty and
> walk with stretched forth necks, and wanton eyes, walking and mincing as
> they go, and making a tinkling with their feet: therefore the Lord will smite
> with a scab the crown of the head of the daughters of Zion." (Isaiah 3.16–17)

Should the daughters of Zion get pregnant out of wedlock, it never occurs to
Isaiah's God to smite with a scab the young men who made them pregnant.
Instead, the ignominy and punishment are reserved only to the female:

> And in that day seven women shall take hold of one man, saying, "We shall eat
> our own bread, and wear our own apparel: only let us be called by thy name,
> to take away our reproach." . . . And the Lord shall have purged away the filth
> of the daughters of Zion . . . by the spirit of judgment, and by the spirit of
> burning. (Isaiah 4.1–4)

In 1984 at a convention entitled "Tradition and Transformation: Women
in Jewish Culture," Ozick challenged the male supremacy in her cultural
heritage. Linda Zatlin, a member of the audience, asserts that Ozick's address, "on the Depth of Loss and the Absence of Grief: The Missing Minds,"
compellingly "argued the urgent need for the formal inclusion of Jewish
women into Orthodox Judaism—precisely because of the Holocaust."[13] But
unhappily, not even the Holocaust is safely beyond the range of gender-
based controversy. Miriam Cooke, an expert on war and gender, puts her
grievance in the form of a rhetorical question: "Does it matter that Claude
Lanzmann represses women survivors' testimony throughout his 9-hour
film on the Holocaust [*Shoah*]?"[14] Perhaps Ozick's best answer to sexism
occurs in her fiction after all, not so much in sardonic broadsides like
"Virility" as in her more subtle portrayals of female vindication. Barbara
Gitenstein, for example, notes how mother-daughter partnerships prevail
over the befuddled male protagonists of *The Cannibal Galaxy* and *The
Messiah of Stockholm,* to which we perhaps could add Rosa and her daughter (though she is just a figment of memory) standing off Persky in *The
Shawl.*[15]

For Ozick herself there was the striking example of her own emancipated
mother, a flamboyant ceramic artist who "wore red hats and called herself a
gypsy. In her girlhood she marched with the suffragettes and for Margaret
Sanger and called herself a Red."[16] Although not an activist in the same
way, Ozick in her turn has used her power of the pen to wreak devastation

upon the adversaries of women's equality, those of both the Old Right and the New Left. Taking on the Old Right in "The Hole/Birth Catalogue" (first published in 1972), she makes hash of Freud's notorious "anatomy is destiny" formulation—

> If anatomy were destiny, the wheel could not have been invented; we would have been limited by legs. . . . Anatomy is only a form of technology—nature's engineering. . . . A person—and "person" is above all an idea—escapes anatomy.(AA 252)

Norman Mailer and Robert Graves supplant Freud as purveyors of the Ovarian/Testicular Theory of Literature in Ozick's most substantial feminist essay, "Previsions of the Demise of the Dancing Dog" (first published in 1971). Whereas Graves relegated Woman to the role of Muse—inspirer of art rather than creator—in *The White Goddess* and *Man Does, Woman Is,* Ozick insists that the human mind is "androgynous, epicene, asexual," and that "the muse—*pace* Robert Graves—has no settled sex or form, and can appear in the shape of a tree *(Howards End)* or a city (the Paris of *The Ambassadors*) or even—think of Proust—a cookie" (AA 264, 272). She is particularly contemptuous of the notion that women's creativity is subsumed within childbearing:

> Literature cannot be equated with physiology, and woman through her reproductive system alone is no more a creative artist than was Joyce by virtue of his kidneys. . . . A poem emerges from a mind, and mind is, so far as our present knowledge takes us, an unknowable abstraction. (AA 271)

By a perverse irony of the times, Ozick found it necessary to battle against the Ovarian Theory of Literature not only on the Old Right flank, manned by Freud and Graves and Mailer, but equally on the New Left rampart defended by radical feminists. In "Literature and the Politics of Sex: A Dissent" (first published in 1977), she disputes the "woman writer" designation advocated by Ellen Moers and Molly Haskell and predicated on the inherent "difference" between male and female states of intellect and feeling. "In art," Ozick insists, "feminism is [that is, should be] that which opposes segregation. . . . I am, as a writer, whatever I wish to become. I can think myself into a male, or a female, or a stone, or a raindrop, or a block of wood, or a Tibetan, or the spine of a cactus" (AA 285). The radical feminist position gives her the opportunity to state an antiseparatist general creed:

> There is a human component to literature that does not separate writers by sex, but that—on the contrary—engenders sympathies from sex to sex, from

condition to condition. . . . Literature universalizes. Without disparaging particularity or identity, it universalizes; it does not divide. (AA 285)

Ozick's most compelling argument against the feminists' Ovarian Theory
is her procession of vividly realized male protagonists. Presumably, if her
feminist adversaries are correct, Ozick should go back and debase these
characters or erase them from her fiction—though one wonders how meaningful her stories would be without Isaac Kornfeld in "The Pagan Rabbi,"
for example, or Lushinski and Morris in "A Mercenary," or Joseph Brill in
The Cannibal Galaxy. In the total framework of her career, feminism has
been a consistent presence but not a central fact of Ozick's artistic vision.
Early on, from the Crazy Lady period through the creation of *Trust*'s repressed narrator, her feminism was a contingency imposed by the immediate presence of a sexist literary establishment. Since then, she has maintained her course between Old Right and New Left without yielding her art
to "the language of politics."

Judaism

The true center of Ozick's art, as it unfolded, turned out to be not biological/
political but cultural: not female but Jewish identity. In sharp contrast with
her rejection of "gender difference"—the idea that women necessarily think
and feel differently from men—Ozick insists with bone-deep conviction on
the importance of Jewish "difference." In "Toward a New Yiddish" (first
published in 1970), she writes: "My reading has become more and more
urgent, though in narrower and narrower channels. . . . I read mainly to find
out. . . . what it is to *think* as a Jew" (AA 157). To Philip Roth's disclaimer
"I am not a Jewish writer; I am a writer who is a Jew," she warns ominously
that "Roth's words do not represent a credo; they speak for a doom" (AA
158). That doom, she explains, is written in the historical record of assimilated Jews who, after their moment of fame, have inevitably declined into
oblivion: "there never yet lived a Jewish Dickens. There have been no Jewish
literary giants in Diaspora. . . . There are no major works of Jewish imaginative genius written in any Gentile language, sprung out of any Gentile
culture" (AA 167–68).
     Ozick's analysis of this cultural dilemma does not, as some might expect,
point to Gentile oppression as the reason for Jewish literary failure. Her
reasoning instead points entirely inward, toward Jewish neglect of a worldwide cultural imperative:

Why have our various Diasporas spilled out no Jewish Dante, or Shakespeare, or Tolstoy, or Yeats? Why have we not had equal powers of hugeness of vision? These visions, these powers, were not hugely conceived. Dante made literature out of an urban vernacular, Shakespeare spoke to a small island people, Tolstoy brooded on upper-class Russians, Yeats was the kindling for a Dublin-confined renascence. They did not intend to address the principle of Mankind; each was, if you will allow the infamous word, tribal. Literature does not spring from the urge to Esperanto but from the tribe. (AA 168)[17]

Rejecting "a literature that is of-the-nations, relying on what we have in common with all men" (AA 168), Ozick goes on to explain why Philip Roth courts eventual "doom" and Norman Mailer figures to end up as "a small Gentile footnote, about the size of H. L. Mencken" (AA 170). "Esau gains the short run," Ozick concedes, "but the long run belongs to Jacob"—and that long run, already four thousand years in the running, depends on the ongoing force of biblical revelation:

> The fact is that nothing thought or written in Diaspora has ever been able to last unless it has been centrally Jewish. . . . By "centrally Jewish," I mean, for literature, whatever touches on the liturgical. . . . Liturgy has a choral voice, a communal voice: the echo of the voice of the Lord of History. (AA 168–69)

It is clear that a proper understanding of Cynthia Ozick's art requires a grasp of its bedrock religious sensibility.

In her review of *Bech: A Book,* Cynthia Ozick rebukes John Updike for creating a "Jewish" protagonist who lacks the very essence of Jewish identity: "It is as if he [Updike] cannot *imagine* what a sacral Jew might be" (AA 122). Her correction of this deficiency—which is doubly grievous in a writer noted for the power and tenacity of his religious consciousness—comprises a rebuke not only to Updike but to Bech's real-life models, the "disaffected de-Judaized Jewish novelists of his generation" (AA 117):

> Being a Jew is something more than being an alienated marginal sensibility with kinky hair. Simply: to be a Jew is to be covenanted; or, if not committed so far, to be at least aware of the possibility of becoming covenanted; or, at the very minimum, to be aware of the Covenant itself. . . . If to be a Jew is to become covenanted, then to write of Jews without taking this into account is to miss the deepest point of all. (AA 122–23)

Because of its vital importance, it is worth taking a moment to rehearse the terms of the Covenant between God and Abraham, which makes its first appearance in Genesis 12:[18]

> Now the Lord had said unto Abram, Get thee out of thy country, and from thy
> kindred, and from thy father's house, unto a land that I will shew thee:
>   And I will make of thee a great nation, and I will bless thee, and make thy
> name great; and thou shalt be a blessing:
>   And I will bless them that bless thee, and curse him that curseth thee: and in
> thee shall all families of the earth be blessed.
>   So Abram departed, as the Lord had spoken unto him. . . .

In his next message to Abraham, God associates the Covenant with His gift
of the Promised Land to the descendants of the founder: "For all the land
which thou seest, to thee will I give it, and to thy seed for ever" (Genesis
13.15). For their part, the seed of Abraham are to keep the Covenant by
worshiping only the one true God and obeying His commandments faithfully.

In Jewish thought, the contest for legitimacy between the two sons of
Abraham, Isaac and Ishmael, has come to represent the rift between Judaism and Islam; and the struggle between Isaac's two sons, Jacob and Esau,
prefigures the friction between Jews and Christians.[19] Within the House of
Israel itself, the Diaspora later imposed a further separation, between Ashkenazic and Sephardic Jews—terms that refer to homelands in Eastern Europe (literally, "beyond the Rhine") and Spain, respectively. For Ozick, this
latter distinction—a recent cause of great friction in Israel—has minimal
importance. Although herself a Yiddish-speaking Ashkenazic Jew, born of
parents who migrated from the Minsk area of Russia, Ozick has displayed
the same affinity for the Sephardic heritage as she has shown for her indigenous area of the Diaspora.

Because the division between Christian and Jew is the oldest and most
important of these dichotomies, covering half of Judaic history, we shall
begin our definition of Judaism with Ozick's own sense of difference. Although a Judeo-Christian continuity must be credited—she says, "All the
varieties of Christianity and Islam are inconceivable without the God of the
Jews" (AA 182)—it is the contrast that matters, a contrast that Cynthia
Ozick remarked after reading (in her twenties) Rabbi Leo Baeck's essay
"Romantic Religion." From this essay, which she says "in some way broke
open the conceptual egg of my life" (Ltr 1/14/82), we may infer not only the
difference between Christian and Jew but also that rootlike thrust of art into
real life which is the essence of Ozick's literary credo. As opposed to the
Jewish "Classical" religious sensibility, Romantic Religion as Baeck defines
it makes an ideal of flight from the world:

> it seeks its goals in the now mythical, now mystical visions of the imagination.
> Its world is the realm . . . which lies beyond all reality. . . . The desire to yield to
> illusion . . . here characterizes the entire relation to the world. . . . Romantic

religion is completely opposed to the whole sphere of existence with which the social conscience is concerned. Every romanticism depreciates the life devoted to work and culture. . . . Romanticism therefore lacks any strong ethical impulse, any will to conquer life ethically.[20]

Together with commitment to the Covenant, Baeck's "will to conquer life ethically" is the chief characteristic of Ozick's own definition of Judaism. Calling Jewish history "a series of intellectual movements," she insists that "even given the diversity and sometimes mutual antagonism of all these ideational currents, they never depart very far from the original Abrahamitic insight: what we nowadays call ethical monotheism" (Ltr 4/22/90). What one needs to know about Judaism, she contends, "can be very briefly stated. So, while standing on one foot, maybe I can try to sum up as follows":

> Judaism is not equal to the Bible alone; the Bible plus the rabbinic tradition—i.e. the sea of commentary—make up Judaism. . . . Jewish ethical monotheism is conceived of as a direct channel (beginning with the principle of the Covenant) between humankind and the Creator, without necessitating a mediator. . . . Another way of stating this is that Idea (or meaning) is imposed on Nature, as in the invention of the Sabbath, or as in the designation of an inherited bit of land (Israel) as the fount of conscience. I might add that in rabbinic Judaism (which *is* Judaism) there aren't any miracles or bizarre contrary-to-nature beliefs, that inquiry is encouraged, that rationalism rules, that textual study is primary, an absolute *sine qua non*. (Interestingly, the high point of Jewish rationalist philosophy was during the so-called Dark Ages.) And that's all there is. . . . (Ltr 8/11/90)

To explain the conflict within the great religions—including Judaism—regarding rationalism versus mysticicism, Ozick refers, much as William James did in *The Varieties of Religious Experience,* to the mystery of temperament. Her reasoning incidentally makes a strong case for the conflicted art of Cynthia Ozick:

> I am persuaded that all this means . . . an inherent split in the human psyche: those temperaments that thrive on mysticism (immanence, incarnation) and those that thrive on rationalism. Dionysus versus Apollo. The hasidim versus the mitnagdim. The split occurs in Judaism, Christianity, Islam. . . . And sometimes both sides are present in the same mind! As in Spinoza, who uses geometrical formulations to espouse pantheistic doctrines. (Ltr 7/20/91)

So far as her conscious intention can resolve the question, Ozick sides absolutely with Orthodox rationalism. Thus, when asked to judge Faulkner's comment that "no writing will be too successful without some conception of God,"[21] Ozick replies that the "'Concept of God' strikes me as an idolatrous phrase. . . . We can't presume to give a face or a name or a shape to the Creator, or set any limits of our own, or presume to define or imagine qualities or attributes. That utterly rules out God in the representation of a human figure, of course." This view undergirds one of the sharpest distinctions between Judaism and Christianity, with its "gnostic inclusion of declared attributes and actual figural representation in the idea of God-Man." In this respect, she says, "Judaism famously has no theology at all. It is not a 'faith' in the Christian sense. Above all, it doesn't have 'a concept of God.'"[22]

Among the biblical verses that she cites in support of this argument are Isaiah 40.18 ("To whom then will ye liken God?") and 40.25 ("To whom then will ye liken Me, that I should be equal?"); Deuteronomy 10.12–13 and its echo in Micah 6.8; and—as "the greatest summary statement of all"—Deuteronomy 29.29 (in the King James Bible; 29:28 in the Jewish Pentateuch): "The secret things belong unto the Lord our God; but the things that are revealed belong to us and to our children for ever, that we may do all the words of this law." Her explication follows:

> What this verse tells us is that what God *is* (the whole kit and kaboodle of mysticism) is not our human business. *Our* business is to go about trying to make an ethical civilization. That's why we say "*ethical* monotheism," not just "monotheism." An idolatrous "concept" of God can't produce civilized conduct, and never has, beginning with Canaan, whose women were "socialized," as we say nowadays, into throwing their babies into the fire to please the idol and thereby "serve" society. It's in the name of theologies, in the name of such "concepts," that people eat one another alive. (Ltr 8/11/90)

With this mention of human sacrifice in ancient Canaan, we arrive at the central precept of the Judaic ethos, as Ozick sees it—namely, that taboo against idolatry which has distinguished this religion from all others since the time of Abraham. In her essay on Harold Bloom (originally titled "Judaism and Harold Bloom"), Ozick clarified her thoughts as follows:

> The single most useful, and possibly the most usefully succinct, description of a Jew—as defined "theologically"—can best be rendered negatively: a Jew is someone who shuns idols, who least of all would wish to become like Terach [the father of Abraham], the maker of idols. (AA 188)

Among the characteristics of idolatry that Ozick specifies (AA 189–90), the one that is "most universally repugnant" is its power to overcome human pity:

From this uniquely Jewish observation flows the Second Commandment. The Commandment against idols is above all a Commandment against victimization, and in behalf of pity. . . . Every idol is a shadow of Moloch, demanding human flesh to feed upon. The deeper the devotion to the idol, the more pitiless in tossing it its meal will be the devotee. Moloch springs up wherever the Second Commandment is silenced. . . . Every idol suppresses human pity; that is what it is made for. (AA 190)

Although, in Ozick's fiction, the Holocaust embodies Moloch most horrifically for this age, founded on the pity-suppressing idolatry of Hitlerism, subtler forms of idol making also claim her extended attention.[23] To the question "What is an idol?" she answers, in "The Riddle of the Ordinary," that it is "anything that is allowed to come between ourselves and God. Anything that is *instead of* God" (AA 207). "This is the point on which Jews are so famously stiff-necked," she goes on to say; for Jews there is "nothing but the Creator, no substitute and no mediator. The Creator is not contained in his own Creation; the Creator is incarnate in nothing, and is free of any image or imagining" (AA 207). For an artist, more susceptible than most people to being in love with the world's beauty, on fire with its significance, the materials of art pose a constant deadly temptation vis-à-vis the forbidding imperatives of the Second Commandment:

there is always the easy, the sweet, the beckoning, the lenient, the *interesting* lure of the *Instead of*: the wood of the tree instead of God, the rapture-bringing horizon instead of God, the work of art instead of God, the passion for history instead of God, philosophy and the history of philosophy instead of God, the state instead of God, the order of the universe instead of God, the prophet instead of God. There is no Instead Of. There is only the Creator. God is alone. (AA 208)

From this insight stems "the deepest danger our human brains are subject to," Ozick says, a danger that she formulates into a question (italics hers): *"how can we keep ourselves from sliding off from awe at God's Creation to worship of God's Creation?"* (AA 206). For the artist, it appears, there is no way to cope with the danger. According to her essay on Harold Bloom, her chosen craft is implicated in blasphemy by definition: "Literature, one should have the courage to reflect, is an idol" (AA 196). It is an idol not only because it creates an alternative world to the Creator's, in competition with the Creator, but also because the imagination that invents such a world cannot do so without trafficking in evil. Ozick explains this point in "Innovation and Redemption: What Literature Means":

Imagination is more than make-believe, more than the power to invent. It is also the power to penetrate evil, to take on evil, to become evil, and in that guise it is the most frightening human faculty. Whoever writes a story that includes villainy enters into and becomes the villain. Imagination owns above all the facility of becoming: the writer can enter the leg of a mosquito, a sex not her own, . . . a mind larger or smaller. . . . The imagination, like Moloch, can take you nowhere except back to its own maw. (AA 247)

So sharp was the conflict between her religion and her craft that Ozick began her essay on Harold Bloom with the idea that the phrase "Jewish writer" is "an 'oxymoron'—a pointed contradiction, in which one arm of the phrase clashes so profoundly with the other as to annihilate it" (AA 178). Among her own writings, *Bloodshed* (1976)—which I consider her single most crucial book—is the paramount embodiment of this premise. Its concluding story, "Usurpation (Other People's Stories)," had been so badly understood by earlier readers as to occasion *Bloodshed*'s preface, which may well comprise Ozick's most cogent literary credo. Here she writes: "There is One God, and the Muses are not Jewish but Greek. . . . Does the Commandment against idols warn even ink?" (BL 10). Her answer appears to be Yes, leading to a renunciation of her own powers: "'Usurpation' is a story written against story-writing; against the Muse-goddesses; against Apollo . . . the point being that the story-making faculty itself can be a corridor to the corruptions and abominations of idol-worship" (BL 11).

But yet, in the end, the "artist" half of the "Jewish artist" oxymoron gets the last word, leaving the author bewildered by a set of unanswered questions:

> Why do we become what we most desire to contend with?
> Why do I, who dread the cannibal touch of story-telling, lust after stories more and more and more?
> Why do demons choose to sink their hooves into black, black, ink?
> As if ink were blood. (BL 12)

Although he was the most dreadful issue of the pagan imagination, the cannibal-god Moloch was not the only enemy of the Sinaitic revelation. Perhaps the most subversive enemy of all was the goddess of Sex, variously named Astarte in Canaan, Aphrodite in Greece, and Venus in Rome. For Cynthia Ozick this primeval root of Hellenism, that which produced the pagan gods, has posed so magnetic an attraction as to nearly tear her loose from her Jewish moorings, as she attests in books like *Trust* and *The Pagan Rabbi*. Beginning in her college years, when she read Matthew Arnold on Hellenism and Hebraism, studied "E. M. Forster's Greeky heroes," and "went mad with Gibbon-joy" (Ltr 1/14/82), she gradually came to regard "the issue of Hellenism-versus-Hebraism as the central quarrel of the West" (AA 181).

It is a quarrel that has been keenly appreciated by other contemporary writers, including John Updike in *The Centaur* and Faulkner in his faun-haunted early works like *The Marble Faun* and *Soldiers' Pay*. But the issue has held exceptional interest for Ozick as a Jewish writer. Her essay on Harold Bloom, while demonstrating the centrality of Bloom's Judaism to his literary criticism, also highlights Bloom's argument, via Vico, on the incompatibility of being both a Jew and a writer:

> paganism—i.e. anti-Judaism—is the ultimate ground for the making of poetry. . . . Bloom writes: "Vico understood the link between poetry and pagan theology. . . . Vico says that 'the true God' founded the Jewish religion 'on the prohibition of the divination on which all the Gentile nations arose.'" (AA 181)

To be an artist, then, is to serve pagan gods—"the spontaneous gods of nature" is her term in a remark about E. M. Forster (AA 15)—and to translate those gods into their new births. "Reinvigorating the ideal of the idol in a new vessel, as Astarte begets Venus," is how Ozick describes this process (AA 194); so we can picture "Venus opening her eyes in a dawning Rome to learn that she is Astarte reborn. Astarte will always be reinvented" (AA 197). Such inventions, in turn, displace the true Creator with counterfeit realities: "Terach [the idol-maker] in his busy shop has put himself in competition with the Creator. . . . [He] refuses to accept Creation as given, and has set up counter-realities in the form of instant though illusory gratifications" (AA 191–92).

It is significant that Ozick selects Venus/Astarte as her example of a pagan god who will always be reinvented. As the climactic scene in *Trust* unforgettably attests, sexuality is the issue that most crucially illustrates the Hellenism-versus-Hebraism conflict in Ozick's writing. In her vividly lyrical, liberating dramatization of the sexual Life Force, Ozick directly flouts the deeply rooted taboo that Rabbi Leo Baeck—a great favorite of hers—defines in *This People Israel*. Jewish sexual discipline, Baeck says, is the very thing that most tellingly distinguishes God's People from the "unclean" Canaanites: "Purity, in this people [Israel], primarily means that of the sexual life. . . . The battle which this people's soul, in its covenant with God, waged against the people of Canaan and the peoples nearby was above all a battle for this purity. It continued for centuries. . . ."[24] To judge from Cynthia Ozick's fiction, Baeck's time frame ought rather to have been millennia rather than centuries in this instance.

Fortunately for Ozick, she proved able to flout the demands of the Second Commandment sufficiently to keep herself functioning as a writer. "To observe it is improbable, perhaps impossible," she says of the divine edict; "perhaps it has never been, and never will be, wholly observed" (AA 198). In this essay—renamed "Literature as Idol: Harold Bloom"—her way of resolving the contradiction is to downgrade the status of literature to the level of "shamanistic toys," while reasserting the central truth of her religious heritage: "The recovery of Covenant can be attained only in the living-out of the living Covenant; never among the shamanistic toys of literature" (AA 199). With the toys cleared away, the Judaic ethos regains its original primacy, as described here in words Ozick quotes movingly from Harold Bloom: "There is no recovery of the covenant, of the Law, without confronting again, in all deep tribulation, the God of the Fathers, Who is beyond image as He is beyond personality, and Who can be met only by somehow walking His Way" (AA 198).

Somewhat too late to affect the bulk of her fiction, Ozick in the mid-1980s changed her mind about the spiritual hazards of storytelling. In her *Paris Review* interview, she answered the question "Is writing idolatry?" by retracting her definition of Imagination as "image-making, . . . a sovereignty set up in competition with the sovereignty of . . . the Creator of the Universe" (Teicholz 167). Thanks to "a conversation with a good thinker" (who preferred not to be identified), she developed the perspective that "I'm in the storytelling business, but I no longer feel I'm making idols." To the contrary, the imperatives of ethical monotheism require "the largest, deepest, widest imaginative faculty of all," so that "you simply cannot be a Jew if you repudiate the imagination" (Teicholz 168). Acknowledging that "this is a major shift for me," she revises her theology accordingly:

> I now see that the idol-making capacity of imagination is its lower form, and that one *cannot* be a monotheist without putting the imagination under the greatest pressure of all. To imagine the unimaginable is the highest use of the imagination. I no longer think of imagination as a thing to be dreaded. . . . Only a very strong imagination can rise to the idea of a non-corporeal God. The lower imagination, the weaker, falls to the proliferation of images. (Teicholz 167)

Welcome as it was, this reconciliation of the Jewish writer with the demands of the Creator did not put an end to Ozick's religious quandary. Appallingly implicit in the question whether a Jew has maintained fidelity to the Covenant is the question whether God has maintained His. One of the oldest themes in world literature—it animates the plays of Aeschylus and Euripides and the Hindu *Bhagavad-Gita* equally with the Book of Job—

theodicy is also perennially new, as seen in Ozick's tribute to Saul Bellow: "his whole fiction is a wrestling with the Angel of Theodicy."[25] Because of the Holocaust, a wrestling with that angel stretches across her whole fiction too, preoccupying characters from Enoch Vand in *Trust* to Rosa in *The Shawl*. In her preface to *Bloodshed* she joins her own voice to those of her characters who question the justice of Yahweh. "I am certain there *is* a demon in this tale ["Bloodshed"]," she writes; "who he is I do not know; I hope he is not the Creator of the Universe, who admitted Auschwitz into His creation" (BL 7).

Perhaps it was by way of exorcising this indulgence in theodicy that Ozick later described the preface to *Bloodshed* as a work of fiction comparable to her stories, with its literary credo being voiced by an imaginary character (Scheick 258). If so, the exorcism is ineffectual, because the ground of theodicy in this instance is not ancient myth, as with Aeschylus and Job, but contemporary history; and the voice that contradicts the Creator's is in no wise imaginary. Instead, it is a historically certified fact that on 30 January 1939, Adolf Hitler made this solemn vow to the Nazi parliament:

> Today I will once again be a prophet: If the international Jewish financiers in and outside of Europe should again succeed in plunging the nations into a world war, the result will not be the Bolshevization of the globe and thus victory for Jewry, but the annihilation of the Jewish race in Europe.[26]

Clearly, the chief problem of belief for postwar Judaism lies in the premise that whereas God apparently did not keep his promise to the Jews, Hitler most certainly did keep his. It may be to God's credit that His Chosen People have somehow avoided total annihilation through four millennia, but whether that fact outweighs the appalling record of Jewish suffering is the great recurring question of the Judaic heritage, particularly since the millions of martyred dead strewn across those millennia have not yet sufficed to lodge His Chosen People in secure possession of their Promised Land. If the center of Jewish identity has been the Covenant, its circumference has been the four-thousand-year record of murderous hostility perpetuated by Gentile neighbors. A proper understanding of Cynthia Ozick's art requires an overview of that historic record.

Jewish History

"I suppose my guilty secret as a writer is that I've long preferred to read histories," Cynthia Ozick has stated. "I have [read] and will read any and every history of the Jews" (Ltr 1/14/82). So far as intellectual history goes, few cultures in the world can measure up to the exalted procession of Jewish theologians, philosophers, artists, and scientists who have enriched world civilization with their brilliant and learned contributions. As George Bernard Shaw observed without too much exaggeration, in Western thought it has always been "the Jews who, from Moses to Marx and Lassalle, have inspired all the revolutions."[27] Even Karl Marx, an apostate figure rarely cited in Ozick's writings, accomplished his revolutionary work in the Jewish tradition of bookishness, basing his thought on years of original research performed in the British Museum library. And Freud, for all his hostility to religion, admitted that being Jewish was a crucial condition for his achievement, in the sense that being part of a scorned minority proved salutary in his development of an independent, unconventional intellect. During childhood, Ozick's intellect was doubly sharpened in this respect, as "almost always the only Jew" in public school, and "almost always the only girl" allowed into an aged rabbi's Hebrew class (Kauvar 385).

In her nonfiction, Ozick pays ample homage to Jewish history in essays that range in time from early and medieval thinkers like Rabbi Akiva and Ibn Gabirol to contemporaries like Freud and Harold Bloom. In her fictional art, however, Jewish history occurs most compellingly in descriptions of Gentile persecution, primarily during the Holocaust and secondarily during the High Middle Ages—that period of Christian hegemony in Europe that spawned the Crusades and the Inquisition. In Ozick's personal life it is clear that her moment of trauma regarding Jewish history occurred about midway through college. An aesthete up to that point—"I have lived in the throat of poetry"—she recalls experiencing "another year or so of this oblivion, until at last I am hammer-struck with the shock of Europe's skull, the bled planet of death camp and war" (AA 116).[28] A period of about fifteen years had to elapse before the subject would receive its definitive historical analysis, beginning with Raul Hilberg's *The Destruction of the European Jews* in 1961. From that point on, with Enoch Vand's emergence as the moral center of *Trust,* the Holocaust became a pervading presence in all of Ozick's books, including her reviews and critical essays.

Fed by burgeoning studies in the subject, Ozick's hunger for Jewish history has produced a point of view that sharply distinguishes her from eminent WASP contemporaries, including several who became the subject of her literary criticism. John Updike, the least offensive of these, offends because, in *Bech: A Book,* he fashioned his Jewish persona from random scraps of authorial prejudice that were synthesized in ignorance. Updike's attempt at "putting Bech together out of Mailer, Bellow, Singer, Malamud, Fuchs, Salinger, [and] the two Roths" (AA 115) can not work, she argues, the telltale sign of inauthenticity being Bech's indifference to—or ignorance of—Jewish history, particularly with respect to its record of ubiquitous and unrelenting persecution:

> Emancipated Jewish writers like Bech (I know one myself) *have* gone through Russia without once suspecting the landscape of old pogroms, without once smelling another Jew. . . . [But Bech's] phrase "peasant Jews" among the Slavs is an imbecilic contradiction—peasants work the land, Jews were kept from working it. . . . If there had been "peasant Jews" there might have been no Zionism, no State of Israel . . . ah Bech! . . . despite your Jewish nose and hair, you are—as Jew—an imbecile to the core. (AA 117)

Updike's peasant Jews may be a pardonable imbecility, the figment of an imagination that strayed too far from its WASP Pennsylvanian point of origin. William Styron's imbecility, Ozick's subject in "A Liberal's Auschwitz," is not pardonable, because it engenders a refusal to acknowledge the central meaning of Auschwitz, that towering presence in modern Jewish history which figures so largely throughout Ozick's fiction:

> The two and a half million Jews murdered at Auschwitz were murdered, Mr. Styron recalls for us, in the company of a million Christian Slavs. This is an important reminder. . . . [But] the enterprise at Auschwitz was organized, clearly and absolutely, to wipe out the Jews of Europe. The Jews were not an *instance* of Nazi slaughter; they were the purpose and whole reason for it.[29]

Notwithstanding his Jewish wife and half-Jewish children, Styron thus repeats Shakespeare's vile error of allowing the Jews eyes and ears but not cultural integrity:

> if the Jew is ground into the metaphorical dust of "humanity," or of "victim," . . . if he is viewed only as an archetype of the eternal oppressed, if he is not seen as covenanted to an on-going principle, if he is not seen as the transmitter of a blazingly distinctive culture, . . . or if he is symbolically turned into "mankind"—but here I stop, having stumbled on Shylock's plea again.[30]

By lacking the sense of history that makes Jewish culture "blazingly distinctive," William Styron illustrates the central thesis of another book reviewed by Cynthia Ozick, Mark Harris' *The Goy*. Here a Gentile's attempt to reverse the usual pattern of acculturation occasions Ozick's culminating statement concerning the bond between identity and history:

> How then shall Westrum become like a Jew? What is the Jewish "secret"? . . . What makes a Jew is the conscious implication in millennia. To be a Jew is to be every moment in history, to keep history for breath and daily bread.[31]

Jewish history in turn makes the goy's case hopeless: how can goy become Jew, she asks, when history has made "fear of the goy" a primary feature of Jewish identity? From this point of view the honored phrase "Judeo-Christian tradition" takes on meanings that are not accessible to a man like William Styron, as she reminds him in "A Liberal's Auschwitz":

> Christianity does not stand responsible all alone in the world; nevertheless it stands responsible. The Inquisition was the known fruit of concrete Christian power. That thirteenth-century Pope (his name was Innocent) who ordered Jews to wear the yellow badge was not innocent of its Nazi reissue seven hundred years later.[32]

For Ozick and many other American Jews, there are ominous implications in this failure of comprehension on the part of men as sophisticated as Updike and Styron. If Updike's Bech cannot hear Jewish blood crying out from the Russian soil he treads on, and if, worse yet, William Styron cannot grasp the true meaning of Auschwitz during his visit there, how can one hope that the Gentile world at large will absorb the lessons of Jewish history? And if the majority Christian culture fails to absorb those lessons—fails to acknowledge a millennium of complicity in persecution—can we be sure the old familiar syndrome will not recur here in America?

Unwarranted as it may seem to a Gentile reader, Cynthia Ozick actually does express serious anxiety about American toleration in "Toward a New Yiddish" (first published in 1970). Her sense of marginality as the only Jew in her neighborhood—among houses owned by Italians, Lithuanians, Germans, and Scotch-Irish, with blacks a few blocks away—leads to thoughts of America being their final home in a way that cannot apply to her. For Diaspora Jews, she says, the soil underfoot is "something sweet and deep, but borrowed, transient," reminiscent of other friendly nations that did, of a sudden, turn savage. It is an insight that carries particular urgency for a Jewish artist: "Read, read, read, and read quickly; write, write, write, and write urgently—before the coming of the American pogrom! How much time is there left? The rest of my life? One generation? Two?" (AA 158, 159). Ozick is not unusual, she says, in harboring such ideas:

> No Jew I know is shocked at this pessimism, though many disagree with it. They will tell me I exhibit the craven ghetto mentality of the *shtetl:* "America is different." I go to the public library and I find a book by three clergymen . . . a minister, a priest, and a rabbi, and the rabbi's chapter is called "America Is Different." The rabbi is the author of a study of the French Enlightenment . . . showing how even Voltaire was not different. The rabbi's chapter is full of fear masking as hope. (AA 159)

As late as 1991, when multicultural pluralism might have seemed irreversibly victorious in academe, Ozick described Euro-American literary studies as a scene of "endemic anti-Semitism" where, "if you are an English major, you simply take it as your premise that you are majoring in Christianity and as part and parcel of that . . . in the teaching of contempt."[33] Although she claims that she personally can take literary anti-Semitism in stride—"my feeling is, so what? I'm enough of an aesthete to care about literature for the sentence, the poetry"—she clearly harbors deep bitterness toward the dominance in the classroom of "a tradition that has received deicide and supersessionism and the teaching of contempt with its mother's milk."

From the foregoing discourse on Judaism, it is clear that the Judeo-Christian tradition translates into very different meanings for Jews and Christians—even if we set aside the fact of endless, worldwide persecution. Strictly on the theological level, Christian readers will be unable to make sense of Ozick's cultural ambience unless they comprehend two paramount issues from the Jewish perspective: first, the Jewish rejection of Christ as the Messiah; and second, the Jewish conception of Christianity as a pagan religion. In a talk at Duke University, Rabbi Shemaryahu Talmon—an expert on the Dead Sea Scrolls—discussed the first of these topics, which is doubtless the central theological quarrel between Christians and Jews. Jewish rejection of Jesus as the Messiah, Talmon said, is not a matter of willful stubbornness or perversity. Instead, according to understandings going back to Hebrew antiquity, Jesus failed to fulfill several essential conditions of Messiah-hood, including status as a married man and a patriarch. Most important, the claim that Jesus is the Son of God represents an unthinkable blasphemy for traditional Judaism, which could never imagine the degradation of the Creator of the Universe into merely one of the world's creatures, to say nothing of His incarnation within some pieces of bread and a cup of wine. God is rather a superhuman Spiritual Being who does not incarnate Himself in anything and does not beget Sons or Daughters.

The other issue, Jewish perception of Christianity as a pagan religion, is implicit for Ozick in the idea of a Trinity—three faces of God replacing monotheism—and in the idea of mediation, not only through the role of the Savior but also through that of saints, totems, and even food (bread and wine). In this respect the Christian Church appears to violate the Second Commandment wholesale with its crucifixes, altar paintings, and other representations of the Unnameable One. In one of many similar passages, Ozick regards with dismay the influx of "Spirit"—that is, of the pagan/Christian imagination—into the world around us: "Spirit—or Imagination, which means Image-making, which is to say Idolatry—puts gods into bizarre and surprising places: into stones, plain or hewn; into rivers and trees;

into human babies born under significant stars; . . . into dry bread and wet wine" (AA 234). As with Moloch worship of old, this form of Idolatry has inevitably led to bloodshed—"wars fought [between] . . . those who argued over whether a piece of baked dough turned, when certain words were addressed to it, literally into God" (AA 234). Insisting that "only what is called Spirit—i.e., Idolatry—produces this kind of butchery," she traces the thread in short order to the human sacrifice of recent times:

> Sometimes it [Idolatry] puts God into the form of a man; sometimes . . . it suggests that a whole people personifies evil. . . . In either case it traffics, ultimately, in corpses. . . . [So that] the remaining Jews of Europe—millions— were locked into freight cars, stacked standing together there like cordwood, some dying as they stood, the rest awash in a muck of excrement, urine, menstrual blood, and the blood of violence. (AA 235)

From this perspective, not even the finest fruit of Christian morality, the Sermon on the Mount, may be presumed free of perversion. Speaking of Sabbatai Sevi, the seventeenth-century fanatic whom many Jews (including Sevi himself) took to be the Messiah, Ozick says his career "hints that every messiah contains in himself, hence is responsible for, all the fruits of his being; so that, for instance, one may wonder whether the seeds of the Inquisition lie even in the Sermon on the Mount" (AA 144). And even if, she says, her "fear of an American abattoir . . . may stem from the paranoia of alienation [rather than] . . . a Realpolitik grasp of scary historical parallels" (AA 170), the majority culture threatens American Judaism with extinction through assimilation. "Diaspora-flattery is our pustule, culture-envy our infection," she writes; "in America Exile has become a flatterer; our flesh-pots are spiritual" (AA 171, 172).

To one such instance of culture envy—a *New York Times* article in which a Jewish mother (Anne Roiphe) describes her family's celebration of Christmas—Ozick sent a reply that would curiously foreshadow her novel *The Cannibal Galaxy:* "When we speak of assimilation among amoebas, we mean that the larger substance swallows the smaller; the majority digests the minority."[34] This metaphor does not, for Ozick, imply a revulsion against Christianity; quite the contrary, she asserts, "I am glad to be an assimilationist. . . . Not to have a grasp of Christianity . . . not to know my neighbor's way, is in some fashion not to know myself." What she finds objectionable is the majority culture's unwillingness to reciprocate:

> I want to be known! I want my neighbors to assimilate my perceptions as I have assimilated theirs; I want them to know the real Hanukkah of history. . . .
> I want them to know the real Passover, the real Rosh ha-Shanah and Yom

Kippur, as I know Allhallows Eve and Whitsuntide and Easter and St. Francis
. . . and Martin Luther and George Fox. (Both the founder of German Protestantism and the founder of the Society of Friends were profoundly unfriendly
toward Jews and Judaism. Luther called Talmud "dung.")[35]

Ozick found her answer to the quandary of American Jewish identity in a
historical episode of two thousand years ago: "America shall, for a while,
become Yavneh" (AA 173). Yavneh was the town where, after the Second
Destruction of the Temple, the Romans permitted a small band of Jewish
scholars to found a religious community. "It was out of Yavneh," Ozick
writes, "that the definition of Jewish life as a community in exile was
derived: learning as a substitute for homeland; learning as the instrument of
redemption and restoration" (AA 173n). By accepting English as the "New
Yiddish," Ozick was able to conceive a middle path between total alienation
of Jews from American culture (which Old Yiddish would have maintained)
and total assimilation, such as Anne Roiphe's Christmas celebration implied:

> When Jews poured Jewish ideas into the vessel of German they invented
> Yiddish. As we more and more pour not merely the Jewish sensibility, but the
> Jewish vision, into the vessel of English, we achieve the profoundest invention
> of all: a language for our need, our possibility, our overwhelming *idea*. If out
> of this new language we can produce a Yavneh for our regeneration within an
> alien culture, we will have made something worthwhile out of the American
> Diaspora, however long or short its duration. . . . By bursting forth with a
> literature attentive to the implications of Covenant and Commandment—to
> the human reality—we can, even in America, try to be a holy people, and let
> the holiness shine for others in a Jewish language which is nevertheless gener-
> ally accessible. (AA 176–77)

Unfortunately, about a half decade later Ozick concluded, in her preface
to *Bloodshed* (1976), that "English is a Christian language" in which "there
is no way to hear the oceanic amplitudes of the Jewish Idea in any . . . word
or phrase" (BL 9, 10). And according to current sociological analysis, her
hope has proven equally vain with respect to Jewish resistance to assimilation. In its religion column for 22 July 1991, *Newsweek* magazine cited
studies showing that of all marriages involving Jews, the percentage that
were interfaith rose from 9 to 52 between the years 1964 and 1985. Moreover, three-quarters of the children of these marriages have not been raised
as Jews. Much in the vein of Ozick's prophecy, *Newsweek* cites an
Orthodox rabbi who calls assimilation through marriage a "death knell" of
American Judaism: "There never has been a community of Jews that has
abandoned ritual and survived."[36]

And yet, America has proved something like a Promised Land in providing unparalleled safety, freedom, and prosperity to millions of Jews (including 325,000 Israeli immigrants living in 1992 in New York City alone).[37] Ozick admits as much in ascribing the 1960s rupture between American blacks and Jews to "this difference—America [being] felt simultaneously as Jewish Eden and black inferno" (AA 95). Thinking presumably of her own immigrant parents, she compares "the Jews' pleasure in an America sweet and open to them" with the "miseries in the Russian Pale" a fraction of a century earlier (AA 95). For all her anxiety about future supersession of Jewish culture in America, "Jewish history" in the sense of Gentile oppression has almost always, in Ozick's work, had a European ambience.

The point is important enough to merit substantiation. Of the four sections of *Trust*—her most self-consciously "American" novel—two are set in "Europe" and "Brighton" (England). *The Pagan Rabbi* is filled with European-born characters—the Pagan Rabbi's wife (a death camp survivor); Edelshtein and his whole circle of Yiddish speakers in "Envy"; the German who fought for the Kaiser in "The Suitcase"; Edmund Gate and his aunt (both English-bred) in "Virility." *Bloodshed*'s most memorable characters are likewise not American nationals: Lushinski (a Pole) and Morris (an African) in "A Mercenary"; the rebbe (a Buchenwald survivor) in "Bloodshed"; two Israeli writers in "Usurpation." The protagonist of *The Cannibal Galaxy* is French-born, and his adversary, Hester Lilt, issued from the whole of Europe. The entire script of *The Messiah of Stockholm* is set in Sweden, with a nod to Poland (Bruno Schulz's home). And all the main characters of *The Shawl*—Rosa, her niece, and Persky—are Warsaw natives. The main character in *Levitation* (Puttermesser) is Ozick's most authentically American character, a contemporary New Yorker; but the book also visits Vienna to scan Freud's room, and its title story portrays a man, Feingold, who is obsessed with the Jew killings in Europe from the Middle Ages through the Holocaust.

There is more than a little of Cynthia Ozick in Feingold's obsession. So extensive and detailed is his account that we cannot escape *this* meaning of her postulate that "To be a Jew is to be every moment in history, to keep history for breath and daily bread."[38] Despite her definition of Jewish history as primarily intellectual history—that is, about what Jews have done—her stories define history most vividly as what has been done to Jews:

Feingold wanted to talk about . . . certain historical atrocities, abominations: to wit, the crime of the French nobleman Draconet, a proud Crusader, who in the spring of the year 1247 arrested all the Jews of the province of Vienne, castrated the men, and tore off the breasts of the women. . . . It interested Feingold that Magna Carta and the Jewish badge of shame were issued in the same year. . . . There he was telling about the blood-libel. Little Hugh of

Lincoln. How in London, in 1279, Jews were torn to pieces by horses. . . .
Feingold was crazed by these tales, he drank them like a vampire. (LE 11–13)

It follows, then, that the true focus of Ozick's "Jewish history" is Europe; neither of her two homeland countries, America and Israel, catches her fictive imagination with that kind of intensity. It is true that other American writers have favored foreign settings—Hemingway set his major novels in Paris, Italy, Spain, and Cuba, for example—but the Europe of Hemingway or James was both culturally consanguine with America and deserving of the author's affection. Cynthia Ozick's Europe, in the light of Jewish history, is diametrically different from these precursors, figuring into her work and thought as one titanic ash-speckled graveyard—a map formed (in *Trust*) from vomit and urine.

Because of its crucial importance throughout all of Ozick's work, this concept of history merits a closer examination. Drawing substantially on Heinrich Graetz's monumental, six-volume *History of the Jews, from the Earliest Times to the Present* (1870), the time frame of Jewish history in Ozick's work goes back to the Great Diaspora (Dispersal) ordained by the Emperor Vespasian and his son, the Roman general Titus, after they crushed the Revolt of the Zealots in 66–73. Jews began to appear in Europe at large during the century after the Romans destroyed Jerusalem (70 A.D.) and depopulated Judea, taking many Jews to Rome as slaves. By the year 300 European Jews numbered about three million and lived everywhere in the Roman Empire except Britain, enjoying freedom of religion and exemption from military service.[39] After the Christianizing of the empire under Constantine, however, Gentile-Jewish relations gradually became less agreeable. The Nicaean Council of 692 decreed intermarriage punishable by death and forbade building new synagogues. In 721 Byzantine King Leo III ordered forcible baptisms for all Jews. In 887 Jews in Sicily were the first Jews of Europe forced to wear a "badge of shame"—an invention emulated all across Europe in later centuries. With the onset of the Crusades in the eleventh century, slaughter assumed the force of systematic policy. Despite efforts by local bishops to protect their Jews, soldiers in the German Crusade of 1096 massacred the Jews of Worms, Mainz, Metz, Trier, Cologne, and Prague, completing their work in the Holy City by killing the Jews of Jerusalem in 1099.

Throughout the High Middle Ages, the persecution intensified. In 1266 the Council of Breslau decreed that Jews must live in ghettos "separated from the Christian dwelling-place by a hedge, wall, or ditch." In 1222 an Oxford student who converted to Judaism was burned alive. Elsewhere in England, in 1255, eighteen Jews were executed for the ritual murder of a child, the incident that formed the basis of Chaucer's "Prioress's Tale." In 1290 the Jews of England, having grown to five thousand strong since arriving with William the Conqueror, were expelled to France, not to return until invited into Oliver Cromwell's Commonwealth in the 1650s.[40] When the Black Death ravaged Europe from 1348 to 1350, the massacres and expulsions multiplied as Jews were blamed for the disease, despite the Pope's earnest admonitions to the contrary, noting in his bulls that the Jews themselves were dying like all the other victims. Even so, for having caused the plague, the Jews of Strasbourg were herded into a wooden cage and burned alive. By 1500 Jews had been expelled from large areas of France, Germany, Austria, Hungary, and Spain.

The latter expulsion, in 1492, produced a community of great interest to Ozick, the Iberian "Marranos" ("Pigs," in contemptuous Spanish vernacular), who pretended to be converted so as to escape both expulsion and the Inquisition's flames but ended up being massacred anyway. A more wholesome effect was the escape of some Marranos to Holland and the Americas, where they prospered. The first Jews to arrive in the New World came with Columbus; five of his crew members in 1492 were known to be Jews. When the Inquisition moved into the Spanish and Portuguese settlements of Hispanic America, the Jews in those areas sought a friendlier environment in Protestant America, arriving in New Amsterdam (New York) by 1654— barely a generation after the *Mayflower*.

The one significant counterpoint to the bloody violence in Europe was the Jewish sanctuary provided during the Middle Ages in a territory that overlapped Poland, Lithuania, and Russia, eventually stretching from the Black Sea to the Baltic. Here Jews were allowed to own land in 1203, were granted autonomy in 1356, and were given protective charters by Poland's Casimir the Great in the fourteenth century. When new rulers arose of less friendly mien, the Jews in this area were either trapped or forced to migrate to places like Germany and America. A Cossack uprising of 1648, for example, resulted in more than 100,000 Jews being murdered. Though Peter the Great halted the pogroms in 1708 and allowed Jews to live in St. Petersburg, the partition of Poland in 1795 added 1,200,000 Jews to the Russian domain, creating a "Jewish problem" in the eyes of the czar which was "solved" by confining all Jews within the territory that was now endowed with the title "The Pale of Settlement." Among those so constrained were Cynthia Ozick's ancestors, living in the region of Minsk, in the very heart of the Pale geographically.

Only with the eighteenth-century Enlightenment did European Jews begin gaining emancipation, which was accelerated by Napoleon's decree freeing the ghettos. But this progress was counterbalanced again by a change for the worse in Eastern Europe, typified by the decree of Czar Nicholas I in 1827 stipulating a twenty-five-year military service for Jews—a law that continued until 1874. Extreme poverty also afflicted the four million Jews in the Pale, one fifth of whom in 1900 were living on poor relief provided by other Jews. These conditions, culminating in the great pogrom (the Russian word for "violent mass attack") that followed the assassination of the czar in 1881, drove more than two million Jews out of Russia, many of them to the United States. Among that flood tide of refugees from Russian oppression were the artist's future parents, William Ozick and Celia (Shifra) Regelson.

The aftereffects of the pogrom were evident to Ozick as a child in her correspondence with her grandmother in Moscow, written in Yiddish: "*Nikolay, Nikolay, oif dayn kop ikh shpay* was my grandmother's lullaby to me— Czar Nicholas, I spit on your head" (AA 160). Her parents, however, chose to withhold the gruesome details of family history until the child had become a woman.

> Not until I was grown up was I told about my great-uncle Mottel and his son Raphael. In a pogrom in a Russian village, the Cossacks . . . tied them to the tails of horses, upside down. The Cossacks galloped back and forth over the cobblestones until the heads were dashed to pieces. When at last my mother confessed this story, she whispered it.[41]

In the Russian town of his boyhood, Ozick's father was spared the fate of great-uncle Mottel and his son Raphael, but only by a harrowingly close margin. The setting was at Easter, "when these things often used to happen," and the plot involved a "good priest/bad priest" dichotomy:

> The bad priest organized a mob with truncheons. The Jews ran to the synagogue and locked themselves in. The truncheons were turned into torches, and the mob . . . [was] about to set fire to the synagogue. My father, then a boy of four or five, always remembered the panic inside, families pressed together. But then the good priest came along and persuaded the murderers to go home.

Hatred of Western/Christian civilization—"that pod of muck," Edelshtein calls it in "Envy" (PR 42)—would seem a natural outgrowth of such a heritage, even without a Holocaust. But a more positive aftereffect of the pogrom was something the child could see about her as a daily presence: the creation of New York as a City of Jews—the metropolis that since 1900 has had the largest Jewish population of any city in the world. Jewish population in America as a whole soared from 100,000 in 1855 to 5,720,000 in 1968. By the time Ozick launched her career, around 1960, New York contained over two million Jews who at that time were sustaining one thousand synagogues and three daily newspapers in Yiddish. The vast majority of these were of Russian origin, like herself—brought here with the immigration wave of two million Russian Jews who arrived between 1880 and 1914. Before and after this period, most American Jews came from Germany and Poland (150,000 by 1870), Romania (125,000 by 1914), and Germany again during the Hitler era (240,000 from 1933 to 1945).

The Holocaust

The Hitler era was of course the culmination of "Jewish history" in the perverse sense of the phrase. No disaster since the time of Abraham could be placed beside it: not the enslavement in Egypt (1800–1500 B.C.), though it "remains the great black hole of the Bible" in one scholar's phrasing;[42] nor the destruction of the First Temple and slavery in Babylon a thousand years later (586 B.C.); nor the massacres imposed in their turn by Rome, Islam, and Christendom during the two millennia after that. Among its effects, Ozick says, was a sense of guilt felt by Jews toward "those who were surrogates for us"—a guilt that "is inexpiable" and so deep that "we must question the legitimacy of our very lives."[43] But though its presence profoundly affects all her work, Ozick was unable to address the Holocaust frontally until *The Shawl*, first published piecemeal in the *New Yorker* ("The Shawl," 1981, and "Rosa," 1984). Even then, she withheld the manuscript from the printer for several years, immobilized by doubt over the moral propriety of "making art out of the Holocaust."[44]

There is a special irony about Germany's being the center of the Holocaust. The 5 percent of Europe's Jews who lived there up to the Hitler years, comprising less than 1 percent of Germany's population, were the most privileged Jews on the continent—prosperous, fully emancipated, and largely assimilated into German society. Conversely, the Jewish contribution to German culture and science was greater than that in any other European country. Kaiser Wilhelm, though a fervent Christian, included many Jewish friends and advisers in his entourage; his chancellor, Bismarck, was philo-Semitic enough to recommend counteracting Prussian stiff-mindedness by "crossing the German stallion with the Jewish mare." Through his father's lineage, Hitler himself may have been one-quarter Jewish, to judge from the fact that his grandmother, as a teenaged maidservant, received the standard paternity payments from her wealthy Jewish employer after giving birth to Hitler's father.[45] Although the paternity of Hitler's father has never been established for certain, Hitler took the evidence seriously enough to assign, in the Nuremburg Laws, full Aryan status to persons of one-quarter Jewish blood—a maneuver by which both he and Jesus Christ would pass muster, if we assume the Catholic doctrine that God is the father of both Jesus and his mother, Mary. (Ironically, the Israeli Law of Return assigns full Jewish identity on the same quarter-blooded basis.)[46]

For Cynthia Ozick, the assimilationist character of pre-Hitler Germany is precisely the index by which to measure the evil of Holocaust betrayal. For her and many other Jews, Germany's pre-Hitler philo-Semitism implies a warning about what could happen in other friendly host countries, not excepting America; and it is an ultimate reason why every Jew on earth, down to the most assimilated apostate, should support with all his heart the Israeli land of refuge. When asked whether Germany's Jews can be equated with America's Indians as victims of genocidal slaughter, as is sometimes asserted, Ozick pointed to the German-Jewish assimilation as comprising the crucial moral difference:

> The American settlers were out to conquer the land; they were motivated primarily by conquest, not by killing for its own sake. And they saw the Indians as . . . different from the settlers in . . . manner, dress, language, custom, and everything else under the sun. Whereas the German Jews were, as the famous sneer has it, "more German than the Germans" . . . in their mastery of German Hochkultur. When the settlers killed Indians, they [were] annihilating utterly alien beings—no more justifiable than any other atrocity, but the usual story. The Germans, curiously, did not adhere to the usual story; they were entirely original. When the Germans murdered the German Jews, literally their next-door neighbors, they annihilated an utterly familiar group, part of and parcel of their own culture. And how profoundly a part of their own culture! Heine, as you know, was so completely implicated in German education that, though the Nazis burned his books, they couldn't root out "die Lorelei"—so Nazi schoolchildren went on singing it, though now it was called a "German folksong."[47]

It is plausibly arguable that there would not have been a Holocaust if England had accepted a peace treaty in 1940, the precondition necessary for the Nazis to carry out their plan to deport all of Europe's Jews to Madagascar. Adolf Eichmann, who helped plan this project, described it as a colony where "Jews could live among their own folk and be glad to get a piece of land beneath their feet."[48] Hitler's war aims, centered mostly on regaining the lands lost by Germanic Europe in World War I, did not evoke a definite prospect of genocide until he had reason to believe that his vow of January 1939 to the Nazi parliament had been disregarded. The most likely moment for that to have happened was in November 1940, when Molotov and Stalin rejected the führer's proposals for redrawing the map of Eurasia so as to offer Japan a free hand in the Far East, Stalin in South Asia,

Mussolini in Africa, and Hitler in Europe. With Stalin claiming an interest in the same territories that Hitler had plans for, it was obvious to Hitler that Jewish Bolshevik Russia had now joined Jewish capitalist America in a conspiracy to thwart German war aims, and the result for "international Jewry" would now be what Hitler had predicted.

Six months later his *Einsatzgruppen* killing squads, following close upon the heels of the Wehrmacht's sweep into Russia, began implementing his prophecy with immediate slaughter of one and a half million Jews by machine-gun fire. The public-image problems implicit in this carnage, committed in the open landscape of occupied territory, led in early 1942 to the Wannsee Conference in Berlin, where the Nazi overlords designed the scheme of bringing Jews to secret killing centers instead of sending killer squads out to where the Jews were. So began the four-part sequence of the Holocaust: the exhaustive process of identifying every Jew in the Greater Reich, followed by their concentration in ghettos, transportation in boxcars, and gassing in death camps.[49]

Next to Germany, the country most deeply implicated in the Holocaust was Poland, the setting for Ozick's most harrowing treatments of the subject, notably in "A Mercenary" and *The Shawl*. With the largest Jewish population in Europe—about 3,000,000 people in 1939—Poland became the vastest killing field of the war. Site of the most notorious of all death camps, Auschwitz, this tragic land gave residence to Moloch resurrectus, his power magnified a millionfold by modern transportation and assembly line efficiencies devoted to the mass production of death. Next to the Warsaw ghetto, with 450,000 Jews crowded sometimes ten to a room, the ancient Jewish settlement in Lublin was the major locus of Jewish confinement. Ozick chose to commemorate the martyrdom of its 200,000 Holocaust victims by naming her protagonist in *The Shawl* Rosa Lublin.

Exacerbating still further the Polish-Jewish relationship was the continuing persecution of Jews after the war, doubtless a strong reason for Ozick's ongoing hatred of "Europe" in the 1950s and 1960s. Most surviving Jews fled Poland after a series of pogroms culminated in the killing of 42 Jews in the streets of Kielce in July 1946, a massacre provoked by rumors of ritual murder of Christian children by Jews. The Communist government added new thrust to the postwar *Judenrein* movement by its official actions against Poland's few remaining Jews following the 1967 Arab-Israeli war. A half century after the German invasion, the 3,000,000 Jews of Poland have dwindled to about 10,000. That has been reason enough for Cynthia Ozick "to think of the whole continent of Europe as one vast Jewish graveyard" (Ltr 6/6/91). The phrase "whole continent," moreover, carries no hint of hyperbole. Eastward of Poland and Germany, Stalin planned as early as

1928 to deport 300,000 Russian Jews to an enclave on the Chinese border; in 1952–53, his plan to send all the Jews under his rule to Siberia was cut short only by his death. In a 1971 essay-interview with a victim of Stalin's policies, Ozick depicted the horrors of Soviet anti-Semitism as nearing Hitlerite dimensions.[50]

Westward, in France and the Low Countries, local opportunists and Jew haters abetted the Holocaust as elsewhere. Many puppet regimes, however, appeared to follow the principle that Cynthia Ozick has elucidated concerning America's Indians: the killing of other countries' Jews proved more acceptable than turning on one's immediate Jewish neighbors. The Horthy regime in Hungary protected its 900,000 Jews from its German ally until Adolf Eichmann arrived to take charge in March 1944, after which the local Arrow Cross Nazis went on a savage killing spree. The Romanian army and police murdered scores of thousands of foreign Jews on its soil, but flouted demands from Berlin so as to shelter most of its native Jews from deportation. The Bulgarian government, another nominal ally of Hitler's, finessed his edicts so shrewdly as to give up not a single native Jew to the Holocaust, though they sent the Greek Jews under their control to Auschwitz.

The Europe-wide "Jewish graveyard" does display one major counterexample, in Ozick's work, to Holocaust misery—the Scandinavian countries. Travel to Sweden in "The Suitcase" figures as the honorable alternative to traveling to Germany ("The Swedes . . . saved so many Jews,". PR 126); Nicholas Gustav Tilbeck, the charismatic demigod of *Trust,* is a Swede; and the country contributes an attractively civilized setting to *The Messiah of Stockholm.* And she acknowledges the uniquely heroic status earned by another Scandinavian country, Denmark, which she contrasts with both other European societies and the Allied leadership (read: Churchill and Roosevelt), who knew of the Holocaust and did nothing whatever about it (AA 236). In the words of Holocaust historian Raul Hilberg, the Danes placed "an extraordinary obstacle . . . in the path of the German destructive machine: an unco-operative Danish administration and a local population unanimous in its resolve to save its Jews."[51] In October 1943, as the Gestapo initiated a roundup for deportation, ordinary Danish citizens organized a nation-wide rescue operation that succeeded in sending almost all Danish Jews across the Sound to Sweden. Although subsequent scholarship has somewhat tarnished the altruism of the affair by exposing its commercial dimensions,[52] the Danish-Swedish salvation effort remains a rare bright spot in the terrible Holocaust story.

Modern Israel

Though it comprises the most awesome black hole in Jewish history—a true singularity, in astronomer's jargon—the Holocaust figured largely into the most spectacular comeback, one may reasonably say, in not only Jewish but world history. The Restoration of Israel in 1947–48, barely three years after crematoria chimneys stopped smoking, could not help but evoke schizoid feelings in the generation of world Jewry who experienced both events as they unfolded. Although Cynthia Ozick fully shares the exultation of the Restoration, and has frequently visited "the living breathing vital sovereign state of Israel" (Ltr 6/6/90), it is curiously absent from her imaginative writing. Perhaps her strong sense of the sacred and the profane leads her to put Israel, like the Holocaust, in a realm beyond the idolatrous defilements of fiction. Yet when Israel does come briefly into her characters' consciousness, the context is likely to be ironic or belittling. In "Envy; or, Yiddish in America," for example, Edelshtein thinks bitterly of the Restored nation:

> Yiddish was not honored in Tel Aviv or Jerusalem. In the Negev it was worthless. In the God-given State of Israel they had no use for the language of the bad little interval between Canaan and now. Yiddish was inhabited by the past, the new Jews did not want it. (PR 48)

At the end of the same story, Israel comes into view once again in the crazy slugfest of words between Edelshtein and a Christian evangelist. Here, in any event, is some grounds for pride for the alienated Yiddish speaker:

> "Accept Jesus as your Saviour and you shall have Jerusalem restored."
> "We already got it." . . .
> "You [people] got a wide streak of yellow, you don't know how to hold a gun."
> "Tell it to the Egyptians." (PR 100)

Though losers on the battlefield, the Egyptians, it turned out, had an impressive corps of allies. When Egypt and Syria launched the Yom Kippur War in 1967, Ozick observed in "All the World Wants the Jews Dead," "the United Nations was silent. The day after and the day after and the day after, the United Nations was silent."[53] Only after Israel had turned the war meant to annihilate them into a stunning victory did the U.N. speak, to save the aggressors. For Ozick that lesson infallibly confirmed two precepts: first, that "*Jewish*" and "*Israeli*" are "one and the same thing, and no one, in or out of Israel, ought to pretend differently anymore" (105); and second, that the shame of "Jewish history," no longer a Western phenomenon, had gone global as the non-Western world leaned heavily against the idea of Jewish survival. Even China, historically remote from Middle Eastern affairs, inveighed against the "Zionist imperialism" of the country under attack, not merely with an eye toward Arab oil or influence but—in a surprising turn—with the weight of historic precedent:

> China, until Mao the most traditional of societies, has *this* tradition too. In the ninth century, in Canton, . . . there was a massacre of Jews. Tens of thousands were killed. Mao, who arms terrorists, is no innovator. (209)

Besides consolidating Jewish-Israeli identity and globalizing the Jewish-Israeli struggle for survival, the Yom Kippur War had one other profound effect on Ozick's self-consciousness. Henceforth, her identity as an artist would forever lack any trace of the art-for-art's-sake sensibility. The catalyst for this stance was a telephone call from a friend who, as the war was hanging in the balance, wanted to recite a new poem. Though alive with the urgency of the war, she "shut off the [television] set and listened to the poem," which was "lyrical; infused, as we say, with sensibility." But, she says, "then and there I vomited up literature. I was turned against every posture grounded in aesthetics. Art is indifferent to slaughter" (207). From that time forward—the year after *Trust* was published—Ozick's creed of art-for-life's-sake was to be her standard for virtually every page of writing.

To judge from Israel's precarious wars for survival, it might seem that "Jewish history" is defined less by Hebraic culture than by the hostility of enormous powers and populations bent on ending Jewish history. Ultimately, however, that inference is false. Probably the deepest meaning of Israel—and of Jewish history—in Ozick's imaginative writing comes in her advice to John Updike about converting his pseudo-Jewish Bech into the real thing. To present this advice, she invents a future book for the series, making it a trilogy that she entitles *Bech, Bound:*

> Whither is Bech bound? . . . And what, above all, is binding Bech? The memory of Moriah, Isaac's binding. The thongs of the phylacteries. The yoke of the Torah. The rapture of Return. . . . By now Bech has read his Bible. He has been taking Hebrew lessons; he is learning Rashi, the eleventh-century commentator. . . . Starting with the six-volume Graetz, . . . Bech has mooned his way in and out of a dozen histories. He is working now on the prayer book, the essays of Achad Ha-Am, the simpler verses of Bialik. . . . He is reading Gershom Scholem.
>
> Bech stands on a street in Jerusalem. The holy hills encircle him—they are lush with light, they seize his irradiated gaze. For the first time, he is Thinking Big. (AA 128)

Here for once is Jewish history as it should be, a cosmic-scale feast of the intellect being hungrily ingested in the Promised Land of the Covenant, with no shadow of a Holocaust or Arab war or Christian supersession to impose its menace. This centering of Jewish history on the intellect, displacing history's actual multimillennial span of violence, provides an appropriate transition to our final topic in our Matrix of Art discussion. We turn to the latter half of the "Jewish artist" oxymoron.

L'Chaim! and the Art of Fiction

From the Gentile majority of American writers, twentieth-century literature has brought to birth an indecent plenitude of anti-Jewish caricatures. To cite some of the more celebrated, we have Fitzgerald's Meyer Wolfsheim, the gangster who wears human molars as cufflinks in *The Great Gatsby;* T. S. Eliot's brothel owners, Rachel née Rabinovitch in "Sweeney among the Nightingales" and Bleistein in "Burbank with a Baedeker," along with the slumlord "jew" who "squats" in the window in "Gerontion"; Faulker's "jew owners of sweatshops" in his original version of the appendix to *The Sound and the Fury* (Faulkner's editor—himself Jewish—excised the offensive adjective; we should also credit Faulkner with mocking anti-Semitism in Jason's part of this novel); and Hemingway's Robert Cohn, so smitten with WASP-hunger while watching Lady Brett as to evoke an exceptionally profane analogy: "He looked a great deal as his compatriot must have looked when he saw the promised land."[54]

In a moment, we shall return to this last impasse between Gentile and Jew—between Jake Barnes and Robert Cohn—for closer inspection. In order to do that, I must first propose a theory of culture that figures importantly in this discourse on the Art of Fiction. The theory is that virtually every cultural group formulates its distinctive ethos in a word that summarizes for the group its most crucial, bone-deep (though often unstated) values. Perhaps the most commonly known of these words in American civilization is the word that epitomizes Afro-American culture, Soul. Ultimately indefinable, like all such words, to have soul means having an intense and subtle emotional responsiveness, such as one may experience in the varieties of Afro-American music— gospel songs, jazz, and blues. In *The Bluest Eye* Toni Morrison memorably renders the efficacy of soul music as a signifier too deep for words:

> The pieces of Cholly's life could become coherent only in the head of a musician. Only those who talk their talk through the gold of curved metal, or in the touch of black-and-white rectangles and taut skins and strings echoing

from wooden corridors, could give true form to his life. . . . Only a musician would sense, know, without even knowing that he knew, that Cholly was free. . . . Free to feel whatever he felt—fear, guilt, shame, love, grief, pity. Free to be tender or violent, to whistle or weep.[55]

By contrast with her treatment of Cholly, Morrison employs a voice dripping with sarcasm to excoriate the "brown girls" whose insufficient blackness implies their betrayal of soul values. By pursuing white middle-class virtues such as hard work and education, along with "thrift, patience, high morals, and good manners," the brown girls at last rid themselves of the "Funk" (Morrison's cognate for "soul") that is their true heritage. They "get rid of . . . the dreadful funkiness of passion, the funkiness of nature, the funkiness of the wide range of human emotions. Wherever it erupts, this Funk, they wipe it away; where it crusts, they dissolve it; wherever it drips, flowers, or clings, they find it and fight it until it dies."

For convenience we shall use the generic term "soul-word" to designate this bone-deep verbal nugget in various subcultures. For several decades I have been gathering a necklace of these words from my readings and travels. In order to confirm the depth and range of soul-word psychology, I shall define some of these as follows:

The Japanese soul-word is *yamato-damashi*, which translates literally as "Japanese soul" but means in practice (politely put): "Have manhood! Don't come back till the job is done." The United States learned what that meant when the Japanese kamikaze pilots inflicted appalling losses on American forces near the end of the war. Fully three decades later, a few Japanese soldiers were still carrying on the war in remote jungles of the Pacific, refusing to come back till the job was done. The return of the last such soldier in the mid-1970s occasioned a mammoth parade in Tokyo for this living embodiment of the national soul-word.

The Armenian soul-word is *genutzat,* which translates as "I give you everything I have." For a people who have been persecuted almost as badly and as long as the Jews, *genutzat* implies an ethic of survival: these people could not have made it without the kind of total mutual support implied in "I give you everything I have."

The Serbo-Croatian soul-word is *dom,* which translates as pertaining to Home, Homeland, defense of the Home. Tragically, the word has come to imply bloody violence in recent times as the fractured ethnic groups in the country fall to quarreling over control over home soil; but it also helped foster the fighting spirit that, in Tito's partisans, gave Hitler's legions all they could handle, and later proved more than even Stalin at the height of his power cared to tangle with.

Something similar proved true of Finland, whose soul-word, *sissu*, translates as the ability to endure pain and hardship with absolutely stoic forbearance. The Finnish custom of taking steam baths followed by immersion in snow or ice water is a minor example of *sissu;* a major example was Finland's stunning success in battling hugely superior Russian armies during the war. After the war, Stalin at the height of his superpower status prudently refrained from taking over this enemy territory.

A few other soul-words we may touch on briefly. The Chinese soul-word, *ren,* means "to endure"—a formulation that needs no explanation regarding that long-suffering population. The—or at least *a*—traditional soul-word for Hispanic culture is "machismo," an index to both male honor and, all too often, oppression of women in Latin countries. (Not until 1991 did the Supreme Court of Brazil rule illegal the murder of an adulterous wife by her husband to defend his honor—and the court has since rescinded that ruling under political pressure.)[56] And, returning to the American scene, the two soul-words that concern us most are those of the WASP and Jewish subcultures: "Class" and "L'Chaim!" respectively.

With this mention of WASP and Jew, we are ready to summon back the two cultural ambassadors that we left in limbo a moment ago, Jake Barnes and Robert Cohn. Recent scholarship has discovered two interesting facts about Hemingway's original manuscript: that in it Lady Brett was the primary focus of the opening pages; and that, angrily overreacting to Fitzgerald's advice, Hemingway did not merely condense the opening thirty pages but swept them away altogether. This abrupt maneuver, by thrusting Robert Cohn to the book's forefront, gave Cohn and his Jewishness a special importance.

What were Hemingway's hidden motives for showcasing Cohn as prominently as he does? The first motive is one that Ozick confessed to in her own work: revenge. But Hemingway's revenge was far pettier and more spiteful than Ozick's retaliation against book-hating, Jew-hating P.S. 71. He was settling a score with a sexual rival, the real-life model for Robert Cohn, Harold Loeb (though Loeb had rescued Hemingway's first book, *In Our Time,* from oblivion). Loeb's transgression consisted of his success in bedding the real-life model for Lady Brett, Lady Duff Twysden, who had rejected Hemingway because, she told him, he was a married man.[57] The other motive, using Cohn to exemplify failure to comprehend (never mind enact) the famous Hemingway Code, reveals a fascinating inability to reverse the premises of that code: that is, Hemingway could not comprehend, never mind enact, the Jewish ethos that Cohn expresses with admirable clarity. The scene of mutual incomprehension occurs early on, in chapter 2:

"Listen, Jake," he leaned forward on the bar. "Don't you ever get the feeling that all your life is going by and you're not taking advantage of it? Do you realize you've lived nearly half the time you have to live already?"

"Yes, every once in a while."

"Do you know that in about thirty-five years more we'll be dead?"

"What the hell, Robert," I said. "What the hell." (11)

The ethos that Hemingway half-consciously upholds in this scene is the paramount WASP imperative to show some Class, which is to say, to maintain one's dignity among one's fellows and—of virtually equal importance—to allow others to have their dignity likewise. The latter purpose is Jake's reason for his repeated though futile efforts to correct Cohn's behavior by alerting him to the Code that he keeps violating. This WASP Code of Having Class, or Dignity, goes a long way toward explaining Hemingway's celebrated emotional taciturnity of style: to have Class is to obey an imperative that imposes self-repressing reticence on its practitioners. The code that allows Jake to cry only in private (never, like Cohn, in public) also invokes, in the above scene, a threefold tacit prohibition in the name of WASP class/dignity/reticence: (1) Don't talk too much; (2) If you do talk, don't talk about yourself; and (3) If you do talk about yourself, for God's sake don't talk about your griefs and anxieties. Obviously Jake has shared Cohn's morbid mood "every once in a while," but his "What the hell" is an appropriate putdown, from the WASP standpoint, of Cohn's lack of dignified reticence.[58]

It never seems to occur to Hemingway, however, that Cohn, not being a WASP, may abide by a non-WASP ethos. In fact, Cohn exemplifies perfectly, in this scene, the Jewish ethos, made familiar to us all (though not to Hemingway's generation) by the immense popularity of *Fiddler on the Roof.* In acting upon "the feeling that all your life is going by and you're not taking advantage of it," Cohn embodies the Jewish "L'Chaim!" principle. Spelled Yiddish-wise as "l'khayim" in Ozick's essay "Sholem Aleichem's Revolution" (MM 197), it means, as Topol taught the world, "To Life!"—but it means, so to speak, more than that: it means, To Life As It Actually Is, not as it is cleansed and idealized by such popular forms of wishful thinking as, for example, Romantic Religion.

Another way of putting it is to say that "To Life!" equals "To Reality!" which in turn equals "To Truth!" The Jewish soul-word implies above all else a reality-confronting, truth-seeking ethos, an ethos that has proved a majestic asset in transforming this tiny sliver of the world's population into a force to reckon with in every realm of actual reality: the arts, sciences, politics, business and finance, education, and institutions of justice. It is the bedrock reason for George Bernard Shaw's perception that the world's revolutionaries are always Jews: the hunger for Life/Reality/Truth implied in L'Chaim! helps explain both this people's extraordinary bookishness and their revolutionary adaptability to new ideas.

The correlation between Ozick's thought and the L'Chaim! principle is evident everywhere. "To Life!" prevails over death, the cemetery, and even the Holocaust in her answer to the question why she will not set foot in Germany, not even to visit "sacred sites" like the thousand-year-old Jewish graveyard in Worms:

> In Jewish tradition, a cemetery isn't regarded as a "sacred site" (indeed, a *cohen*—someone in the priestly line descended from Temple times—is forbidden to enter a cemetery), and in any case I have to confess that I think of the whole continent of Europe as one vast Jewish graveyard. And why go look at cemeteries when I can visit, as I have many times, . . . the living breathing vital sovereign state of Israel? (Ltr 6/6/90)

Among Ozick's essays, her most graphic depiction of the struggle between L'Chaim! and Moloch is "The Hole/Birth Catalogue," first published in 1972. In this work, which was occasioned by Freud's notorious formulation that "anatomy is destiny," she accords to Freud the title of "philosopher" but then goes on to observe that "all the truth any philospher can really tell us about human life is that each new birth supplies another corpse." In this light, "to say anatomy-is-destiny is to reverse the life instinct," in the sense that "if the woman is seen only as childbearer, she is seen only as a disgorger of corpses" (AA 255). By correlating "anatomy is destiny" with the death instinct in this way, Ozick finds the secret reason for Freud's attack on religion in *The Future of an Illusion*—and particularly for Freud's rejection of his own religious heritage:

> In the light of Freud's assertion of the death instinct, it is absolutely no wonder that he distorted, misunderstood, and hated religion. . . . He despised Judaism because it had in the earliest moment of history rejected the Egyptian preoccupation with a literal anatomy of death and instead hallowed, for its own sake, the time between birth and dying. Judaism has no dying god, no embalming of dead bodies, above all no slightest version of death instinct— "Choose life." (AA 256)

For Ozick, L'Chaim! is not merely a secular formulation, then—not just a piece of practical advice like that of Strether in Henry James's *The Ambassadors:* "Live all you can! It's a mistake not to." It is rather an ethos that expresses the long Judaic heritage, having risen coeval with the birth of Israel itself out of the centuries of brutal Egyptian oppression. This reverence toward the past—toward those real ancestral lives that have created the Judaic heritage—causes Ozick to repudiate a central feature of literary modernism: its obsession with (in Harold Bloom's phrase) "'undoing' the precursor's strength" (AA 194). "Nearly every congeries of Jewish thought is utterly set against the idea of displacing the precursor," Ozick says, insisting on the "carrying over of the original strength, the primal monotheistic insight, the force of which drowns out competing power systems." Quoting the Passover Haggadah to illustrate this cultural continuity—"We ourselves went out from Egypt, and not only our ancestors"—Ozick measures literary modernism against her Judaic heritage and chooses the latter:

> In Jewish thought there *are* no latecomers.
> Consequently the whole notion of "modernism" is, under the illumination of Torah, at best a triviality and for the most part an irrelevance. Modernism has little to do with real chronology, except insofar as it is a means to dynamite the continuum. Modernism denotes discontinuity. . . . Modernism and belatedness induce worry about being condemned to repeat, and therefore anxiously look to break the bond with the old and make over. . . . The mainstream Jewish sense does not regard a hope to recapture the strength, unmediated, of Abraham and Moses as a condemnation. Quite the opposite. In the Jewish view, it is only through such recapture and emulation of the precursor's stance, unrevised, that life can be nourished. . . . (AA 194, 195)

If modernism courts irrelevance and triviality through valorizing discontinuity, postmodernism falls radically short of Ozick's Judaic standard of historicity. In "Toward a New Yiddish," first published in 1970, and "Literature as Idol: Harold Bloom" (1979), she performs a surprisingly early roundup of what would later become the usual suspects: Robbe-Grillet (the "father" of the new movement), Susan Sontag (its "mother"), Richard Kostelanetz and Richard Gilman (its "foster uncles . . . two de-Judaized American critics"), William Gass, Paul de Man, Stanley Fish, J. Hillis Miller, Angus Fletcher, Jacques Derrida, and Roland Barthes.[59]

In assessing the shortcomings of postmodernism, she chooses Kostelanetz and Gass to exemplify the postmodern divorce of literature from actual life. Kostelanetz's statement "So we learn to confront a new work with expectations wholly different from those honed on traditional literature" reminds Ozick of Henry Ford's dismissive gesture "Or, history is bunk" (AA 243). Equally anti-Judaic, for her, is Gass's assertion that "Life is not the subject of Fiction"—that fictional characters should not "passionately wallow in the human reality which the work of art refers to" but rather "shine like essence, and purely Be" (AA 165). This view of literature has not only "aestheticized, poeticized, and thereby paganized" the contemporary novel,

Ozick says; it has reduced novelistic horizons to the scope of a linguistic playschool with only two games to play—"parody of the old forms, Tolstoyan mockeries such as Nabokov's," or else "a new 'form' called language, involving not only parody, but game, play, and rite. The novel is now said to be 'about itself,' a ceremony of language" (AA 164).

For Ozick, this "pagan aestheticism" will not serve. "The religion of Art isolates the Jew," she declares; "it is above all the Jewish sense-of-things to 'passionately wallow in the human reality'" so as to relate "conduct and covenant" to literature (AA 165). For this reason, to a Jew in America "the Problem of Diaspora in its most crucial essence is the problem of aesthetics." Predicting that the religion of Art will "dominate imaginative literature entirely" in America "for a very long time," she says the Jewish-American writer who wants to stay Jewish will have to "stay out of American literature. . . . [He] will have to acknowledge exile" (AA 165).

Fortunately, there is a place of exile in Ozick's literary world that is immediately accessible, thoroughly Judaized, and inhabited by the most glorious figures in the history of fiction. That place of exile is the nineteenth-century novel, emphatically Cynthia Ozick's favorite period of fiction because of its high correlation with the L'Chaim!—Life/Reality/Truth-seeking—principle. There is, of course, the minor inconvenience that "the nineteenth-century novel has been pronounced dead" by modern/postmodern consensus, and therefore, "since the nineteenth-century novel is essentially *the* novel, . . . the novel itself is dead" (164). Ozick's answer to this challenge is to draw an analogy between the premodern/modern dichotomy in fiction and a cultural dichotomy of far larger proportions, that which separates what Gentiles call the Old and New Testaments. First, says Ozick, we had the Old Testament novel of ethical insight:

> The novel at its nineteenth-century pinnacle was a Judaized novel: George Eliot and Dickens and Tolstoy were all touched by the Jewish covenant: they wrote of conduct and of the consequences of conduct: they were concerned with a society of will and commandment. At bottom it is not the old novel as "form" that is being rejected, but the novel as a Jewish force. (AA 164)

Displacing that Jewish force is the novel of New Testament insight, based not on history and character but on miracle and mystery:

> The "new" novel, by contrast, is to be taken like a sacrament. It is to be a poem without a history—which is to say, an idol. It is not to judge or interpret. It is to *be*. . . . The new fiction is to be the literary equivalent of the drug culture, or of Christianity. It is to be self-sustaining, enclosed, lyrical and

magical—like the eucharistic moment, wherein the word makes flesh. (AA 164–65)

Ironically, Ozick's chief exemplar of such a literature is a Jewish rather than Gentile writer, the flamboyant poet Allen Ginsberg. Noting the prevalence, circa 1970, of "lifestyle" as the touchstone of the new ethos, Ozick carries her New Testament analogy a little further regarding Ginsberg's case: "But revolutionary lifestyle incorporates very literally a eucharistic, not a Jewish, urge. What Ginsberg . . . called 'psychedelic consciousness' is what the Christians used to call grace" (AA 161). We thereby arrive in Ozick's literary criticism at one more battlefield of Jewish versus Christian values, Yahweh versus pagan gods. At the end of the following passage, an interesting resemblance may be discerned between Allen Ginsberg the poet and Tilbeck, the pagan demigod who drowns at sea at the end of *Trust* exactly as Ginsberg does here metaphorically:

[Ginsberg] recapitulates the Hellenization of Jewish Christianity. He restates the justification-by-faith that is at the core of Pauline Protestantism. In dethroning the separate Oneness of God . . . he goes farther than . . . Christianity, even in its Roman plural-saint version. He wades into the great tide of the Orient, where gods proliferate and nature binds all the gods together and the self's ideal is to drown in holy selfhood until nature blots out man and every act is annihilated in the divine blindness of pure enlightenment. . . . Ecstasy belongs to the dark side of the personality, to the mystical unknowingness of "psychedelic consciousness." . . . When a man is turned into a piece of god he is freed from any covenant with God. (AA 162–63)

In contrast to this "pagan" model of fiction, Ozick advances the Judaic model in "Innovation and Redemption: What Literature Means"—a synthesis of three essays she had published earlier over the span of a decade. Two "outmoded" precepts characterize the Judaic model that she here espouses: tradition and didacticism. Openly Judaic about tradition, she subordinates modernist discontinuity to the biblical injunction concerning respect for one's (in this case, literary) ancestors: "more useful cultural news inhabits the Fifth Commandment [Honor Thy Father and Mother] than one might imagine at first glance" (AA 241). The other precept, truly nineteenth-century in character, is the idea that "fiction will not be interesting or lasting unless it is again conceived in the art of the didactic. (Emphasis, however, on *art*)" (AA 245). Her idea of didacticism, in turn, presumes that "literature *is* the moral life," creating "a certain corona of moral purpose" or a "nimbus of *meaning* that envelops story" (AA 245, 246). Those who claim that fiction is "self-referential, that what a story is about is the language it is made of, have snuffed out the corona," she adds. And without that nimbus of meaning, that corona of moral purpose, the novel can not serve the ancient Judaic purpose of redemption.

In saying that literature cannot last if it does not "touch on the redemptive," Ozick is quick to define the word as having nothing to do with "goodness, kindness, decency, all the usual virtues." Redemptive literature deals rather with "the singular idea that is the opposite to the Greek idea of fate: the idea that insists on the freedom to change one's life" (AA 245). Redemption thus comes to resemble a transcription of the L'Chaim! principle, in that both L'Chaim! and Redemption represent "everything against the fated or the static: everything that hates death and harm and elevates the life-giving—if only through terror at its absence" (AA 246). Ozick's quarrel with Freud stems from this insight (as well as from Freud's misogyny). "The Freudians claim that they're not determinists, but I can't see anything else," she told Elaine Kauvar apropos the "prediction from earliness" that ruined Beulah Hilt's chances in school in *The Cannibal Galaxy* (Kauvar 389).

But though her purpose in fiction is thus moral and redemptive—in a word, Judaic—there remains the "Jewish writer" oxymoron to contend with, pitting the writer's imagination and idolatry against the Jewish ethos. Calling the battleground within the Jewish writer a "darkling plain," Ozick portrays this inner struggle as occurring among adversaries as powerful as any of those within the fiction that is born of this process. There follows a memorable instance of the conflicted art of Cynthia Ozick:

> Literature, to come into being at all, must call on the imagination; . . . but at the same time imagination is the very force that struggles to snuff out the redemptive corona. So a redemptive literature, a literature that interprets and decodes the world, . . . must wrestle with its own body, with its own flesh and blood, with its own life. Cell battles cell. The corona flickers, brightens, flares, clouds, grows faint. The . . . Evil Impulse fills its cheeks with a black wind, hoping to blow out the redemptive corona; but at the last moment steeples of light spurt up from the corona, and the world with its meaning is laid open to our astonished sight. (AA 247–48)

The key word, in that final clause, is "meaning"—a postmodern taboo that Ozick sweeps aside without compunction or apology (italics hers): "*What literature means is meaning.* . . . *Literature is for the sake of humanity*" (AA 246–47). Aware that she is contradicting the Zeitgeist in this attitude, she offers the career of Solzhenitsyn as proof that "more often than not the *Zeitgeist* is a lie." Following—however unwittingly—the Judaic model of fiction, Solzhenitsyn shows how "the idea of the novel is attached to life, to the life of deeds, which are susceptible of both judgment and interpretation, and the novel of Deed is itself a deed to be judged and interpreted" (AA 87). The Russian writer's opposite, in this context, is Truman Capote, whose *Other Voices, Other Rooms* exemplifies the "narcissistic" modern novel. The survival of the novel form, she predicts, "depends on this distinction between the narcissistic novel and the novel of Deed" (AA 87). Though admittedly Capote's flair for style and mood outshines Solzhenitsyn's plodding naturalism, Ozick sides with the Russian as the greater truth teller: "Life is not style, but what we do: Deed. And so is literature" (AA 89).

Ozick's insistence that fiction must correlate with external reality—that "Literature (even in the form of fantasy) cannot survive on illusion" (AA 101)—brings harsh judgment to bear on several of her contemporaries. In general, the most damaging thing she can say about any fiction is that it manifests, like Romantic Religion, the flight reflex, choosing to fantasize rather than cope with reality. Reviewing *The Wapshot Chronicle*, she considers John Cheever's praiseworthy talent to be irredeemably defeated by this moral weakness: "Minor writers record not societies, or even allegories of societies, but vapid dreams and pageants of desire. . . . Cheever's suburbs are not really suburbs at all. . . . St. Botolphs . . . is a fabrication, a sort of Norman Rockwell cover done in the manner of Braque."[60] And when Cheever portrays the decay of his Yankee heritage in terms of ethnic snobbery—his Dr. Cameron is unmasked as né Bracciani—no amount of nostalgic rhapsodizing can make amends: "Oh, it is hard to be a Yankee—if only the Wapshots were, if not Braccianis, then Wapsteins—how they might then truly suffer. And we might truly feel."

Another telling example of evading reality that Ozick chooses to discuss is perpetrated by E. M. Forster—otherwise a great favorite of hers—in *Maurice,* his only overtly homosexual novel. Forster's irresponsibility lay in putting a wish at the heart of his work, rather than the will that brings a character up against life's genuine contingencies: "I was determined [she quotes Forster as saying] that . . . two men should fall in love and remain in it for the ever and ever that fiction allows" (AA 64). Ozick's allegiance to reality condemns this concept: "The essence of a fairy tale is that wishing *does* make it so. . . . In real life wishing, divorced from willing, is sterile. Consequently *Maurice* is . . . an infantile book, because, while pretending to be about societal injustice, it is really about make-believe, it is about wishing; so it fails even as a tract" (AA 64).

We may infer, then, that Ozick has chosen a middle ground for her work, rooting it in the hard contingencies of actual life on one hand (unlike those fantasists, Forster and Cheever), while imbuing it all with religious meaning on the other (unlike sociological novelists like Philip Roth or the Updike of

Bech). Talking with Elaine Kauvar, she defended the latter perspective as one that "goes to the root of every civilization":

> There's no civilization that hasn't had a religious aspect; until the world was quite old, there was no way to separate civilization from religion. I would think we can do that only for the last two hundred years. A person's religion *was* his civilization. It was his medicine, his science, his social structure, his politics. (Kauvar 379)

In this broad sense Ozick sees "Judaism in its ontological and moral aspects" as a heritage that "all of Western civilization shares," in that "you just can't have a Christian culture without understanding that it is also a Jewish culture."

Here Ozick appears to be shifting the balance of her longstanding mental conflict, subduing her hatred of Western/Christian civilization to the premise that "to be a Jew in Western civilization is to be part of the foundation." Her aesthetic creed shifts its ground likewise; though "completely torn and in an unholy conflict between moral seriousness and . . . aestheticism," she leans in the end toward Judaic humanism: "what else is a great novel going to be about if it isn't about humanity in society?" She appears to lapse from this standard into further conflict when she admits that "as a writer I absolutely wallow in mystery religion," despite being a rationalist in "both my personal inheritance and my temperamental being," but her ultimate allegiance as an artist is found in propositions reminiscent of Matthew Arnold and Henry James—that "life is nothing without art, . . . that experience, no matter how intense, is nothing at all without the potter's hand!" (Kauvar 380–81, 393, 377).

Ozick's most important early essay on the relation between moral seriousness and art was "The Jamesian Parable: *The Sacred Fount*" (in the *Bucknell Review* of May 1963). Not surprisingly, the essay is as revealing of Ozick herself as of her mentor. Crediting James's "perception of moral beauty" with an "influence . . . almost as forceful and definitive nowadays as Freud's," she relates James's work to "the Talmudic and Chassidic class of the parable" as well as to Gospel usage (58). In parable, she says, "the moral is *in* the tale, directly and immediately; without the moral, the tale is nothing" (59). Whereas Kafka is "an allegorist," in her view, "James is a teller of parables; and for him there must be so tight a fusion of object and meaning that the two resolve into an integer" (59). Thanks to this "unfissionable method of parable," James was able to rely "on direct insight, on instantaneous attestation, on primary apperception, . . . wherein the moral beings *are* the moral lesson" (68).

Two specific corollaries of this technique effect a lasting Ozick-James correlation. First, their use of parable works most often through negative example—that is, their main characters (as she says of James) are typically "negative moral beings—the values they espouse are evil because they are self-contradictory" (68). And most important, the evil they perpetrate consists primarily of some form of imposture. For Ozick as well as James, this is so vital a theme as to correlate *The Sacred Fount* with her total oeuvre as well as with its author's:

> What, then, in the parable, is the meaning of the sacred fount? . . . It is the natural balance of things, the human personality unmarred and untampered with. It is (and here again we recognize the full great chord of *the* Jamesian theme) self-realization, the completion of the potentialities of the self. He who desires to change himself, to become what he is not, contradicts himself, negates the integrity—the entelechy—of his personality. The self, like the fount, must always remain full; for once it is robbed or distorted or molested, it cannot replenish itself. . . . The drinker is seeking to become what he is not, and in this he is immoral. (69)

As against "the inherent urgency in his novels toward a celebration of life" (a Gentile L'Chaim! principle, we might say), Ozick thus construes James's parabolic method as showing us "his abhorrence of the 'unreal' in all those persons who are false to the code implicit in the conditions in which they find themselves—Madame Merle, for example, Merton Densher, Charlotte Stant, Ralph Pendrel, *et alia*" (70). Ozick's corresponding abhorrence of the unreal is shown in her characterization of apostate Jews who betray their heritage throughout all her fiction. As with James, her parables produce a procession of "negative moral beings" who seek to become what they are not.

This classic standard concerning the purpose of literature is further illuminated in two brief commentaries. In a Round Table discussion entitled "Culture and the Present Moment," Ozick rejected the Susan Sontag school of high camp with the claim that "artists themselves must stand up against [Sontag's book] 'Against Interpretation.' . . . There's not enough judgment— and by 'judgment' I mean not simply opinion, but bringing to bear on a work history, character, and other speculation."[61] Her adversary on the highbrow side is the playfully self-reflexive novel, a pure art object, against which she holds up the model of Thomas Hardy: "Hardy writes about— well, *life* . . . life observed and understood, as well as felt. A society . . . is set before us: in short, knowledge; knowledge of something real, something *there*" (AA 238). Hardy's high seriousness in turn imparts a permanent efficacy to his work: "Though Hardy was writing one hundred years ago,

. . . Hardy speaks to me now and I learn from him. He educates my heart, which is what great novels always do."[62] Although we cannot "turn back to the pre-Joycean 'fundamentalist novel,'" she goes on to say, that fact cannot excuse contemporary writers for having "led away from mastery . . . and from seriousness"—in a word, from Henry James's Art of Fiction and Matthew Arnold's Criticism of Life. With the loss of those qualities, she feels, the contemporary novel has ruinously vitiated that sort of suspense which comprises the novel's appeal to the intellect: "Suspense occurs when the reader is about to learn something, not simply about the relationship of fictional characters, but about the writer's relationship to a set of ideas, or to the universe" (AA 241). Or, as she put it in her preface to *Bloodshed*, "a story must not merely *be*, but mean. . . . I believe that stories ought to judge and interpret the world" (BL 4). Having now looked at this writer's "relationship to a set of ideas," we may be better prepared to see how her stories "judge and interpret the world." We turn now from the Matrix of Art to the art work itself.

2

Readings

Early Pieces

I used to submit a ms. every year to the Yale Series of Younger Poets, until I passed the age limit—40—and quit.

(Ltr 6/6/90)

In her mixed judgment of *Trust,* the huge novel that grandly wasted her youth, Ozick's one constant stance over the years has been her claims for its style. "I wanted to include a large range of *language,*" she wrote in 1982 (emphasis hers): "a kind of lyric breadth and breath" (Ltr 1/14/82). A decade later she recalled: "the energy and meticulous language-love that went into that book drew on sources that were never again so abundant. In certain ways it is simply an immensely long poem" (Ltr 7/20/91). Whether the sources were "never again so abundant" might be questioned; virtually all of Ozick's critics agree concerning the sustained mastery of style that permeates every part of Ozick's work. Her remark does serve as a reminder, however, of the poems she compiled during her earlier life as an artist. Space limits us here to a few representative specimens, beginning with a cluster written when she was about thirty.[1]

"Cant won't. Wont can't." Those four words, each given a full line, comprise the entirety of a poem entitled "Morals and Mores." Although the poem suits its title, its distaste for the nouns "Cant" and "Wont" (i.e., habit and custom) also defines Ozick's artistic creed of independence. In forms that range from rhyming quatrains to free verse, she displays her debt to mentors such as Blake, Dickinson, Whitman, and T. S. Eliot while still moving toward her eventual place among the most original voices of her generation. Of special interest are poems that adumbrate the central concerns of her later fictional oeuvre.

The conflict between gender and artistic needs is one of those themes, implicit in fiction such as *Trust* and "Virility" and explicit in the essays on women writers such as Virginia Woolf and Edith Wharton (two childless artists, as Ozick was until age thirty-seven). In "Five Lives" Ozick ruefully contrasts her persona's life—"I stayed at home and stuck to bed / and wrote and wrote and read and read"—with those of four acquaintances who "stuck to bed" more productively: Helaine, who cunningly snared "husband cot and cradle"; Vera, who married smart ("chose the brain worth dollars"); and two Carols, who "all have sons" as well as successful husbands. Another poem, "Terrain," uses landscape imagery and Emily Dickinson's hymnal stanza to defend this life of apparent deprivation for the sake of artistic struggle: "Those others call my life plateau / and cry me to their plain / as if a peak were point too low / to gain."

Perhaps the most interesting of these early poems are those that describe the psychology of the narrator of *Trust,* which was then in progress. "The Intruder" begins with "I am a voyeur of your loves: / outside, a neuter," and concludes with a series of sexual puns: "What armor [should I] give you against what arms? // O little sweated god Amor who watches over the tangled suitor." Another poem, "Fire-foe," portrays the conflict between Eros and Thanatos in terms of fire and ice, with the narrator turning the argument of "To His Coy Mistress" backwards: "You [the lover] snatch, I flee; / you thrive, I fail; / yet ice will trail / through you and me / equally." Because "The lustful and the tame / come to just the same," the speaker thinks it "easier by far to go / under the exacting snow / when the blaze is ashes-low / in the barren bush of No." Another losing battle of Love versus Death is dramatized in "Vision me old-age grief," whose narrator previsions herself as old and sexless with "body-sap suckled," enjoying "no immortality / of skin to skin" but rather enduring "shriveled sex and silent rooms." Even the immortality of having children will yield in the end to "filial shrieks among our tombs."

In a similar mood, "The Syllable"—a title referring to the pronoun "I"— evokes the prophet Isaiah's cry "All flesh is grass" in its master image of personal mortality: "The hale specked tower / of me, fretwork self I made— / this blade / arranged / upward—the mower / bent, / and frailed and changed to freckled hay." With the upper world deleted (the hay has been "taught / to be burned"), the grassblade-speaker turns to the underworld: "I have turned, // turned downward to the cruel / root-webbed well, / down to the nodule-thing of all, / down to the earth's eye." Here in the dead underground the lesson motif concludes as the speaker "learned: / I." A similar morbidity attends the speaker's birth in the cryptic "Apocalypse," published in *Commentary* in September 1959: "In my father's wife I grew like a worm.

Enslimed / I climbed from her grave. All the rest / is a dirty search for a dry crib." The infant-narrator then proceeds to satirize the idea of Original Sin by relating it to the narrator's loaded diapers: "On the twelfth day of the apothegmatical month I am asked what word / 'wipes out the sins of innumerable aeons.' I reply 'Your nose.'"

Sometimes the mood lightens, even in poems about death, thanks to Ozick's recourse to magic and parable that would later turn up in works like "The Pagan Rabbi" and "Usurpation." Nature-magic dominates "In the Yard," where the speaker's dead parents spectrally visit her fever-dream, their life and youth gloriously restored, but in the end the nature god reclaims them like Tilbeck's greenish sea: "they slyly faded out, becoming all little leaves / and grass and bush and everything green." A more realistic version of the pastoral mode is "Boston Air," which achieves its welcome to spring by sardonically reconceptualizing the grubbiness of the modern city: "the soot / will wisp like blown-seeds in the town," while the crush of cars become "Silver / herds" that crowd the thoroughfare. In "Urn-Burial," a poem that conjoins a lyric style with a narrative design, death assumes benignity through an extended religious parable. Here God allows men to live immortally in exchange for letting their possessions die, and they gradually lose precious or useful objects ranging from jewelry and money to clothing and plumbing. But in the end God accepts their appeal to reverse His edict, as the life of eternal stasis without possessions proves unbearable.

Various aspects of Ozick's Jewish sensibility find strong expression in three poems that suggest Enoch Vand's conversion in *Trust*. In "Diaspora" the Holocaust is evoked by so innocent an action as painting the front gate, an ironwork grill that had undergone previous repair work by an ethnic salad of Gentile owners—Fantelli, Schlaempfe, Hudson, and "Earliest, LeComte the Huguenot / [who] built the fence around the lot." The idea of Christmas wreaths hung on the gate by those owners rounds a sudden grim corner—"Santa sits by the fire, he likes to stoke / and watch the Jew go up in smoke"—and in no time flat the gate brings us up against the image of Auschwitz: "This fence has spikes and staves / like a pen." Like Enoch Vand working his way through Holocaust-despair, the poem nonetheless ends on a triumphant note: "Zion's seed / can wait and wait / for the holy fall / of every gate." Pending that messianic apotheosis, the gate does tease out one positive meaning from its Hitlerian shadows: "My grandfather's rags laugh to see me propertied." The struggle of American Jews to climb out of ancestral poverty, here capped by Ozick's status as a homeowner, produced in Cynthia Ozick a sensitivity to class identity that was to echo powerfully across her writing career.

Predictably, several poems of the early 1960s portrayed the frustrations,

sacrifices, and surprises of the artist's life—another recurrent theme of
Ozick's fiction. "Visitation," in the fall 1962 *Prairie Schooner,* recalls Hawthorne's "The Artist of the Beautiful" in its depiction of the artwork as a
beautiful fragile cobweb that is "shattered / by the crass gross army-footed
blunt blind tap / of boots." But like Owen Warland, Ozick's spider-artist
will shrug off this callousness of a philistine public: "My decimated web,
like a city of war, / will summon hidden spittle for rebuilding." "The Artist,
Ha Ha," in the *Literary Review* of spring 1962, recalls Henry James and
Yeats in its rueful portrait of the artist as an encaved hermit, trading her life
for her work: "So do not linger now to live: / turn your back within the cave. /
At its mouth a stone is hurled. / Turn your back: it was the World." But
another poem, "Stile," in the *Virginia Quarterly Review* of winter 1962,
defines the artist's reward—an unexpected beauty that can suddenly irradi-
ate the humble artwork: "The filigree of snow / That is my neighbor's fence /
(An ordinary rail, with staves) / Suggests a secret immanence." (Ozick's
other poem on this page appears startlingly prophetic in view of its 1962
date: "While in the Convention they were nominating the Next President of
the United States, / I thought of death: / . . . Death the dark, dark horse.")

The final two poems we shall consider were printed in *Voices within the
Ark: The Modern Jewish Poets* (Pushcart Press: Yonkers, 1980)—a book
that includes generous samplings of Ozick's favorite Yiddish and Hebrew
poets, including Hayim Bialik (of "Bialik's Hint"), Jacob Glatstein (Edelshtein in "Envy"), and Shaul Tchernikhovsky (in "Usurpation"). Here Ozick's
"The Wonder-Teacher" confirms her preference for rational rather than
romantic religion, for ordinary life over the extraordinary, as her epony-
mous rabbi impresses his pupils not when he levitates, "[waiting] in air for
the unknotting of the Name," but rather when he "slept like any one of us,
as if to scorn / all prodigy. We huddled near the marvel of his lung."[2] The
other poem, "A Riddle," describes a creature with two disparate feet—"The
right wears a tough boot and is steadfast. / The other is got up in a Baby-
lonish slipper of purple laces." The answer to the riddle discloses Ozick's
dualistic concept of Judaic biblical commentary, which points a contrast
between "Aggada (legend, tale, and lore) and Halachah (law and code)."

An engaging instance of this double-footed approach to art—and the
final early work we have space to consider—is "The Sense of Europe," a
story published in the *Prairie Schooner* of summer 1956, at about the same
time as the genesis of *Trust.* Early as it is, appearing when the writer was
twenty-eight, it nonetheless displays an absolutely distinctive voice—only
Cynthia Ozick could possibly have written this story—and it presents a
preview that reaches from *Trust* to Puttermesser. The title, belying its Jamesian urbanity, refers instead to the "terrible and corrupted heritage" of the

Nazi era with its "old throbbings of fear and flight" (135, 133). Making the
sense of Europe worse is the sense of America as a place of Jewish alienation, thanks to the assimilationist craving of the narrator's Allegra Vand-
like mother:

> My mother despised my face, studying it daily and lamenting over the heavy
> curly hair that broke the comb as she combed it, over my dark thick oily
> features, brooding like a Persian's or an Arab's. . . . Even the placid plainness
> of the other [Christian] girls would have pleased my mother, their blue-eyed
> looks full of confidence and pleasant things. . . . I might as well have been an
> East European ghetto Jewess or, which was after all the same thing, a New
> York East Side Jewess (my mother always said "Jewess," just as our Gentile
> neighbors did)—and my father would say . . . "well, she's a throwback, I guess
> she's a throwback to the scissors-grinder . . . my stepgrandfather Lester." (129)

The scissors grinder's rise to affluence in the hardware trade is a familiar
American-Jewish story, though its setting in the Deep South, however historically valid, is not so familiar. What makes this story distinctively Ozick's
is the parable she contrives with the marriage of this deracinated narrator
and a boy-man from "Europe." The husband, a Frenchman studying at
Heidelberg, was himself victimized by German brutality in the 1930s, so
badly that his mother committed suicide over it, but neither that experience
nor the subsequent war and Holocaust have enlarged his moral stature—a
stature symbolized by his dwarflife appearance ("tiny and beautiful like a
perfect little mannikin," 127). On the contrary his ("Europe's") narcissism
indicates arrested development as he opens the story fixated on his face in
the mirror: "scrutinizing his molars [he] looks like a nine-year-old-boy"
(126). Not only boylike, he has become girllike in his obsession with having
an immaculate appearance—"he shaves under his arms like a woman and
cares for his skin with fragrant white soap . . . [and] now he will tweeze his
eyebrows with me in the same room" (126).
   Of course the marriage fails as he abandons his heavy, homely "Jewess" in
favor of someone like himself, a "chattering bird-like exchange teacher from
France" (137). In this gesture Jacques reminds us—rightly, I would say—of
Paul de Man, writing in 1942 that Europe was culturally better off without
its worthless Jews. But the point of the story is that the Jews *were* "the Sense
of Europe," and their absence reduces "Europe" to the status of a pretty art
object, diminutive and narcissistic and culturally impotent under the charming surface:

> For in spite of his perfection, in spite of his exquisite and museum-like duplica-
> tion of some rare, half-sacred, and beautiful semblance of life, the bridegroom

was impotent. He was impotent and effete, as a wax image is without the possibility (and without will or desire for the possibility) to make life. (136)

In addition to the golemlike character of the bridegroom (a golem also cannot create life), his vampirish nature gradually becomes manifest, "Europe" having subsisted all along on its Jewish bloodstream: "Only then I did not know he was using me up, draining me like a flask of magic serum to keep him alive and moving." The Holocaust thus destroyed both Europe and its Jews, the apparent survival of both being a surface appearance only:

> we began to decay together. It was a horrible, weird decay. . . . like two painted corpses which are not allowed to be dead in which the sign, but not the meaning, of life is perpetrated by a mechanical device compelling the two hearts to pump, to continue to pretend hollow aliveness. (136)

With this story, the path was open for Ozick's seven-year apprenticeship to *Trust*, the huge novel in which this deadly weight of Jewish history plays off against a contrary impulse toward L'Chaim! and Sacred Beauty. In the end, I shall argue, the conflicted mind of the artist tilts toward the latter pole of her thought in that masterwork of her middle career, but "The Sense of Europe" is a strong reminder of how close a margin obtains.[3]

Trust: A Kunstlerroman

> *Trust* went on and on for so many years [seven] that I was able to achieve, during its composition, wholesale revisions of self, vast turnabouts of personality and character.
> (Ltr 1/14/82)

American literature has featured a number of major novels in which the search for a father forms the essential plot line. Faulkner's Charles Bon comes to mind, in *Absalom, Absalom!*, as does Jack Burden in Robert Penn Warren's *All the King's Men*, and for that matter the actual gist of the Horatio Alger stories (as opposed to their rags-to-riches surface theme). Perhaps it was Thomas Wolfe who stated the idea of father hunger most compellingly:

> The deepest search in life, it seemed to me, the thing that in one way or another was central to all living was man's search to find a father, not merely the father of his flesh, not merely the lost father of his youth, but the image of a strength and wisdom external to his need and superior to his hunger, to which the belief and power of his own life could be united.[4]

Particularly as related to the concluding part of this statement, there have been many novels, written by men, about fathers and sons; rather few, written by women, about fathers and daughters. *Trust* is just such a book, whose quite remarkable climax fixes upon the way a young woman's "belief and power" are united with a long-sought father image.

For its originality and evocative power, that climactic scene of *Trust* is a piece of great literature, something to justify the preceding five hundred pages where Ozick pursued her plan "to write a novel about Everything, about politics, love, finance, etc. etc." (Ltr 1/14/82). The ground theme that unifies these disparate motifs, including the father hunger, is the venerable theme of self-discovery. Through most of her twenty-one years, the book's narrator does not know her own name. Because "her [mother's] aim was to re-father me" (58), she has borne the name of her mother's first husband while living under the roof of the second, only to be informed in the year of her majority that she is "illegitimate issue" because her mother and her biological father never married. That natural father is the mystery man whose identity the narrator must uncover before she can know herself. Until then, she remains a nameless narrator, like Ellison's Invisible Man.

The four sections of *Trust* are titled after the place-names most relevant to her self-knowledge. "Part One: America" describes her present sojourn with mother in the New York area where, while planning postgraduation travel in Europe, she receives word that her Prodigal Father has demanded her presence at Duneacres, the abandoned "marine museum" her maternal grandfather established. "Part Two: Europe" recalls the girl's first encounter with her father at age ten, when he visited her mother in Paris to extort money from her. "Part Three: Brighton" describes the mother's vagabond youth, with major focus on the seaside resort in England where the narrator was born. "Part Four: Duneacres," picking up the narrative thread suspended since Part One, describes the last fateful encounter of father and daughter over a two-day period.

Together, the three father figures in *Trust* represent Ozick's three cultural matrices—WASP, Jewish, and pagan Greek. William, her mother's first husband, appears to be a model of WASP order and rectitude (it is he who calls her "illegitimate issue"). Enoch, the second husband, is a Jew whose keenly original intellect appeals strongly to the narrator. And Gustave Nicholas Tilbeck is the illicit lover who fathered the narrator, thereby dissolving her mother's first marriage. Although he appears by conventional judgment to be utterly disreputable—an irresponsible hedonist, runaway father, vagabond, ne'er-do-well, sponge, and blackmailer—in the end Tilbeck becomes the role model his daughter has longed for and the unlikely repository of her "Trust": a man of spontaneous passion, of faunlike immersion in the moment, of Greek/pagan heresies, suggesting the "spontaneous gods of nature" that Ozick has associated with E. M. Forster.[5]

The heresy that Tilbeck lives by and which in the end engages his daughter's allegiance is the subject of an essay written by her stepfather, Enoch Vand: "It's called Pan versus Moses. It's about Moses making the Children of Israel destroy all the grotto shrines and greenwood places. . . . It's about how Moses hates Nature" (557). What produces the turn toward Pan, or more precisely the return to Pan, is the crisis in culture that Ozick portrays in exceptional breadth and detail. Like Henry James, she juxtaposes Europe and America, but with a view of the subject that Henry James was spared because of his death in 1916. It is true that James was incredulous and heartbroken to have to witness, after a lifetime of treating the "international theme," the outbreak of World War I; but his agony must seem positively enviable compared with Ozick's view of the scene following the Holocaust. In *Trust* the two characters who represent the before and after of that unspeakable fragment of history are the narrator's mother and stepfather, Allegra and Enoch Vand.[6] The year the war ends, Allegra brings her young daughter to Europe in a Jamesian rage to ingest its superior culture while Enoch Vand is pursuing his job, as a functionary for the State Department, of listing the names of death camp victims:

> She had brought me to see the spires . . . and minarets like overturned goblets, and . . . she promised from this fountain of the world (she called it life, she called it Europe) all spectacle, dominion, energy, and honor. And all the while she never smelled death there. . . . But it was deathcamp gas . . . that plagued his head and . . . swarmed from his nostrils to touch those unshrouded tatooed carcasses of his, moving in freight cars over the gassed and blighted continent. (78)

Even though too young, at age ten, to understand the Holocaust, the narrator leans toward her stepfather's rather than mother's view of Europe. On approaching the German border, she vomits on a German tank and makes a map of Europe with her vomit (63), and later she repeats the motif with another map of Europe traced in the stale urine and blood left on her hotel mattress (116).

An admirer of Europe, Allegra Vand is a compendium of American errors and follies representing the bankruptcy of her native culture. In politics, art, religion, and family life, her immense wealth as heiress to a trust fund has turned her life into a series of pathetic gestures. In her youth, a binge with a radical political organization led her to write a bad novel, *Marianna Harlow*, that became a best-seller in Stalin's Soviet Union. As an older person, she has been contriving to get her husband appointed ambassador to a country with an aristocratic tradition. In the eyes of her daughter, Allegra's two sexless/childless marriages are the worst thing of all, proving the failure of love.

The root of corruption is of course her money, which in Jamesian fashion has stirred predatory instincts among her acquaintances. As a would-be artist, Allegra is patroness to a poetry magazine called *Bushelbasket* and its poet-parasite editor who boasts: "I am an instance of private enterprise. The Edward McGoverns of the world are luxuries which only the very rich can afford" (41). And her two husbands—to say nothing of her blackmailing ex-lover—are deeply conscious of her financial well-being. Even after the divorce, her first husband, William, is willing to stay on as Allegra's trustee and lawyer: "They were all bought, after all, as Ed McGovern has not been afraid to express it . . . even the incorruptible William, who had put her away as his wife, . . . was bought and paid for" (41). So surrounded, the narrator, wearing a silver and gold graduation dress specially ordained by her mother, feels rank with vicarious corruption: "There was the sick breath of money upon all of us; it rushed out dirtily, as from a beggar's foul mouth . . ., full of waste . . . trivial and tedious" (36).

As that sickness metaphor indicates, the failures of the parents infect the next generation. Thus the narrator is altogether adrift through most of the text, her keen intelligence mainly devoted to skepticism, distrust, and revulsion concerning every aspect of her cultural nurture. Her sole instance of passion is an ephemeral flaring up of love toward William's son, but this seems occasioned by fellow-feeling in that he too abjures his parents and their bankrupt way of life. His fiancée, Stefanie, is a brainless chatterbox whose interest in him appears motivated by his prospective moneyed future, so that in the younger generation the cycle of mercenary marriage looks likely to repeat itself.

Ultimately, the crisis of culture pervading *Trust* is a religious one, caused by the contemporary inability of parents or society to provide beliefs to live by. *Trust* is trellised throughout with allusion to religious figures—Christ, Buddha, Moses, Poseidon, Pan, even Allah—and to religious myth and imagery. And this is where Tilbeck, for all his disreputable ways, proves the answer to the "quest for consequence" (519) as the various threads of the novel lead to his concluding apotheosis. In virtually every respect, Gustave Nicholas Tilbeck is a contrapuntal opposite to the book's perverted ideologies. Named after Swedish and Russian royalty, such as Allegra Vand pines after, he chooses to flaunt his descent from a common Swedish sailor who "died frozen drunk in the streets of Seattle" (457)—a world-wandering grandfather as free-spirited as Tilbeck himself. His disdain for social status is matched by his Thoreau-esque disinterest in having money or its symbols.

The narrator's earliest memory of Tilbeck, when as a girl she eavesdropped on a conversation in the adjoining hotel room (she never saw his face), focuses on the ancient bicycle, leaning splashed with mud and rain, that marked his arrival. (Contrapuntally, that same weekend Allegra wrecked her limousine during a stint of illegal and dangerous driving.)

Tilbeck's blackmailing of Allegra, it turns out, is a matter of amusement and curiosity for him, and of contemptuous protest, rather than a serious extortion scheme: he wants to measure just how much her spurious respectability means in her life. He always throws away the hush money she sends on prostitutes or other frivolities, and when the opportunity arises for real extortion—he could ruin the prospective ambassador's appointment by disclosing his own fathering of the love child—it is clear that for this score of years the whole process has been a bluff she could have called at any time without retribution. It is noteworthy that Tilbeck was her faithful companion during the only period of poverty in Allegra's life, while she was waiting in England for her child to be born and for her trust fund to begin yielding its opulence. When, after the child's (our narrator's) birth, he wandered off toward the Mediterranean, he seemed to be testing whether she would give up all she had and follow him. Instead, despite her passionate yearning for him, she took her child and dowry back to the shelter of married respectability, with her first husband staying on as her trustee and her second one opening up superior access to "Europe."

Concerning this theme, too—of "Europe"—Tilbeck plays a role of contrapuntal reversal. Whereas Enoch Vand (though born in Chicago) comes out of the Europe of unspeakable horror, which Allegra never sees, Tilbeck as a Swede represents a Europe untainted by the Holocaust; and as a neo-pagan he embodies the freely expressed life force of the Europe of classical times, before either Christ or Moses imposed their Puritan denials. Moreover, while Allegra hearkens toward the Old World of palaces and pageantry, Tilbeck reverses this motif of Jamesian pilgrimage by flying an American flag on his bicycle in Paris, a reminder of the energy and adventurousness of that Europe whose denizens journeyed abroad to create America. Tilbeck, in sum, is a singular example of Europe at its best, made all the more attractive by the book's otherwise ruinous expanse of cultural negations.

In *Trust* those negations cover the most fundamental issues of any culture: money (as we have seen), sex, and God. Sex—including marriage and the family—is the first of these issues to appear overtly. In chapter 1, as the rites of graduation are concluding, a little girl tells the narrator, "My sister's getting married tomorrow," thereby evoking that greater rite of passage that normally is indispensable to any young woman's sense of identity: "There was a shimmer of mass marriages. . . . Envy . . . ought not be accounted sinful, for sinning is what we do by intent, and envy . . . desires us against our will" (3). But in this novel of the Eisenhower-Kennedy years, marriage is virtually moribund. Most of the husband figures—Purse, Enoch, William, William's son—are either literally or emotionally cuckolded (by Tilbeck, in each instance), and even apart from this prevalence of sexual mistrust, marriage is an institution of social-economic convenience rather than a form for the containment of passion.

The ultimate negations are those that pertain to religion. For the narrator, a Gentile, Christianity has become meaningless if not actually harmful, mainly because it is for her a "Romantic Religion," as Leo Baeck described it.[7] Its otherworldliness turns Christian doctrine into gibberish, as seen in the narrator's response to the Trinity. "I had once actually confused the Holy Ghost with a new kind of candy bar," she says (59); the Son for her is "the bitter and loveless Christ" of "redemption, that suspect covenant" (38); and the Father actually delivered a piece of excrement rather than a Savior with regard to perhaps the most celebrated of all New Testament verses (John 3.16): "God so loved the world that he gave his only begotten dung" (279). For the narrator this world cannot be so wishfully dealt with: "the irretrievable can never be returned to us; and there is no alternative but to go on with the facts exactly as they are" (38).

Enoch Vand, a Jew, theologizes this view of Christianity as a version of the flight reflex. After correcting Jesus' promise of paradise—"The house of death hath many mansions" (80)—he states the main Jewish objection to it:

> Christ was one of Enoch's great villains . . . not merely for his cruelty in inventing and enforcing a policy of damnation, but more significantly for his removal of the Kingdom of Heaven to heaven, where, according to Enoch, it had no business being allowed to remain . . . and ought instead to be brought down again as rapidly as possible by the concerted aspiration and fraternal sweat of the immediate generation. (375)

To complete the negation of Christianity there remains only the travesty of Christian charity expressed by William's new wife, who speaks of "Christian mercy" and contempt for non-WASPS (the Irish) in almost the same breath (360–61). And William himself finally reveals beneath his Presbyterian facade nothing more than old-time Calvinist confusion between God and Mammon, "his preoccupation with ownership being a further example of his Calvinist probity" (59).

In the person of Enoch Vand, the Jewish faith is as bankrupt as Christianity, but at a much higher level of intellectual integrity. What has ruined modern Judaism is its recent encounter with "Lady Moloch," with "her diadem of human teeth and ankle-ring of human hair," who has substituted for Torah Enoch's Book of the Dead, "the black canvas of that ledger held on that priestly spot [Enoch's heart] like a tablet of the Law" (102). So Enoch, and apparently the narrator with him, leans toward atheism: "Kein Gott ist" (136). Even the Holocaust, to him, is just a prototype of "the magnificent Criminal plan" for the whole species: "Who can revere a universe which will take that lovely marvel, man (. . . aeons of fish straining toward the dry, gill into lung, paw into the violinist's and dentist's hand), and turn him into a carbon speck?" (373). For a time he had held to the Jewish belief "that whatever you come upon that seems unredeemed exists for the sake of permitting you the sacred opportunity to redeem it"; but now he has learned that "God [is] the God of an unredeemed monstrosity," and "the world isn't merely unredeemed:—worse worse worse, it's unredeemable" (397, 398). So Enoch is not so far removed from the Christian flight reflex after all, as the narrator reminds him: "'You're waiting for the Messiah then,' was all I ventured. He strangely did not deny it" (191). Until that inconceivable supernatural intervention, there is for Enoch only a deepening revulsion against the world's monstrous uncleanness: "'The trouble is the brooms don't work. Nothing works,' he said. . . . 'There's no possibility of cleaning up. . . . It's the whole world that's been dipped in muck. . . . You can't clean murder away'" (191).

For the narrator, the question that Enoch's attitude defines is how, or whether, one's life can be sustained in a world "not only unredeemed but unredeemable." It is a question that other Jewish writers have spent a lifetime raising and answering, most notably Saul Bellow—whose "whole fiction," Ozick says, "is a wrestling with the Angel of Theodicy."[8] For Ozick, unlike the others, the answer comes from pagan antiquity. For the modern religious sensibility, she suggests, recovery of the L'Chaim! ("To Life!") principle must come by a Hellenic rather than Hebraic access, for it was the old Greeks who most deeply immersed their religious imagination in the natural world, seeing a divine essence in sun and sea, tree and mountain, and—above all—in the immense creative force of sexuality.

In *Trust,* that last element of nature is far and away the most crucial, evoking celibate Christ and taboo-promulgating Moses—both serving a God who created life without sex—in radical contrast to the pagan worship of Venus/Astarte. In treating this theme with a power and seriousness that are rare—perhaps unique—among Jewish writers, Ozick contributes to a major tradition in American literature. One thinks of John Updike pitting the last Christian, George Caldwell, against the horde of neopagan hedonists in *The Centaur* (they celebrate their total victory in *Couples*); of Faulkner running his doomed worshipers of Aphrodite to their defeat by a "Christian" society in *The Wild Palms;* of Henry Adams musing over the Virgin's unaccountable victory over Venus in *The Education;* of Ralph Waldo Emerson owning the supreme power of Love ("Men and gods have not outlearned it") in his poem "Eros." Ultimately, they all hearken back to actual pagan literature in antiquity, of which a chorus in Sophocles' *Antigone* is an excellent example. "Where is the equal of Love?" they chant—

> In the farthest corners of the earth, in the midst of the sea,
> He is there; he is here
> . . . .
> And the grip of his madness
> Spares not god or man. . . .
> At the side of the great gods
> Aphrodite immortal
> Works her will upon all.[9]

Tilbeck's role as avatar of a pagan fertility god enables him to lift his daughter from the mire of Christian/Mosaic "uncleanness" that would otherwise enclose her identity as "bastard" or "illegitimate issue." Her path to enlightenment is thus the path from the (Mosaic) "clean" to the (Bacchic) "dirty"; her gain in wisdom is measured by juxtaposing the girl in the white dress of chapter 1, fearing to get her shoes muddy, and the same girl ecstatic amid the filth, rust, and decay of Town Island, where the liberating god himself is last seen, after his death by water, smeared with his own green vomit. It is dirt, in the end, that fosters life and nourishes it—as the nine Purses so engagingly illustrate—leaving the "clean" people like William and Enoch marooned in their sterile and deathsome sanctity.

The importance of this transformation of the religious sensibility—the most momentous thing in the book—is borne out by the elaborate web of allusions and images that threads through the text. Scattered across that web we find fragments suggesting those that T. S. Eliot shored against his ruins: Yahweh, Buddha, Norse and Greek deities, and scenes from *The Golden Bough* fade in and out like the bass line of a melody. Initially, in her "clean" period, the narrator correlates sexuality with Evil, as Semitic myth teaches: "presumably those rivalrous siblings [Cain and Abel] were not yet born while their parents were innocent; that indeed is the point of the story. The connection between Evil and the birth of the next generation is intimate" (446). From this standpoint, she regards her father, with shame, as resembling a primitive sea god, reptilian (with "the patient lids of a lizard"), crudely sexual (lying "among shells with their open cups waiting"), and cruelly rapacious for his blackmail:

like a terrible Nile-god Gustave Nicholas Tilbeck invaded, vanished, and reap-
peared. Nothing could assure his eclipse but propitiation . . . and my mother,
as enraged as any pagan by a vindictive devil, had to succumb. . . . Money
came to him at last where he lay, and he blinked his torpid jaundiced lids and
was content. (11–12)

Even so, the god's allure also breaks through from the beginning, investing
her gold-and-silver graduation gown, originally a symbol of her mother's
crass opulence, with her father's nature imagery: "the dress she had bought
for me singed my skin with a blaze of gold and silver, the hot gold of my
father's beach and the burning silver of his sea" (23).

Throughout *Trust* the sea is a crucial motif. For Allegra, the sea's murk
and slime harbor not a sea god but a sea monster who comes, rapacious and
unclean, to invade her shelter—"that Tilbeck who rose from the murk like a
half-forgotten creature of the strait to claim his tribute (I was educated
enough in myth to know that in every tale of this sort it is a daughter who is
taken to feed the slime)" (186). Allegra's father, however—the superrich
founder of her trust fund—had been a compulsive mariner who bequeathed
his seaside estate to establish a marine museum. He meant this place, Duneacres on Town Island, to illuminate the religious-scientific truths that con-
join myth and biology: "I'll give the place to the sea. Every room to be a
mansion for Neptune—sea-nymphs everywhere. . . . Let it be a History of
the Origin of Life" (296); and again:

> People are wrong, you know, when they talk of Mother Earth. It's Father
> Neptune who takes us in our last days. . . . Blood is salt water, like the sea,
> which never left us though we left it. . . . All of mankind's wrung with
> drunkard's thirst for the sea. In my view that's the explanation for religion.
> (295)

Apart from so honoring the prime matrix of life and myth, the marine
museum becomes a master metaphor for the crisis of culture that undergirds
this novel. Disdained and ignored by Allegra and Enoch (the modern and
secular), closed up and left to decay by William (a Presbyterian Calvinist),
Duneacres while serving as Tilbeck's habitation gradually gathers its force
of psychic retaliation, foretelling a return of the repressed in the offing:
Tilbeck's Dionysian backlash against the contemporary Apollonian. Beneath
the surface realism of style a current of allegory thus becomes manifest:
"Surely my father, constituting present evidence of a buried time, was a sort
of museum," the narrator muses; "he housed matters which had to be dug
after, collected bit by bit, and reconstructed" (56). This imagery, which
adumbrates precisely the central theme and plot line of the whole narrative,

leads to further allegorical meanings whereby, apropos of the reduction of Duneacres to "fossil museum" status, Tilbeck reveals that his real motive for blackmail is not money but recognition:

> "I see it does you good," the visitor said softly, "to think of me as a fossil."
> "I never think of you at all."
> "Never?"
> "You're not there. You don't exist," she repeated.
> "I'm perfectly willing not to exist . . . for someone else . . . as long as I can manage to exist for *you*. . . . Well, put it that one wants a little acknowledgement. . . . Of who one is; of what one is." (condensed from 120–22)

Who and what Tilbeck is—a question as central as who and what Gatsby or Kurtz or Moby Dick is—gradually comes clear by means of allusions and imagery from pagan antiquity. For his daughter the earliest hint of her father's true character lies in the book that drops from his rain-soaked bicycle during the encounter in Paris. Immediately before this moment—one page earlier—the scene was set by the young girl's religious speculation: "I was wondering if there's a God. . . . If there *is* a God, is it the same God for everywhere? I mean, the same in America as here? . . . I wish there were a different one for America" (150). With an American flag flying from his bicycle—"a sort of glorious and healthful omen of America," his daughter thinks (165)—this avatar of a different god drops his "ENCHIRIDION: OF WOODLAND FLOWERS" for his daughter's perusal, in which one flower in particular rivets her attention: "'Jewelweed; Wild Touch-Me-Not,' said the caption. . . . 'The name Touch-Me-Not almost certainly derives from the quick, spasmodic action of its ripe seed-pods which instantly erupt at a touch and spurt their seeds in every direction'" (151–52). Seed-spurting flowers are not the only clue to Tilbeck's identity. "Ah, you're clammy. You don't feel clean," her mother says (164); in lifting Tilbeck's book from the mud the girl makes her first step in the long trek from the clean to the dirty. Meanwhile, in the background of this encounter with her father, a quartet of honeymooners engage in open sexual play (they may have been bride swapping) with a zest that offends Allegra and the landlady but evokes for the narrator the old amphorae: "They raced across the dewy grass like Greek runners" (163).

The conflict between Pan and Moses concerning sex reaches maximum intensity in the scene where William's painful euphemisms for the narrator's illegitimacy ("the circumstances of my birth—how indecently priggish and Dickensian that sounds," 274) place Tilbeck's role invitingly in focus, "as though, while standing solemnly in court, about to be sentenced, I had caught sight of the god Pan at the window, clutching a bunch of wild flowers . . . and laughing a long and careless jingle of a laugh, like bicycle bells" (274). In this context the fall of Pan measures well the failure of the Western religious imagination. Worshiped in antiquity as the god of spontaneous life—of wine, sex, the dance—Pan was appropriated by the Christian fathers and so transformed that his faun shape became identified with the Christians' devil. Tilbeck's role is to reverse that epoch-making error. To Allegra, of course, Tilbeck retains the conventional devil's penumbra, leaving "an unmistakable cloven hoof eloquently delineated in slime" (153), and his nickname—Nick—reminds us of one of the devil's common appellations. But Tilbeck says the name Nicholas represents his "part Greek" ancestry, which combines with the Norse to open multiple possibilities: "'Nick?' he said. 'Why not Thor? Why not Loki? Why not Apollo? . . . Well, in my time they didn't call babies Zeus—' 'Or Pan' [I offered]" (474).

As the narrative advances toward its climax, a Dionysian procession of pagan figures appears to be gathering, leaving all manner of verbal traces: "the goat-hooves of Venus and Pan" (334); "religious processions for Dionysus and Demeter" (343); "the divine . . . Bacchus" (519); "Poseidon . . . Cupid" (536); "Circe and her pale herd" (450); "Thor at the clavier" (511); "a god of the Nile" (511); "He [Tilbeck] has an island right off Greece" (435); "He [Tilbeck] looked like a faun" (473). Tilbeck's domain at Duneacres, when finally approached, appears suitable for such an inhabitant. Ritualistically commanded to appear alone with no guide or escort, the narrator travels a "road as buried now as Caesar's" (424), then is rowed to the island by a Charon-like youth with "eye-glasses twinkling light like semaphores" (426)—though we come to see that this is a reversal of the classical passage: the world she has left behind, that of Enoch's Moloch and William's Mammon, is the realm of the dead, while the island before her harbors, like an Eleusinian mystery, nature's deeply immanent Life Force.

Bespeaking this Life Force, and radiant with its kabbalistic power, is the tree that guards the way to Tilbeck's island. Gathering vast affinities in its branches—to the Golden Fleece, the Burning Bush, the Tree of Life and Tree of Knowledge, the Buddha's bo tree of Enlightenment, the druid's sacred oak—it signals the beginning of the narrator's apprehension of Sacred Beauty, a term that her mother had defined during *her* initiation (with Tilbeck at Brighton) twenty-one years ago: "If you want to know what I mean by Sacred I mean anything that's alive, and Beauty is anything that makes you want to *be* alive and alive forever, with a sort of shining feeling" (337). (Allegra's short-lived phase as "an ancient Greek" also centered upon a "holy looking" tree outside their cottage window: "Most trees are atheists, but not this one," 337). Which is to say, Sacred Beauty is what makes Enoch Vand's "unredeemable world" not only redeemable but redeemed. First described as bushlike, with a "comb of yellow leaf stained through by sunlight . . ., the whole blown head of it coruscating like a transparent great net of caught fishes"—an image linking the tree to Tilbeck's sea realm—the tree soon becomes animate with religious meaning:

> Lens upon lens burned in the leaves with a luminosity just short of glass and nearer to vapor; the veins were isinglass ducts swarming with light. . . . A radiance lifted itself from the shoulders of the tree and hung itself, by some unknown manner of passage, close against my face, so that, to see, I had to stare through a tissue of incandescence. . . . The tree was an eye. It observed me. The tree was a mind. It thought me. . . . It burned for me, it leaped all whiteness and all light into being, and for me. . . . I was its god, my gaze had forced its fires, the sanctity of my wonder had quickened its awe. . . . I appeared like a god or goddess . . . as once the Buddha sat and stared, and, seeing, showed himself divine; I was nymph, naiad, sprite, goddess; I had gifts, powers. . . . (424–25)

Although the vision collapses—"Then it was snuffed. The light went out of it. The sun slid down and away" (425)—her passage to Tilbeck's island brings fresh epiphanies through the agency of some surprising companions. Her boatman, "a sort of Norse centaur, the top half human, the lower half presumably the parts of a boat" (426–27), is one of seven siblings in the Purse family, whom Tilbeck has invited to stay at Duneacres a few days while they wait for their plane flight to Pakistan. There, Purse senior will dig for "humanoid bones" on a Ford Foundation grant; in the interim Tilbeck's "fossil museum" should satisfy both his professional interest and a serious need to save money.

The nine Purses contribute three elements to the novel's climax: they emanate a Dickens-cum-Marx Brothers comic flair; they function as ancillaries to the initiation rites on Town Island; and they step into the role of ambassadors from America that Enoch and Allegra fail to fulfill. In a novel replete with Jamesian echoes—it even quotes verbatim the opening sentence of *The Portrait of a Lady* (451)—this portrayal of America's real representatives becomes in itself an initiation motif for the narrator, who was born in Europe and has known only Allegra's wealth-insulated leisure-class America. Like Tilbeck, the Purses constitute a counterpoint to the book's opening cultural negations.

As a compendium of both the strengths and petty vices of Middle America, the Purse family (from New Rochelle, New York—Ozick's hometown) exhibits a checklist of representative American traits. Adventurous (the whole family is moving to Pakistan), resourceful (they live mainly by their wits), high-spirited (they are inveterate game players), mildly acquisitive (as befits their name), and pragmatic (they profess no ideology), the Purses realize the middle-class ideal of self-improvement through the "diffusion of competence" that Eric Hoffer thought the most distinctive characteristic of American culture. The mother, for example, is a superb auto mechanic, and even the small children are studying Urdu. Unlike Allegra and Enoch, they will make fine ambassadors.

Amplifying their quintessence of Americanism are the names of the Purse children, four of which refer to the great transcendentalist writers—Manny, Sonny, Throw, and Al being Whitman, Emerson, Thoreau, and Bronson Alcott respectively. The only daughter is Harriet Beecher Stowe Purse, and the other two boys are named after exceptionally admirable religious leaders— Dee and Foxy being Mohandas K. Gandhi and George Fox Purse. Of these names, Emerson's appears most significant, partly because it turns up elsewhere in the novel (e.g., 319), but mostly because it clarifies the religious meaning of this episode.[10] In the end it is the Purse family that certifies what the narrator had envisioned as a young girl, "a different God for America."

Nominally the Purses are Quakers, or Friends—which is to say, members of a peaceable sect unstained by Christendom's history of bloody violence and hypocrisy—but in practice they radiate a pagan mentality, savoring each moment with passionate vitality. Theirs is the stance Emerson calls for in his essay "Circles": "In nature every moment is new; the past is always swallowed and forgotten; the coming only is sacred. Nothing is secure but life, transition, the energizing spirit."[11] And their God is actually the "spontaneous gods of nature" that Ozick associated with E. M. Forster but which also evoke the Emerson of "Experience": "Nature, as we know her, is no saint. . . . She comes eating and drinking and sinning. . . . We must set up the strong present tense against all the rumors of wrath, past or to come" (263). Even the Quaker Inner Light suggests Emersonian rather than orthodox theology: "Jesus Christ belonged to the true race of prophets," Emerson said in his notorious "Divinity School Address"; "He saw that God incarnates himself in man, and evermore goes forth anew to take possession of his World" (105). Certainly the Purses are doing their best to emulate this model.

So the Purses become part of the Dionysian procession that moves into Tilbeck's magic island, with Mrs. Purse taking the role of Circe, and her youngest cherub—who is usually nude and hyperactive to an airborne degree—serving as a Cupid surrogate. Circe's fabled powers of transformation are in this instance limited to the junk that litters the island (she gets castaway engines running); her nightly trysts with Tilbeck signify her larger importance as a sort of love goddess whose previous adventures may well have bred illegitimate issue: "Was he really Purse's son, the splendid savage child . . .? Or had Circe coupled with a hero while Purse lay bound in the snores of an aging athlete?" (481). At the same time she evokes other pastoral/sexual nuances, including "Eve in Paradise on the world's sixth day, surrounded by the forms of nature" (441); Prospero, Miranda, and Caliban (479); and those two famed Latin poets of love, "Ovum and Virgin" (494). With the Purses on board, the scene is almost set for the grand rite toward which the whole narrative has been heading. There remains only one crucially missing actor, or actress, that being a young woman to enact and celebrate the mystery to which the narrator will become witness-initiate. That role is filled when the last two visitors arrive at the island, William's son and his fiancée, Stefanie, who expect to find a private retreat for prenuptial lovemaking.

Its cast now complete, this final epiphany scatters allusions like leaves from a Golden Bough. To begin, this ground—this sacred grove—was consecrated to Love years ago when an Armenian youth killed himself here rather than give up his beloved; that was why it became a "fossil museum," closed to the public and given over to the wild growth of nature. Now the tomb of Allegra's parents has come to resemble a scene from ancient Attica, featuring "in the center of a sort of grove an astonishing stone ruin, broken like a Greek shrine" (452). Here, as the narrator arrives, ritual games are in progress exempt from conventional rules and standards: Purse and Tilbeck are playing tennis without court lines or net. Later, the children would appoint Stefanie their "mistress of games."

Appropriately, the narrator recognizes which of the two men is her father through his Dionysian quality. Tilbeck's first words on behalf of his visitor are "Show her the wine cellar" (452), which she correctly regards as a sort of password: "At once I knew him. Tilbeck was the one who needed wine" (453). His first question of his daughter is priestly rather than fatherly—"You religious?" (454). To this crucial question Ozick brings a wide range of possibilities significantly exclusive of the Judeo-Christian tradition. The chief reference to Christianity in these pages is a joke: Tilbeck's "Last Supper"—he calls it that because his presence makes thirteen at the table (499)—is correctly designated; however, it prefigures not crucifixion but sexual consummation preceding his death by water. Further belittling the faith are the twelve chairs for his guests, each chair topped by the carved head of a reprobate Christian king. Those same countenances, recurring on the mansion walls, indicate why Tilbeck has so cheerfully burned most of the furnishings: "The kings matched the kings on the chairs under the trees. Grotesque noses, awkward rough little snarls, wicked wicked foreheads leering with the minute grain of the crafty wood. . . . 'See?' he said. . . . 'That whole row up there? . . . Those are the Six Philips of France. . . . On the other side . . . those are the Five Philips of Spain. Murderous, hah?'" (455).

Buddhism, by contrast, appears to great advantage, as Tilbeck evokes the Buddha's smile (466), the Buddhist "Man without Ego" ideal (468), and the Buddha's teaching of desirelessness: "Not wanting anything is what makes me perfectly free. . . . There's not a thing in the wide world I want. Or ever wanted" (468). Allegra later confirms through her mockery this facet of Tilbeck's role: "The Man of No Desires. I know the whole thing. . . . Just like the Buddha after nirvana. A holy man" (548–49). And the pagan ambience continues to thicken. When Nick/Zeus/Pan licks his daughter's blood from a cut finger, emanating "the floweriness of wine in his shoulder," she becomes half initiate, then yields to the flight reflex: "Strange and new, I breathed the minotaur. Then ran . . . to the panicked kings, to the table dense with civilization, ran, ran from the faun" (474). But she already knows there is no going back to innocence: "Following slowly up out of the beach, a small laughter came from the beautiful man" (475).

Philosophically, the ideology that undergirds this interlude appears to derive from the teachings of Gnosticism, that longstanding rival of Christianity which fostered the Catharist Court of Love in the twelfth century. Like Denis de Rougemont in *Love in the Western World* (and like his disciple John Updike in *Couples* and *Marry Me*), Ozick postulates a redeeming knowledge at the heart of this episode—a knowledge attainable only through sexual consummation. In this instance, the narrator's undeveloped state—young, virginal, small-breasted—imposes the need for vicarious learning: she will be witness to the rite of love, not participant. Yet her knowledge is sure and transforming, as her affinity with the celebrants grows stronger: "I was initiate. I knew it. I knew the taste of complicity. Nick had put it on my tongue like a pellet—complicity, amazing first-hand knowledge of the private thing" (520). There follows the sense, hitherto unimaginable in her "hollow man" condition, of deep change pending: "knowledge is the only real event in the world, and something had happened. . . . In me the private thing turned: knowledge turned, love turned, what my mother knew I knew" (521). Again, in Gnostic/Catharist fashion, the knowledge in question is ineffably sensual:

> Taste; no word. Yet there was no memory of a physical flavor. . . . It is never sensuality that remains (I know now and glimpsed then), but the idea of sensuality. . . . Feeling cannot be stored. . . . The nerve gives only the now, and is improvident. (520)

Brought to this level of enlightenment, the narrator is fully prepared at last for transcendence, as the Purses are not; unspiritual, conventional-minded sluggards, they snore through the final epiphany. On the brink of transcendence, the narrator enters the lovers' circle:

The lovers had touched. The lovers had touched at last. Their skins had touched; the friction had begun; the Purses were expunged: something had happened. Love. The private worm; the same. What my mother knew I knew.
—I loved my father.
And the union of the lovers was about to be. (526)

The key phrase here is "I loved my father." Her mother's purpose from the beginning had been "to re-father me" (58) to William or Enoch, and that purpose had struck away the girl's identity, bringing on her Hamlet-like mood of world-weariness. Without roots, money, career, respectability, or even a family circle, Tilbeck seems eminently suitable for defathering. What redeems him as father is his life's proof that all the above desiderata are obstacles to his daughter's freedom and subversive of her search for self-knowledge. Initially, the encounter between father and daughter appears to magnify her identity problem. As though being illegitimate issue were not enough, her father's youthful appearance engenders still deeper humiliation:

There was still something unrecounted about the stink of my first cell. Dejection seized me. Shame heated my legs. Not even William, sordid puritan, had had the courage of this sordidness. I viewed my father. He might have been a decade younger than my mother. . . . Then and there I had to swallow what I was: the merest whim. . . . It surpasses what is decently normal. A boy of seventeen had made me. (453–54)

The narrator's movement from this depth of shame to unconditional love of father thus marks a transformation that in the end makes possible her own self-acceptance. Tilbeck's Catharist practice of free sexuality, performed so she might know she "had witnessed the very style of my own creation" (531), wipes away every trace of taboo and stigma.

It is important that what our narrator witnesses is free sexuality, not "free love." Ozick underscores this distinction in the setting of the scene (the floor), the dialogue, and the action. Throughout their dalliance the lovers mock each other verbally—she calling him "Cockroach" and suggesting that he starch his soft member—and, most important, the narrator notes that "From the beginning they never kissed" (53). Moreover, the very style of her creation, she observes, is doglike: at the last moment, "brutally, and before she can sprawl, he flips her over. And penetrates. A noise of pain creaks from her . . ." (530). Which is to say, the distinctly human tenderness of face-to-face sex has been abjured in favor of more primitive, more purely erotic conjunction: Zeus choosing the form of a swan or bull for his fleshly encounter. (Zeus—as commander of the thunderbolt—is also evoked here by the background storm's thunder and lightning.)

From this nexus of nymph and demigod we may infer three crucial insights, commonly hidden behind a veil of sentimentality: (1) that sexuality, the Life Force, emanates with irrepressible power from the uncivilized, prehuman depths of the human psyche; (2) that in the male lover of any age the sexual being—the faun—is always a seventeen-year-old boy; and (3) that such sexual conjunction as is described here is not sordid or "dirty" but expressive of Sacred Beauty. The narrator's perfect agreement with these principles, and her newfound contentment with her status as "illegitimate issue," are shown in her subsequent taunting of William's son, who is determined to marry Stefanie despite her infidelity, "so as not to embarrass the families" (533). "'I,' I said, 'am issue of the floor. You,' I said, 'are issue of the nuptial couch'" (534). Plainly, she flaunts the richer heritage.

There remains the sine qua non of style, in this book a momentous presence. "[In *Trust*] I wanted to include a large range of *language:* a kind of lyric breadth and breath," the author has stated (Ltr 1/14/82), and in her preface to *Bloodshed* she says that *Trust* "was conceived in a style both 'mandarin' and 'lapidary,' every paragraph a poem" (BL 4). Some inkling of such a style may be evident in certain passages I have cited, such as the "enchanted tree" episode, but no critical analysis can do justice to this feature of her six-hundred-page novel. In this limited space, I shall rest the case on two excerpts, choosing one for its lyric effect and the other for its masterly organization. The lyrical excerpt, describing the union of lovers, is a sunburst of prose poetry reminiscent of D. H. Lawrence for its quasi-mystical mood and of James Joyce for its fusion of graphic precision with rhythmic cunning. In the gradual shortening of her phrases we may detect a resemblance to the quickening, panting rhythm of foreplay:

> a bridge of strength grows from the root of her neck to her calves, her buttocks strain into squares, she seems to hang upward from the cord of her side, . . . his touch which has risen with her, turned and fallen with her, clings for its life to the cliff, . . . her voice runs with a moist sluggishness, the surfaces of her eyes are leathery as callouses, he has tripped some strand linked to other strands, some voluptuary wire in her brain tightens, he has caught the drawstring of her frame, her thighs knot and shift, the wicks of her nipples tighten . . . her upper lip is hoisted, her nostrils knead themselves. . . . (528)

The other passage I have selected is the opening sentence of the novel, evocative of Henry James for its craftsmanship in making design subserve meaning:

> After the exercises I stood in the muddy field (it had rained at dawn) and felt the dark wool of my gown lap up the heat and din of noon, and at that instant,

while the graduates ran with cries toward asterisks of waiting parents and the
sun hung like an animal's tongue from a sickened blue maw, I heard the last
stray call of a bugle—single, lost, unconnected—and in one moment I grew
suddenly old.

While the sentence strikes us at once for its complex trelliswork—the paral-
lelisms branching into subordinate particles—its full artistry becomes clear
only on second reading of the novel, which reveals that we are looking at a
thick cluster of the book's most important motifs and issues. The "exer-
cises," for example, though a major rite of passage to the other graduates
who "ran with cries toward . . . waiting parents," produce only a Hamlet-
like melancholy in the narrator, whose own "graduation" will require a rite
of passage with her own "waiting parent" some five hundred pages hence.
The rain and "muddy field," in turn, indicate the narrator's transition from
"clean" to "dirty" which that rite of passage will entail. Whereas here in
chapter 1 she "took off my white shoes to save them from the mud," the
epiphany on Town Island is associated with rusted junk, mud, and (after
Tilbeck's drowning) slimy green vomit. The fulcrum of that shift from
Moses to Pan, the book's climactic sexual encounter, is presaged in the
unconsciously sexual phrase, "[I] felt the dark wool of my gown lap up the
heat and din of the sun," while her conscious mind regards the sun and sky
with a sick soul's revulsion ("the sun hung like an animal's tongue from a
sickened blue maw"). The "last stray call of a bugle—single, lost, unconnected" represents her own alienated condition, from which—together with
its resulting condition of growing "suddenly old"—Tilbeck would ultimately
rescue her, with his Pan-like spirit of perpetual youth and his gift of intimate
connections.

In its cumulative effect, the "mandarin" and "lapidary" style of *Trust*
points up a final meaning. Cynthia Ozick, who wrote an MA thesis entitled
"Parable in the Later Novels of Henry James," has here framed her own
parable: *Trust,* which began in the initiation mode of *What Maisie Knew,*
ends in a parable of the artist. Like Melville's "Bartleby the Scrivener" (a
"most cherished" favorite of Ozick's, Ltr 1/14/82), *Trust* forms its analogies
around the figure of an artist-rebel; unlike Bartleby, the narrator of *Trust*
escapes her sick soul condition at last through her transfiguring experience
of Sacred Beauty. This liberation, however, is conditioned by the narrator's
ongoing namelessness, which implies a final inability to resolve the artist's
conflicted identity. In effect, *Trust* clarifies the issue by eliminating two of
the cultural options portrayed in the narrator's four parent figures. In Ozick's
future fiction, we shall not see Allegra's Europhiliac aesthetics reappear as a
serious option, nor will America's dominant Christian culture ever magnify

its allure beyond William's cold and hypocritical paradigm. The remaining two father figures, however—pagan and Jewish—will continue their battle for possession of the artist's soul from *The Pagan Rabbi* and *Bloodshed* through *The Messiah of Stockholm* and *The Shawl*. As *Trust* ends, Tilbeck's victory is genuine but temporary, as Enoch Vand prepares himself for renewed combat by total immersion in Orthodox Judaism.

Tilbeck's final metamorphosis, after his death, greatly enhances the parable. "A male Muse he was. Nick" (539), says the narrator, overriding the objection that "the Muse is a woman." In "Women and Creativity: The Demise of the Dancing Dog," Ozick defines what a Muse, of either gender, does. As against the "sentimentalists" who "believe in money, in position, in a marriage bell"—incidentally a good description of Allegra Vand—the Muse says "'Partake,' it says, 'live,'" reminding us "that the earth lies under all." In its deployment of this *Kunstlerroman* ending, *Trust* resolves its deepest theme, that search for self-knowledge or identity which originated in the book's opening pages. Clearly the male Muse, though biologically unprogenitive (Stefanie was using contraceptives), has dropped germinous seeds into his daughter's soul, thereby transforming her bridal hunger of chapter 1 into an easy jest in the novel's closing paragraph: "What I was and what I did during that period I will not tell; I went to weddings."

Even Nick's exposure as a "tawdry Muse," with dyed hair and a laurel of vomit ("tender putrid greenish flowers," 545), only enhances the parable. "It is no light thing to have intercourse with the Muse," the initiate says of her newly insatiate thirst for beauty; "The planet's sweetmeats fail after a nibble at vatic bread" (539). But the tawdry Muse teaches his offspring to spurn any celestial city; grubby, earthbound Town Island is the soil from which will spring art's Sacred Beauty. From this standpoint the bridal hunger of chapter 1 may be seen, in hindsight, as the artist's passion for the world's body:

> I looked out at them with envy in the marrow, because I was deprived of that seductive bridegroom, . . . of his shining hair and the luster of his promised mouth. . . . I did not wish to envy them, . . . but greed for the world had bitten me. I longed to believe, like these black-gowned brides, in pleasure, in splendor, in luck; in genius, in the future, most of all in some impermeable lacquer [i.e., art] to enamel an endless youth. (3)

That final phrase, "to enamel an endless youth," is what art can promise in its Keatsian mode: forever wilt thou love and she be fair. But for Tilbeck, the enamel comes at a high cost. By dyeing his hair, this apostle of Buddhist desirelessness does disclose one desire after all, to preserve his youth; and nature answers his need with the only preservative it has, an early death.

The Orphic ambience of his death at sea suggests an immolation to Sacred Beauty, perhaps a willing surrender to the nature gods he serves. For now, to Ozick's narrator, Tilbeck's example suffices. But the moral vacancy of those pagan gods, tracing back to rambunctious Olympic fable, is reflected in Tilbeck's stunted ethical development: he has achieved "eternal youth" in the sense of immaturity of character as well as in beauty worship. Tilbeck's irresponsibility, not his mortality, would provoke the recoil of the Hebrew conscience in Ozick's later writings. Even so, the Tilbeck phase is a necessary period in the growth of the artist, who will be forever changed by that taste of the world's beauty.

At the end of *Trust*, the male Muse imparts one last gift to his neophyte, that being his own example of the virtue cited in the book's title. "The title 'Trust' was of course ironic, and signified distrust in every cranny," Ozick has said (Ltr 1/14/82). This distrust notably extends to the novel's fake artist figures: Edward McMahon, the poet-parasite; Eugenia Karp, the punster; Allegra Vand, authoress lionized in the Soviet Union. The novel's epigraph, however, poses the choice between "a mammoth trust fund" and "a minuscule fund of trust," and in leaving her mother's domain for her father's, the narrator has chosen the latter legacy. However minuscule the fund, self-trust is perhaps more necessary for the artist than for any other calling. "To believe in your own thought, to believe that what is true for you in your private heart is true for all men,—that is genius," said Ralph Waldo Emerson (a presence in *Trust*) in "Self-Reliance"; and again, "In self-trust all the virtues are comprehended," he declared in "The American Scholar" (147, 74). To the narrator of *Trust*, these precepts bear significant correspondences. To think and feel independently, seeking Sacred Beauty; to follow new gods, pursuing Gnostic knowledge; to believe in her calling, emulating the male Muse's "cult in himself. . . . The cult of art . . . the cult of experience" (325)—these are the salient features, in the end, of Cynthia Ozick's portrait of the artist as a young woman.

Three Story Books: From Pan to Moses

A fugue of antagonisms. One cannot even be sure of Agnon's definitive passion, whether he leans finally to the side of lyrical sorcery or of Torah.

"Agnon's Antagonisms"

The Pagan Rabbi and Other Stories (1971)

Obviously a collection of short stories can not be expected to display the coherence or unified focus that we expect to find in a novel.[12] In her three collections Cynthia Ozick gathers a rather disparate group of writings, ranging from brief sketches to novella-length narratives, in which her literary modes vary from conventional realism to parable and fantasy. To a surprising degree she imposes a web of coherence upon the stories, nonetheless, through her continuous process of "reinvigorating" (a favorite word in her literary criticism) her central themes and obsessions. By imagining radically new sets of characters and dramatic situations, and employing fresh ways of approaching her material—especially in the comic/ironic mode—she extends and deepens her ground themes rather than merely repeat them from one book to another.

The themes that predominate in her three story collections are familiar to readers of *Trust,* but their interaction now assumes an altogether different profile. The Pan-versus-Moses theme continues to sustain a *basso continuo* presence in the time frame that stretches from "The Pagan Rabbi" (1966) through the Puttermesser-Xanthippe stories of *Levitation* (1982), but this central theme of *Trust* gradually loses ground to two themes that were subordinate in the novel: problems of the artist, particularly the Jewish or female artist; and the exigencies of Jewish identity. This latter theme, relegated to Enoch in *Trust,* eventually emerges as the transcendent issue of the story collections, evoking the author's deepest emotional and artistic power.

Illustrating the new balance among her triad of ground themes is a brief quantification: of the seven stories in *The Pagan Rabbi,* only two make the Pan/Moses dichotomy their central theme, while two others touch on the issue. By comparison, five of the tales focus upon the figure of the artist, and six of the seven amplify the theme of Jewish identity, leaving only "The Dock-Witch" to carry forward the Gentile cultural ambience of *Trust.*

Although the pantheistic element thus seems downgraded from its paramount status in *Trust,* it still rated enough importance to justify making "The Pagan Rabbi" the title story for the whole volume. In this tale the Pan/Moses conflict attains a new intensity, in part because the story is a more concentrated form than the novel, but equally because the adversarial ideologies are more clearly drawn: not Tilbeck versus the general modern malaise, but Pan versus orthodox Judaism. Moreover, the conflict now occurs within a single individual, the learned rabbi whose suicide occasions the story.

As in *Trust,* a vital symbol in "The Pagan Rabbi" is the tree that functions as both totem (for Hellenic nature worship) and taboo (for Hebraic forbidden knowledge). Sex and death, the two modes of forbidden knowledge associated with the Semitic myth of the Fall, do in fact pertain to the rabbi's tree: sex, when he couples with the tree's dryad; and death, when he hangs himself from its branches. Yet it is Pan who prevails over Moses in this encounter. Death here becomes (as Walt Whitman called it) a promotion rather than a punishment in the light of the rabbi's pantheistic insight: "The molecules dance inside all forms, and within the molecules dance the atoms, and within the atoms dance still profounder sources of divine vitality. There is nothing that is Dead" (20). From this Spinozan heresy—Spinoza is cited by name on page 32—arise two intolerable consequences for traditional Judaism. First, the Second Commandment is nullified by the immersion of the Creator in his creation: "Holy life subsists even in the stone, even in the bones of dead dogs and dead men. Hence in God's fecundating Creation there is no possibility of Idolatry" (21). And second, as a final outrage against the Hebraic ethos, the concept of holiness, of being separate from the unclean, becomes meaningless. Even more than Town Island in *Trust*, the setting of "The Pagan Rabbi" is thus befouled with corruption, so that the rabbi's ecstatic sexual union occurs in an environment of "wind-lifted farts" and "civic excrement" created by the city's sewage polluting the nearby seashore (33, 37). Even so, the vitality of Nature overrides the authority of Torah. When the Law undertakes direct competition with the senses, claiming to sound "more beautiful than the crickets," to smell "more radiant than the moss," to taste better than clear water (36), the rabbi on the instant chooses to join his dryad-lover, hanging himself from the tree with his prayer shawl.

Because the narrator of "The Dock-Witch" is a Gentile, neither the Jewish horror of idolatry nor the ideal of holiness stands in opposition to his pantheistic enticement. (The Gentile is sufficiently Holocaust-haunted, however, to notice the cleansing of a German ship, which "smelled of some queer unfamiliar disinfectant, as though it were being desperately scoured into a state of sanitation," 139). So the protagonist, originally a midwestern churchgoer (131), yields immediately and guiltlessly to the impulse that brought him to New York to live within sight of the East River. Here the pagan goddess of Nature is connected, like Tilbeck in *Trust*, with the sea and pagan Norsemen (her final metamorphosis puts her on the prow of a Viking ship), as well as with the original Canaanite seagoers, the Phoenicians whose tongue she speaks. Between seeing off a shipload of Greeks to their homeland and another vessel packed with Orthodox Jews to theirs, the Dock-Witch so affects the narrator's view of nature that even a pair of penguin-sized rats on the dock appear "sacerdotal" to him, "like a pair of priests late for divine service" (147). And as with Tilbeck and the Pagan Rabbi, the speaker's immersion in nature is consummated in a sexual union of insatiable magnitude—"she made me a galley slave, my oar was a log flung into the sea of her" (156). The parable ends, like Keats's "La Belle Dame Sans Merci," with the narrator immersed in the grief of abandonment.

The hunger for the world's beauty that underlies these extraordinary sexual encounters relates the tales of Pan worship to both the theme of Jewish identity and that of the portrait of the artist. An engaging example of all three themes working in concert is "The Butterfly and the Traffic Light," a sketch that shows the artist toying creatively with her material. Here the thematic triad begins to form when a character named Fishbein talks with a young woman about the "insistent sense of recognition" that can attach to so mundane a thing as a street in their small city:

> Big Road was different by day and by night, weekday and weekend. Daylight, sunlight, and even rainlight gave everything its shadow, winter and summer, so that every person and every object had its Doppelganger, persistent and hopeless. There was a kind of doubleness that clung to the street, as though one remembered having seen this and this and this before. (213)

To see this doubleness is the beginning of metaphor, so that an unneeded traffic light over Big Road becomes, for the young woman, "some sort of religious icon with a red eye and a green eye" (214), and this in turn becomes a new version of the Hellenism/Hebraism dichotomy. It is Fishbein who argues in favor of plural gods and Isabel who maintains the Orthodox Jewish position (215):

> "What kind of religion would it be which had only one version of its deity—a whole row of identical icons in every city?"
> She considered rapidly. "An advanced religion. I mean a monotheistic one."
> "And what makes you certain that monotheism is 'advanced'? On the contrary, little dear! . . . The Greeks and Romans had a god for every personality, the way the Church has a saint for every mood. Savages, Hindus, and Roman Catholics understand all that. It's only the Jews and their imitators who insist on a rigid unitarian God. . . . A little breadth of vision, you see, a little imagination, a little *flexibility,* I mean—there ought to be room for Zeus *and* God under one roof. . . . That's why traffic lights won't do for icons! They haven't been conceived in a pluralistic spirit, they're all exactly alike.

Two other metaphors give this sketch a behind-the-scenes candor, the impression of the author's mind disclosing the way it works. One is the butterfly of the title, a metaphor for the death-bound beauty of actual life. It is a prettier creature but less significant than the caterpillar (art in the process of creation): "The caterpillar is uglier, but in him we can regard the better joy of becoming" (217). The other metaphor is that of the immortal city, like Jerusalem, Baghdad, or Athens—mythologized by millennia beyond any sense of utility. America, in this sense, has no cities; and that, we may surmise, is why Town Island is the crucial setting in *Trust:* it was hopefully christened Dorp Island a mere three hundred years ago, like Gatsby's Manhattan, by Dutch sailors.

Whereas "The Butterfly and the Traffic Light" creates a positive impression of artistic creativity, two other sketches of the artist render a feminist protest in one instance and a nightmare vision of failure in the other. The feminist satire is "Virility," an attack against male supremacy in art that correlates largely with Ozick's ridicule of the Testicular Theory of Literature in her essay "Women and Creativity: The Demise of the Dancing Dog." So manly has the poet Edmund Gate become, after his meteoric rise to success in "Virility," that his very shape now resembles a "giant lingam" (244), and his reviewers search for appropriate imagery to describe his verses: "The Masculine Principle personified," "Robust, lusty, male," "Seminal and hard." When it turns out that an elderly aunt actually wrote the poems, the praises turn to abuse ("Thin feminine art," "A spinster's one-dimensional vision," 266), and Edmund Gate does penance for his impersonation by faking his death at age twenty-six and spending his remaining half century going in drag.[13]

"Virility" was written with a classic novella about a failed artist in Ozick's mind. Like the employer-narrator in "Bartleby the Scrivener," Ozick's narrator is much put-upon by his lowly proofreader, who usurps, in turn, the employer's name (Edmund), his home (the attic becomes Gate's study), his sister (by whom Gate fathers illicit offspring), and finally his personality (the editor haplessly mimics Gate's alliteration of the "p" sound, like Bartleby's employer mimicking "I would prefer not to"). Just as Bartleby's role as a burnt-out writer is reflected in his dogged perfectionism at the mechanics of longhand copying ("he seemed to gorge himself on my documents . . . [writing] on silently, palely, mechanically"), so Gate's ambition as a poet is sublimated into unparalleled mechanical skill on the typewriter, which "was so consistent, so reliable, so intelligible, so without stutter or modest hesitation—it made me sigh. He was deeply deadly purposeful" (242). And Bartleby's reputed sojourn in the Dead Letter Office—the final repository of failed artwork—is matched by the motif of the dead aunt's letters, which sustain Gate's spurious role as the poet of *Virility* for three years after Aunt Tivka's death.

If such artistic fraudulence is contemptible, there is one thing even worse: having talent without the strength of character to realize it. In "The Doctor's Wife," Doctor Silver's failure to realize his talent resembles that of Hemingway's persona in "The Snows of Kilimanjaro":

he thought how imperceptibly, how inexorably, temporary accommodation becomes permanence, and one by one he counted his omissions, his coward-

ices, each of which had fixed him like an invisible cement. . . . At twenty he
had endured the stunned emotion of one who senses that he has been singled
out for aspiration, for beauty, for awe, for some particularity not yet dis-
closed. . . . At forty he was still without a history. (187–88)

Apart from Hemingway and the later Henry James who feared a wasted
life ("The Beast in the Jungle" is especially relevant here), one other writer—
an Ozick favorite—makes a curiously negative contribution to "The Doctor's Wife." The success of Anton Chekhov, another bachelor-doctor-artist
like Doctor Silver, stands as a reproach to the latter's arrested development
while at the same time representing something like Harold Bloom's "Anxiety of Influence" thesis. In fact, the story is a perfectly Chekhovian paradigm of waste and futility, vividly illustrating the banality of marriage (a
theme carried over from *Trust*), the illusiveness of happiness, and the human incapacity to achieve or even formulate a meaningful purpose in life.
The Chekhovian tone is especially strong concerning this last motif: "his life
now was only a temporary accommodation, he was young, he was prepar-
ing for the future, he would beget progeny, he would discover a useful
medical instrument, he would succor the oppressed, . . . he would be saved"
(182–83).

Although his sympathy informs his practice in saintly proportions, the
Doctor's spiritual ministrations avail nothing, especially regarding the hos-
tilities he tries to anneal. His patients—poor Negroes and Italians whose
nonpayment leaves him poor also—display unrelenting ethnic hatred in his
waiting room; his sisters radiate contempt toward their husbands, who in
turn loathe each other; and his aged father, a dependent now living in the
Doctor's apartment, seethes with "incessant fury." Nor can he help his
brother-in-law, who presses questions with a manic-depressive's urgency:
"How do you get to be happy?" "Tell me what I'm alive for" (185). The
black mood engendered by his quandary leads to the central conflict of the
tale, between actual life and art, reality and fantasy. Given the circumstances, reality faces an unequal battle: "[To himself] he confessed . . . that
the human race—husbands, wives, children—was a sink, a drainpipe, a
sewer, that reconciliation was impossible, that his waiting room would
remain divided, that his brothers-in-law would remain divided, that his
sisters were no more than ovum-bearing animals born to enact the cosmic
will, that he himself was sterile" (189).

The counterpoint—"that all the same it was possible to be happy" (189)—
depends solely on the efficacy of art, defined here in connection with the
photograph of a woman pictured with Chekhov around the year 1890.
"Too late"—the Doctor is now fifty—"he made up his mind to marry, but

fell in love . . . with a picture" (188). By now, in actual life, "this eternally dimpling girl" has become "a withered old woman . . . or, more likely, dead, dead, dead!" (189), but in Keatsian fashion he chooses this image of eternal youth and beauty over the older woman his sister tries to match him with—"a sunset, it was the last hour before her night" (203). Implicit in this scene is Ozick's own ambiguity about the issues: though resolutely "Judaic" in her aim to correlate art with actual life, she has also expressed a deep ongoing infatuation with photography for its power to preserve the passing moment from decay. In the end, because Doctor Silver has not lived, he preserves not a scrap of his life in art, nor does he even manage to define what mode of art might suit his need. Bewildered by the chaos of it all, he leaves the capturing of his own time to another brother-in-law, a commercial photographer, while he takes the woman in the photograph as his imaginary wife in a final Chekhovian lapse into protective illusion.

The remaining two tales in *The Pagan Rabbi* also portray artistic failure, but their central concern is Jewish identity. Both "The Suitcase" and "Envy; or, Yiddish in America" define the Jewish ethos by contriving a memorable confrontation between Jew and Gentile. In "The Suitcase," the adversaries at first seem totally assimilated into the larger American society. The Gentile, formerly a pilot in the Kaiser's air force, has lived in America so long that he "no longer thought of himself as German" (103). Apart from naming his son Gottfried—he later wishes it were John—his only connection to his native land has been a sister whose eleven-year-old daughter died in the bombing of Cologne. The Jew is Genevieve, a brilliant woman who has become mentor and mistress to the German's son, though both lovers are married to others. She too has become assimilated, preferring the art world of New York to her dull Jewish husband (a CPA) and four daughters back in Indianapolis. For her Gentile lover, a painter, she has even culled through German literature, selecting comments from Beethoven, Mann, and Goethe for Gottfried's exhibition program. (The program features a talk by one "Creighton MacDougal" of the *Partisan Review,* a pretentious fraud who gives Ms. Ozick occasion for some wicked satire of the eminent pundit Dwight MacDonald.)

The color yellow, however—innocently visible in a brick house, in buttercups, in curtains, in a field, in a girl's hair—inevitably portends the Star of the Holocaust, and thus confrontation. When these two characters meet—the painter's father and mistress—their layers of assimilation rapidly peel away, exposing the ethnic granite at the core of each personality. Her innate Jewishness rises to the mention of Carl Gustav Jung as "some famous Jewish psychiatrist" (107), to which she replies, "He isn't a Jew. . . . That's why he went on staying alive" (108). His ethnicity thereupon reacts in a surge of defensiveness.

He knew what she meant him to see: she scorned Germans, she thought him a
Nazi sympathizer even now, an anti-Semite, an Eichmann. She was the sort
who, twenty years after Hitler's war, would not buy a Volkswagen. . . . Who
could be blamed for History? It did not take a philosopher . . . to see that
History was a Force-in-Itself, like Evolution. (109)

Of course he is not a bad fellow. All he wants, as a German, is to forget
History, which is exactly what she, as a Jew, cannot permit. Ostensibly
he gets the best of her by breaking up the miscegenational dalliance and
sending Genevieve back to her Jewish family. But the final victory is hers. At
the end of the tale, when Genevieve's purse is reported stolen, he com-
pulsively proves himself innocent by opening his suitcase and demanding
that she search it. It is a paradigm of his much larger and unanswerable need
for innocence, brought to exposure by his remark that tomorrow he sails
abroad:

"To Germany?"
"Not Germany. Sweden. I admire Scandinavia. . . ."
"I bet you say Sweden to mislead. I bet you're going to Germany, why
shouldn't you? I don't say there's anything wrong with it, why shouldn't you
go to Germany?"
"Not Germany, Sweden. The Swedes were innocent in the war, they saved
so many Jews. I swear it, not Germany. It was the truckmen who stole your
purse, I swear it." (125, 126)

A similar confrontation of Jew versus Gentile concludes "Envy; or, Yiddish in America," where the aging Yiddish poet Edelshtein gathers together
the familiar thematic triad: problems of the artist, Jewish identity, and the
pagan enticement. What defeats the artist in this story is not lack of will or
talent but entrapment within a minority culture that is dying from worldwide loss of interest within modern Jewry. Edelshtein has found that even
the nation of Israel has no use for "the language of the bad little interval
between Canaan and now" (48), and with Yiddish eradicated from Europe
by the Holocaust, there remains only America as a site where Yiddish might
survive. Here, however, to his dismay, the younger generation of American
Jews actually refers to its elders as "you Jews" while disdaining the Jewish
obsession with history as "a waste" (92). Meanwhile, America interprets
Jewish culture through novelists who were "spawned in America, pogroms
a rumor, . . . history a vacuum. . . . They were reviewed and praised, and
were considered Jews, and knew nothing" (41).
    Yet Edelshtein himself exhibits telltale signs of cultural betrayal. Emanat-
ing from the same reflex that makes him envy "natural religion, stones,

stars, body" (86), his dream life hovers about Canaanite temptations, such as homoerotic desire for Alexei, a friend of his boyhood, and similar lads spotted in the subway: "The love of a man for a boy. Why not confess it? Is it against the nature of man to rejoice in beauty?" (80). And his lapse into wishing "he had been born a Gentile" (68) must mitigate the cultural betrayal he ascribes to others. Moreover, the Gentile preference for flesh over spirit—"Our books are holy, to them their bodies are holy," the Pagan Rabbi had said (12)—gains new appeal when measured against the decrepitude of the Yiddish speakers. Together, Edelshtein and Baumzweig comprise a catalogue of decay featuring a dripping nose, a urine-stained fly "now and then seeping" (9), "Mucus the sheen of the sea" (58), "thighs . . . full of picked sores" (76), and a recurrent "vomitous belch."

The status of Yiddish in America seems analogous to this decrepit condition, but in the end it is not Yiddish so much as Jewish history that Edelshtein struggles to preserve from oblivion. Like the face-off between Jew and German in "The Suitcase," Edelshtein's confrontation with the Christian evangelist focuses upon a vein of history that the Gentile prefers to dismiss. To Edelshtein's list of historic villains—"Pharaoh, Queen Isabella, Haman, that pogromchick King Louis that they call in history Saint, Hitler, Stalin"—the evangelist responds with the sort of fancy that Leo Baeck classified as Romantic Religion: "You're a Jew? . . . Accept Jesus as your Saviour and you shall have Jerusalem restored" (99). As in "The Suitcase," the thrust and parry of dialogue quickly strikes ethnic bedrock, as Edelshtein places his adversary among his list of historic villains—"Amalekite! Titus! Nazi!"—when the majority culture bares its teeth in familiar fashion: "You people are cowards, you never even tried to defend yourselves. . . . When you were in Europe every nation despised you. When you moved to take over the Middle East the Arab Nation, spic faces like your own, your very own blood-kin, began to hate you. . . . You kike, you Yid" (99–100).

By way of transition to the next book, it should be noted that Edelshtein's closing outcry, "On account of you I have no translator!" obscures a fundamental precept stated earlier in the story, that Yiddish is untranslatable. Even without the indifference of young Jews and the contempt of Gentiles to contend with, Edelshtein's poetry would remain hopelessly incommunicable to a non-Yiddish readership:

The gait—the prance, the hobble—of Yiddish is not the same as the gait of English. . . . *Mamaloshen* doesn't produce *Wastelands*. No alienation, no nihilism, no dadaism. With all the suffering, no smashing! NO INCOHERENCE! . . . The same biblical figure, with exactly the same history, once he puts on a name from King James, COMES OUT A DIFFERENT PERSON! (81, 82)

In her preface to *Bloodshed* Cynthia Ozick amplifies this statement with an exposition of her own problems with the English language—"A language, like a people, has a history of ideas. . . . English is a Christian language. When I write English, I live in Christendom. But if my postulates are not Christian postulates, what then?" (BL 9). The specific story to which she relates this problem is the next one we shall consider, "Usurpation (Other People's Stories)" in *Bloodshed*. Having written this preface, she says, solely from frustration over a critic's comment that "Usurpation" is unintelligible, she explains why it may have seemed so:

> There is no way to hear the oceanic amplitudes of the Jewish Idea in any English word or phrase. "Judaism" is a Christian term. . . . English . . . cannot be expected to naturalize the life-giving grandeur of the Hebrew word—yet how much more than word it is!—"Torah." . . . So it came to me what the difficulty was: I had written "Usurpation" in the language of a civilization that cannot imagine its thesis. (BL 10)

We turn next to the book that is at once the most profoundly Jewish and the closest to the midpoint—in several meanings—of Ozick's career as an artist.

Bloodshed and Three Novellas (1976)

As these fragments of her preface indicate, *Bloodshed* is the book in which Cynthia Ozick most markedly stakes her claim to being a Jewish author— more profoundly Jewish, I should say, than the more celebrated names like Saul Bellow and Philip Roth. Because all four of its tales take as their governing theme the betrayal of Jewish identity, *Bloodshed* is the most coherently unified of her collections, Taken together, the four stories comprise a form resembling that of a classical symphony, with the first and last movements ("A Mercenary" and "Usurpation") being monumental expositions of her theme, the second movement ("Bloodshed") having the mood and pace of a slow movement (like the funeral march in Beethoven's *Eroica*), and the third movement—the quasi-farcical "An Education"—taking the role of a mood-lightening scherzo (Beethoven's "Joke" movement). The preface, in this scheme, would be the coda, coming first in the book but invented last.

As in her earlier writing, Jewish identity forms part of a thematic triad that includes the appeal of paganism and the portrayal of the artist torn by self-conflict. With its artist persona and its renewal of the Pan-versus-Moses conflict, "Usurpation (Other People's Stories)" is the entry in *Bloodshed* that best illustrates this continuing thematic interplay. Subserving this portrait of the artist mired in self-conflict are two issues the author discussed at length in her essay "Literature as Idol: Harold Bloom." The first issue is Bloom's "anxiety of influence" thesis, here taking the form of Writer's Envy; and the other is the conflict between Judaism—specifically the Second Commandment—and art. This latter question evokes the most forgivable and yet—to the author—the most worrisome instance of cultural subversion in the volume. As her preface states it: "the worry is this: whether Jews ought to be story-tellers! . . . There is one God, and the Muses are not Jewish but Greek. . . . Does the Commandment against idols warn even [against] ink?" (10).

Because this story has caused more confusion than any other in the Ozick canon, a brief synopsis may be helpful. "Usurpation" is unified throughout by its narrator, who succumbs to Writer's Envy on hearing a famous writer (Bernard Malamud) give a reading of his "The Silver Crown." Among the crowd is a would-be writer who asks her to bring his manuscript ("A Tale of Youth and Homage") to Malamud for his help. She instead reads it and usurps it for her own narrative, which further incorporates two disparate Hebrew writers—Agnon (a pious Jew) and Tchernikhovsky (a pagan apostate)—into her story. Claiming that incoherence is, "as you know, the fash ion," the narrator slyly plies a technique of postmodern playfulness as she repeatedly apologizes to the reader about her raggedness of form: "I see you are about to put these pages down. . . . I beg you to wait. Trust me a little"; "Here I will interrupt the goat's story to apologize"; "I will have to mend all this somehow. Be patient. I will manage it"; "oh, how I despise writers who will stop a story dead for the sake of showing off!" (139, 142, 147, 158). Culminating this violation of the story's frame is a critique by one of the characters: "'I looked up one of your stories. It stank, lady. The one called 'Usurpation.' . . . Boring! Long-winded!" (175).

But though the author is accused of plagiarism—"Half of it's swiped, you ought to get sued"—the narrator's usurpation of other people's stories shortly becomes a minor issue. In this most openly confessional of Ozick's stories, the essential usurpation encompasses a much larger prize: the appropriation of an alien culture, which alone can make storytelling permissible: "Magic— I admit it—is what I lust after. . . . I am drawn not to the symbol, but to the absolute magic act. I am drawn to what is forbidden" (134). Because "the Jews have no magic," she goes on, "I long to be one of the ordinary peoples . . . oh, why can we not have a magic God like other peoples?" (135).

The answer to that question comes through another usurpation, borrowed from the manuscript of the "goat."[14] In it, our narrator finds the concept of the writer as "self-idolator, . . . so audacious and yet so ingenious that you will fool God and live" (141). The writer who has done this is Tchernikhovsky, a Jew who has lapsed into "pantheism and earth-worship . . . pursuit of the old gods of Canaan" (144). Despite this apostasy, which culminates in his "most famous poem, the one to the god Apollo" (143), he ascends after death into the Jewish paradise, where our narrator glimpses him wickedly at ease in Zion, hobnobbing with his pagan gods, savoring his faunlike pleasures, and ignoring with impunity his Jewish obligations of worship:

> Tchernikhovsky eats nude at the table of the nude gods, clean-shaven now, his limbs radiant, his youth restored, his sex splendidly erect . . .; he eats without self-restraint from the celestial menu, and when the Sabbath comes . . . as usual he avoids the congregation of the faithful before the Footstool and the Throne. (178)

The story's last sentence, however, makes it clear that though he could fool the Jewish God, neither he nor any other Jew can ever fool the gods of that alien culture in whose praise he wrote his poetry. They will always know he is not one of theirs: "Then the taciturn little Canaanite idols call him, in the language of the spheres, kike" (178).

If "Usurpation" portrays the least blameworthy betrayal of the Jewish heritage, "An Education" treats the most blameworthy, which may explain why it emanates the most sardonic tone of these four stories, and is the most immediately comprehensible. Written about the time *Trust* was completed, it extends several of the novel's themes, as is evident in the heroine's (Una's) initial interest in the classics (she earns two graduate degrees) and her ultimate uninterest in marriage (she refuses to marry her lover). In the opening scene, a Latin class, Una is called to explain the genitive case—a term that becomes a key to the story, both as a description of marriage and as a foreshadowing of Una's total possession by a singularly irresponsible married couple.

That married couple, in turn, illustrates the central theme of the story, the cultural vacuum that ensues when they try to assimilate to the Gentile majority. Having changed their name from Chaims ("But isn't that Jewish?") to Chimes ("Like what a bell does"), they further de-Judaize themselves by eating ham, naming their daughter "Christina," and making a joke of the Holy Ghost/Holocaust pun (80). The retaliation for this betrayal of their heritage comes when Clement Chimes, a would-be artist, is unable to progress beyond the title page of his masterwork, "Social Cancer/A Diagnosis in Verse/And Anger." Leaving aside his lack of talent, we may read this story as the obverse of "Envy; or, Yiddish in America." Contrary to Edelshtein, who fails because his art is rooted in a dying minority culture, Chimes fails because, having renounced his Jewish birthright, he faces the dilemma of trying to write literature without any cultural enrootment whatever.

Whereas "An Education" presents an essentially comic view of Jewish deracination, "A Mercenary" projects a tragic instance of this governing theme—tragic in the old sense of portraying grievous waste. The tale begins rather shockingly with an epigraph from Joseph Goebbels—"Today we are all expressionists—men who want to make the world outside themselves take the form of their lives within themselves." Whatever else we may make of this remark, it comprises a perfect definition of idolatry as Ozick portrays it: a man making the outer world over in his own perverse image. The tale proper applies Goebbels' remark to three characters representing the civilizations of three disparate continents. The two main characters have in some sense exchanged birthrights: Lushinski, a native of Poland, by becoming the United Nations representative of a small black African country; Morris, his assistant, by submerging his African past under a European veneer acquired at Oxford. A third character, Louisa—Lushinski's mistress in New York—is American, and hence too innocent to either require or comprehend a multiple identity; but she, like the others, follows Goebbels' expressionist standard in so far as she prefers her innocent inner picture of the world to the reality defined by actual history.

Lushinski is the "Mercenary" of the title, an eloquent "Paid Mouthpiece" for his African dictator both at the U.N. and in television talk shows featuring "false 'hosts' contriving false conversation" (20). In his latter role he makes a televised confession of murder, but he never tells anyone who his victim was—not even Morris or Louisa. Instead he tells his audience of other violence: how the Germans took Warsaw on his sixth birthday, causing his wealthy parents to buy him a place with a peasant family, after which the parents, though Aryan in looks and manners, were identified as Jews and shot. It is not very entertaining stuff, commercially speaking, and soon the mercenary in the man rises to meet the mercenary medium; he makes his tale out to be a jest, a fabrication to entertain his listeners: "All this was comedy: Marx Brothers, . . . the audience is elated by its own disbelief. . . . Lushinski is only a story-teller" (29).

In thus making a travesty of his tragic past, Lushinski is not solely interested in commercial advantage; he mainly wants to exorcise the self he was, the child who "had survived the peasants who baited and blistered and beat and hunted him. One of them had hanged him from the rafter of a shed by the wrists. He was four sticks hanging" (37). Telling Louisa he is "the century's one free man," he explains: "every survivor is free. . . . The future can invent nothing worse" (37). Having chosen to use his freedom establishing a new identity, he has largely succeeded. Though "born to a flag-stoned Warsaw garden," he now feels himself "native to these mammalian perfumes" of African flowers, in token of which he long ago immersed his being in this culture's pagan hedonism ("these round brown mounds of the girls he pressed down under the trees," 16). To further underscore his freedom from that Jewish child in his past, he has taken a crypto-German mistress in America: "They spoke of her as a German countess—her last name was preceded by a 'von' . . . though her accent had a fake melody either Irish or Swedish" (21). At the same time he has done all in his power to offend Jews everywhere: "Always he was cold to Jews. . . . In the Assembly he turned his back on the ambassador from Israel. . . . All New York Jews in the gallery" (41).

Yet the Jewish child in the man is not wholly expungeable. For all his sophistication, words like "peasant" and "Jew" evoke visible fear in Lushinski; and most important, he reveals that telltale sign of Jewish identity, a passion for Jewish history. The history in question—Raul Hilberg's monumental work *The Destruction of the European Jews* (1961)—opens a breach between Lushinski and his mistress, who sees no purpose in this masochistic morbidity:

> "Death," she said. "Death, death, death. What do you care? You came out alive." "I care about the record," he insisted. . . . He crashed down beside her an enormous volume: it was called *The Destruction*. She opened it and saw tables and figures and asterisks; she saw train-schedules. It was all dry, dry. . . . (38)

Paradoxically, his affinity for Jewish history only strengthens his need for exorcism, as his Gentile mistress correctly infers: "You hate being part of the Jews. You hate that. . . . Practically nobody knows you're a Jew. . . . *I* never think of it" (40).

In the remainder of the tale Lushinski accelerates his flight from his Jewish past by becoming "a dervish of travel" as he speaks about Africa on the television and lecture circuit and by cementing his ties to his African "homeland." Morris, the real African, meanwhile moves in a direction exactly opposite to that of Lushinski, gradually shedding his European veneer so as to recover his tribal birthright: "the dear land itself, the customs, the rites, the cousins, the sense of family" (33). Pushed in this direction by his revulsion against the Tarzan movies—"Was he [Morris] no better than that lout Tarzan, investing himself with a chatter not his own? How long could the ingested, the invented, the foreignness endure" (46)—Morris tries to push Lushinski likewise. From New York, "a city of Jews" (49), he sends a letter to the seacoast villa in Africa where Lushinski is enjoying his employer's gratitude. The letter describes a Japanese terrorist, jailed for slaughtering Jews in an air terminal, who in his prison cell has converted to Judaism.

Unlike Lushinski, the Japanese convert is not a mercenary. Lushinski reads the message as an unmasking: "It meant a severing. Morris saw him as an impersonator. . . . Morris had called him Jew" (51).

Thus a familiar pattern recurs: a Jew who tries mightily to assimilate is in the end forced back into his native Jewishness. Like Tchernikhovsky in "Usurpation," whom the Canaanite gods called kike though he had fooled the God of the Jews, Lushinski will finally be pronounced Jew no matter how far he may flee into the hinterland. As the tale ends, the blue-and-white colors of his African surroundings comprise a double reminder of his Jewish identity, evoking memories of Holocaust Poland and of the Israeli flag at the United Nations. His very cigarette smoke, with its blue-white haze, now calls him "Jew" and so thrusts him away from the pleasures of his new country and toward the land of his birth, and thence to a closing revelation: the name, in the last two lines, of the man Lushinski had killed and buried in Warsaw:

> And in Africa, in a white villa on the blue coast, the Prime Minister's gaudy pet, on a blue sofa . . . smoking and smoking, under the breath of the scented trees, under the shadow of the bluish snow, under the blue-black pillars of the Polish woods, . . . under the rafters, under the stone-white hanging stars of Poland—Lushinski.
> Against the stones and under the snow. (51–52)

Up to this point, the stories in *Bloodshed* have portrayed the deracination of Jewish identity in terms of art ("Usurpation"), sociology ("An Education"), and politics ("A Mercenary"). In her title story, "Bloodshed"—and doubtless this is why it *is* the title story—Ozick brings forward her most momentous mode of deracination, the theological. In this instance the theology does not involve a conflict between Judaism and some alien system (e.g., Pan versus Moses); rather, its focus lies wholly within a Jewish matrix. Cleared thus of goys and pagans, the narrative measures a New Yorker named Bleilip, a middling sort of Jewish American, against "the town of the hasidim," an Orthodox village within range of Bleilip's neighborhood that is inhabited almost entirely by survivors of the death camps and their close relatives. Ostensibly, he has come hither to visit his cousin, but in reality he is in flight from a despair so deep that he has been toying with the idea of suicide—toying, literally, in that he carries in one pocket a toy gun ("to get used to it. The feel of the thing," 70) and in another pocket a real pistol. Thus possessed by the Kierkegaardian Sickness unto Death, Bleilip has undertaken this sojourn among the faithful as a last feeble grasp for beliefs to live by.

Fundamentally, the issue in "Bloodshed" is the most crucial dichotomy that fractures the Judaic ethos—the contradiction between sustaining unbearable suffering, as predicated by Jewish history, and the L'Chaim! or "To Life!" principle, which holds that life is always worthful. The cause of Bleilip's despair is his enclosure within the far side of that contradiction, so that his religious belief fails in the face of recent Jewish history—the bloodshed of the story's title. Regarding the Holocaust even the Orthodox rebbe, a survivor of Buchenwald, apparently shares Bleilip's sick soul condition. At worship he describes the appalling transference wrought by that monstrous event upon the ancient idea of the scapegoat:

> For animals we in our day substitute men. . . . we have the red cord around our throats, we were in villages, they drove us into camps, we were in trains, they drove us into showers of poison. . . . everyone on earth became a goat or a bullock, . . . all our prayers are bleats and neighs on the way to a forsaken altar. . . . Little fathers! How is it possible to live? (65, 66–67)

Now when it most seems that the rebbe is Bleilip's alter ego, he suddenly turns on Bleilip: "Who are you?" (67). To Bleilip's answer—"A Jew. Like yourselves. One of you"—the rebbe retorts: "Presumption! Atheist, devourer! For us there is the Most High, joy, life. . . . But you! A moment ago I spoke your own heart for you, emes [true]? . . . You believe the world is in vain, emes?" (67). This exchange leads to the rebbe's final divination: "Empty your pockets!" Even before the guns come to view, the rebbe—a death camp survivor speaking to a New York intellectual—says the key sentence: "Despair must be earned" (69).

Other Jewish writers have threaded forth a similar response to the Suffering/L'Chaim! dichotomy—Saul Bellow's *Herzog* is a masterly example—but Cynthia Ozick remains distinctive for her theological rather than philosophical orientation. In "Bloodshed" her confrontation of Jewish opposites concludes in a kind of theological dialectic. Bleilip, the hater of bloodshed, admits he once used the pistol to kill a pigeon. The rebbe, defender of the faith, admits that "it is characteristic of believers sometimes not to believe" (72). What they hold in common, as Jews, at last takes precedence: first, a belief, if only "now and then," in "the Holy One. . . . Even you [Bleilip] now and then apprehend the Most High?"; and second, the blood kinship, including the most dreadful meanings of the term, that the Most High has seen fit to impose upon His people. The rebbe's last words, "Then you are as bloody as anyone," become Bleilip's final badge of Jewish identity in this most severely Jewish of the book's four tales. They also make a convenient bridge from this title story of *Bloodshed* to the title story of *Levitation*, where Jewish history again transforms bloodshed into a singular mark of this people's identity.

Levitation: Five Fictions (1982)

As its title indicates, *Levitation: Five Fictions* is a collection that ventures into fantasy, fable, and allegory. Beneath these novel tactics, however, Ozick's earlier triad of ground themes continues to inform the new book. Behind her fresh slate of characters facing new dramatic situations in widely different settings, the essential issues remain the familiar concerns with Jewish identity ("Levitation"), the pagan enticement ("Freud's Room," the Puttermesser-Xanthippe stories), and the struggles of the artist ("Shots").

In her title story, Ozick tries a new tactic: adopting the point of view of a Christian minister's daughter. Her (Ozick's) task is eased, however, by the woman's desire to marry "Out of my tradition," which makes her eligible for marriage to Feingold, a Jew who "had always known he did not want a Jewish wife" (3). A psalm her father recites from the pulpit leads her to resolve the problem of a mixed marriage: she will become "an Ancient Hebrew." After her conversion, the marriage seems unusually companionable; they are both novelists, as well as "Hebrews," and they love their professional intimacy: "Sometimes . . . it seemed to them that they were literary friends and lovers, like George Eliot and George Henry Lewes" (4). As writers, they share a view of literature that makes them feel "lucky in each other. . . . Lucy said, 'At least we have the same premises'" (6).

The central point of "Levitation," however, is that they don't have the same premises. Whereas her concept of "Ancient Hebrew" leads inevitably to Jesus as her stopping point—that supersessionist attitude of Christians so infuriating to Ozick—his concept of "Hebrew" begins in the Middle Ages and ends in World War II. Which is to say, Feingold is a Jew, not a Hebrew; and as such, he is obsessed with Jewish, not biblical, history: "Feingold's novel—the one he was writing now—was about [the] survivor of a massacre of Jews in the town of Estella in Spain in 1328. From morning to midnight he hid under a pile of corpses, until a 'compassionate knight' (this was the language of the history Feingold relied on) plucked him out and took him home to tend his wounds" (4–5).

When they throw a party to advance their professional interests, this dichotomy between "Jew" and "Hebrew" widens enormously. To Lucy's dismay, her husband insists upon pouring out his obsessions upon the company: "Feingold wanted to talk about . . . the crime of the French nobleman Draconet, a proud Crusader, who in the . . . year 1247 arrested all the Jews of the province of Vienne, castrated the men, and tore off the breasts of the women" (11). Eventually, she is driven to cut him off: "There he was, telling about . . . [h]ow in London, in 1279, Jews were torn to pieces by horses. . . . How in 1285, in Munich, a mob burned down a synagogue. Feingold was crazed by these tales, he drank them like a vampire" (12–13). In a Christological maneuver resembling a priest administrating the sacrament, Lucy "stuck a square of chocolate cake in his mouth to shut him up" (13).

There is one guest, however, who does not want Feingold to shut up: a man who updates Jewish history. A Holocaust survivor, he describes in a whisper the slaughter at (apparently) Babi Yar, gripping the other listening Jews with hypnotic power but leaving Lucy alone and bewildered: "Horror; sadism; corpses. As if . . . hundreds of Crucifixions were all happening at once . . . bulldozers shoveling those same sticks of skeletons" (14). As the whisper rasped on, the "room began to lift. It ascended . . . levitating on the little grains of the refugee's whisper. . . . They were being kidnapped, these Jews, by a messenger from the land of the dead" (15). Eventually, they levitate beyond her range of hearing, rapt in their necrotic visions, leaving her alone with her revulsion:

> A morbid cud-chewing. Death and death and death. . . . "Holocaust," someone caws dimly from above; she knows it must be Feingold. . . . Lucy decides it is possible to become jaded by atrocity. She is bored by the shootings and the gas and the camps. . . . They are tiresome as prayer. (19)

As the Jews soar up and away, she comes to a realization. Essentially she is not Jewish nor Ancient Hebrew nor Christian: she is a pagan, a believer in the Dionysian gods of the earth. What evokes this insight is her recollection of Italian peasants dancing, shouting "Old Hellenic syllables," and ringing bells like those "the priests used to beat in the temple of Minerva" (17). In this scene "she sees what is eternal: before there was the Madonna there was Venus, Aphrodite . . . Astarte. . . . the dances are seething. . . . Nature is their pulse. . . . Lucy sees how she has abandoned nature, how she lost the true religion on account of the God of the Jews" (18). Despite their intentions, then, neither partner can assimilate to the other: he tries to cease being a Jew, but cannot; she tries to cease being a Gentile, and cannot.

Of the three recurring themes in "Levitation," two (paganism and Jewish identity) are treated seriously, and one (the Feingolds as artists) is handled with levity. (They comically subvert the tale in which they appear, for example, by agreeing "on the importance of never writing about writers," 4). In "Shots," the portrayal of the artist is the central theme, calling up Ozick's most serious intentions. The art form in "Shots" is photography—a subject she has touched upon with great sensitivity in many writings but most notably when she discusses biography (see her essay on Edith Wharton, for example, AA 11–12). "When I read biographies," she told Elaine Kauvar, "I simply fall into those pictures. I think I spend more time drowning in old photographs in biographies than in the text" (Kauvar 397).[15] She is "drawn to the eeriness of photography," she says, because of "the way it represents both mortality and immortality. It both stands for death and stands against death because it's statuary" (396). Far from fostering illusion, a photograph exposes "hidden reality." It is a net that can snare "absolutely total reality. It's the capturing of what is, and in the is-ness there is God knows what"—a mysterious quality that makes a photograph "an impenetrable comment on reality" (397–98).

In "Shots" photography shortly becomes an analogue for Ozick's own vocation as a writer. The tale ranges into allegory along the way, but with the saving virtue of being meaningful both on a symbolic plane and on the level of immediate realism. The allegory begins with the motif of infatuation, initially with the art form itself. What the camera (or literature) offers its devotee is the power to raise the dead ("Call it necrophilia. . . . Dead faces draw me," 39), to preserve youth ("time as stasis . . . the time . . . of Keats's Grecian Urn"), to touch eternity. For the camerawoman who narrates "Shots," these powers are summed up in two images. One, from her childhood, is an ancient photo of "the Brown Girl," showing the face in youth of a patient at the nearby Home for the Elderly Ill—which face has since become one with the Home's "brainless ancients, rattling their china teeth and . . . rolling . . . their mad old eyes inside nearly visible crania" (140). The other image is her own handiwork, a happenstantial photograph of an assassination that blinks in an instant from life to death: "I calculated my aim, . . . shot once, shot again, and was amazed to see blood spring out of a hole in his neck" (43).

Here is witnessed the "eeriness of photography, the way it represents both mortality and immortality." But the infatuation grows beyond her embrace of a magic box. While on assignment to cover a public symposium, she becomes enthralled to one of its speakers, a professor of South American history. If Ozick's mode in this story were realism, doubtless the professor's subject would be Jewish history; for her portrayal of the artist, his subject doesn't matter. What does matter is the photographer's compulsive immersion in the professor's subject, which brings her into open rivalry with his wife, Verity. Though she is a perfect wife, a paradigm of multiple abilities, "He didn't like her. . . . His whole life was wrong. He was a dead man . . . ten times deader than [the assassin's victim]" (47).

Here the symbolism becomes complicated. If Verity (Conventional Realism) is unable to bring her husband out of his rigor mortis condition, she nonetheless has little to fear from her photographer rival, who has her own handicaps. Though she gets deeply into Sam's sphere (as Verity can not), and though she does revitalize him, hers must at best be a partial claim on his favor: she (Art, Imagination) may be History's off-hours paramour; Verity is his lawful and permanent companion. For all their affinities, the ways of Art and History are not finally compatible. "You really have to wait [for the picture to develop]," she tells him; "What's important is the waiting." It is during the wait that art happens: "If you have a change of heart between shooting your picture and taking it out of the developer, the picture changes too" (52).

Like so many other Ozick tales, "Shots" ends in a flare of combat. Verity and her historian husband, for their part, overcome the narrator by dressing her in archaic brown clothes, making her a "Period piece" (in Verity's phrasing). The period piece cannot resist this inevitability; eventually even the artist must submit to time and history. "I am already thirty-six years old, and tomorrow I will be forty-eight," she says (56), and thereby completes a circle: "I'm the Brown Girl in the pocket of my blouse. I reek of history" (56). But in one respect she registers a final prevalence of art over history. With all the intensity of the sex drive, she captures the image of her adversary for eternity: "I catch up my camera . . . my ambassador of desire, my secret house with its single shutter, my chaste aperture. . . . I shoot into their heads, the white harp behind. Now they are exposed. Now they will stick forever" (57).

As though to confirm the theme of "Shots," the next fragment of *Levitation*, "From a Refugee's Notebook," derives from photography its primary illumination. "Freud's Room," the opening section of "From a Refugee's Notebook," subjects the creator of psychoanalysis to his own invention via pictures of the famous studio in Vienna. What most engages the narrator is Freud's collection of primitive idols in the background, "hundreds of those strange little gods" which "represent the deep primitive grain of the mind Freud sought" (61). Had he looked deeply enough, Freud would have discovered that primitive grain in himself, notably in his simultaneous role as both Moses and Pan—the rationalist supervisor of the psyche subject to the Dionysian dream-life that those idols imply. In the end Freud's idols evoke a link with the golem-making propensity of the subsequent "Puttermesser and Xanthippe" narrative: "Is the doctor of the Unconscious not likely to be devoured by his own creation, like that rabbi of Prague who constructed a golem?" (64).[16]

The other link to Puttermesser in "From a Refugee's Notebook" is the utopia/dystopia motif of "The Sewing Harems," a heavy-duty satire on the antimaternal fringe of contemporary feminism. By sewing shut their labia, thereby suppressing reproduction, these women make the planet less polluted and crowded while giving themselves "greater opportunities to add to their goodness via self-improvement and self-development" (70). Because the attitude being lampooned is so obviously untenable, it is not clear why Ozick spent her talent on such a target. Perhaps, as she remarked about "Virility," it is because subtlety risks failure to be understood; or perhaps in this case she wanted to offset the arguably antimaternal implications of her "Hole/Birth Catalogue" essay, in which she demolished the "anatomy-is-destiny" argument.

The ongoing motif of Jewish identity is carried through "From a Refugee's Notebook" by the narrator. Though uncommonly vague—the epigraph of the piece ascribes "European or perhaps South American origin" to this otherwise "unidentified" figure—the narrator discloses Jewish identity in three stages. First, we are told that the Refugee-narrator must rely on pictures of Freud's room because he/she will not visit "any land which once suckled the Nazi boot" (59). More telling still is the narrator's expertise with bolts of cloth (like that of the Miamians in *The Shawl*), which suggests a long sojourn within the largely Jewish garment industry of New York: "I can, with eyes shut, tell you which is rayon and which silk, which the genuine wool and which the synthetic . . ." (62). And finally, there is the dead giveaway of the role of Moses, cited here as Freud's counterpart in overriding the spontaneous rule of nature (63). This last motif in particular forms a link with the final, major entry of *Levitation,* "Puttermesser and Xanthippe."

Puttermesser

In the "Works in Progress" column of the *New York Times Book Review* of 6 June 1982 (page 11), Cynthia Ozick gave a brief preview of the work that would soon comprise the centerpiece of *Levitation.* "Here are 54 pages of a novel begun some time ago, still breathing, with a live protagonist," she writes, adding that when she abandoned the project years ago, the protagonist "seemed old; now I am creeping up on her age." An odd resistance emanates from the author toward her story—"I'm afraid of it. I see how much I don't want this woman who wants me"—but she does admit a powerful affinity with her theme: "Oh, admit it—the dream of happiness! I want to invent virtue and happiness!"

More than half of *Levitation* is given over to Ozick's model seeker of virtue and happiness, an urbanite named Ruth Puttermesser who is thirty-four in the prefatory segment ("Puttermesser: Her Work History, Her Ancestry, Her Afterlife"), forty-six in the novella-length "Puttermesser and Xanthippe," and mid-fiftyish in "Puttermesser Paired"—a sequel that appeared in the *New Yorker* of 8 October 1990. Apart from her marital status (single) and job (a lawyer), Puttermesser is clearly an alter ego of her maker.

Possessing "one of those Jewish faces with a vaguely Oriental cast" (23), she is devoutly loyal to New York, guilty over piano lessons fudged in child-hood, angry at her subjection to job discrimination, exultant over her studies in Hebrew grammar, and so hungrily intellectual that her dream of the afterlife is an eternal reading binge featuring Ozick's favorite subjects and authors:

> She reads anthropology, zoology, physical chemistry, philosophy, . . . about quarks, about primate sign language, . . . what Stonehenge meant. Putter-messer . . . will read at last . . . all of Balzac, all of Dickens, all of Turgenev and Dostoevski (her mortal self had already read all of Tolstoy and George Eliot); . . . and the whole *Faerie Queene* and every line of *The Ring and the Book* . . . at last, at last! (33)

From that heavenly list, George Eliot would later prove the most consequen-tial, providing the basis for the 1990 novella "Puttermesser Paired."

Meanwhile, although Ozick wrote in 1976 that "Literature-as-game was exactly what I had been devotedly arguing against" (BL 8), the most distinc-tive feature of the first Puttermesser story is its postmodern sense of litera-ture as artifice and play. The modernist realism of *Trust* and *Bloodshed* now gives way to open authorial intrusion into the text: "Now if this were an optimistic portrait [Ozick writes at mid-point] . . . [her] biography would proceed romantically . . . to a bower in a fine suburb." But the postmodern uncertainty principle will not permit so tidy a plot line: "Perhaps she will undertake a long-term affair with Vogel; . . . perhaps not" (31). At times the author interrupts her writer-persona with strident objections: "Stop. Stop, stop! Puttermesser's biographer, stop! Disengage, please. Though it is true that biographies are invented, not recorded, here you invent too much" (35). The sketch ends in a similar fashion, with a postmodern confession of artistic aporia: "Hey! Puttermesser's biographer! What will you do with her now? (38).

The author's postmodern presence can also be readily detected behind Puttermesser's ethnic feelings—in her disdain for the assimilated Jew who rules her workplace ("a blue-eyed Guggenheim, a German Jew" who had gone to Choate), and in her distrust of her WASP bosses in the law firm, blue-eyed, close-shaven, and with "such beautiful manners even while drunk" (30, 31). A familiar reason why those beautiful manners remain unavailing relates to her name ("Puttermesser" being Yiddish for "Butterknife"), as it is expounded for her by her Orthodox Uncle Zindel:

> By us we got only *messer*, you follow? By them they got sword, they got lance, they got halberd. . . . So help me, what don't one of them knights carry? Look

up in the book . . . you'll see cutlass, pike, rapier, foil, ten dozen more. By us a pike is a fish. Not to mention what nowadays they got—bayonet stuck on the gun. . . . But by us—what we got? A *messer*! *Puttermesser*, you slice off a piece butter, you cut to live, not to kill. (34–35)[17]

The revelation that Uncle Zindel does not exist (he died before Puttermesser was born) just adds to the postmodern fun.

In the same "Works in Progress" column of the *New York Times Book Review* mentioned above, Ozick reveals a major shift in aesthetic theory between the two "Puttermesser" segments of *Levitation* (the briefer of which was written earlier). Inasmuch as the postmodern playfulness of "Puttermesser: Her Work History" had led to a dead end—"Hey! Puttermesser's biographer! What will you do with her now?"—Ozick proceeds to renounce the postmodern in favor of an earlier, better concept of fiction:

I am thinking about the old lost power of "having a subject," . . . about the malaise of subjectlessness, which leads to parody or to nihilism: esthetic "distance," distaste, the "absurd," affliction, dead ends, death. Oh, happiness without parody! Why not, why not? To drill through the "postmodern" and come out on the other side, alive and saved and wise as George Eliot.

Although the wisdom of George Eliot would have to wait for the grand impersonations of "Puttermesser Paired," her novella of 1990, "Puttermesser and Xanthippe" has substance enough to carry the quest for virtue and happiness to mock-epic proportions, broken into the epic's obligatory twelve sections ("books," we might say) that are numbered with Roman numerals. It likewise upholds the epic mode by making the destiny of a whole society (New York City) depend on the wisdom, courage, and resourcefulness of its epic heroine, Ruth Puttermesser. To this ancient Greek narrative form Ozick conjoins the medieval Jewish legend of the golem of Prague (the subject of a 1920s silent movie made in Austria). Though she violates the Jewish tradition for the feminist purpose of making her golem a female, Ozick in most respects follows the pattern of the Grand Rabbi of Prague. Made of earth and breathed into life through the speaking of the Name, the golem is raised up to save its creator's people from mortal danger: a forthcoming pogrom for the Jewish community of medieval Prague; an imminent total collapse into utter civic, social, and economic chaos for New York City.

Like her medieval predecessor, Xanthippe—named, with feminist ardor, after Socrates' supposedly overbearing wife—is marvelously effective at her task of redeeming the doomed and damned metropolis. Wearing a toga

(136), or a "sari brilliant with woven flowers" (141), Xanthippe the Jewish golem elides into a Greek goddess risen from earth, thereby giving a new twist to Ms. Ozick's old Hellenism-Hebraism dichotomy. Here our female Pan and Moses work in harmony, as it were, with Puttermesser using the golem's magic to effect a transformation of New York City. (While it lasts, this Jewish/Greek collaboration comprises a triumph of the "Dual Curriculum" that Joseph Brill dreams of effecting in Ozick's next book, *The Cannibal Galaxy*.) Elected mayor, Puttermesser rids the city of its crime, ugliness, and debt: "Everyone is at work. Lovers apply to the City Clerk for marriage licenses. The Bureau of Venereal Disease Control has closed down. The ex-pimps are learning computer skills. . . . The City is at peace" (135).

But as we would expect in an Ozick story, the collaboration between Pan and Moses is short-lived as Xanthippe turns out to be not merely a Greek goddess but a sex goddess, who in the end has to be dissolved into the earth again because of her uncontrollable nymphomania. Succumbing to the unruliest of gods ("Eros had entered Gracie Mansion," 138), Xanthippe becomes Puttermesser's adversary, consuming the mayor's entire slate of city officers in her sexual fire; and when the golem returns to the earth, her magic goes with her, leaving the city in its normal ruined condition. With Puttermesser's closing outcry—"O lost New York! . . . O lost Xanthippe!" (58)—*Levitation* as a whole attains a circular structure: it began with a levitation and ends with a collapse back to ordinary reality.

Postscript 1990: "Puttermesser Paired"

Perhaps because her public life had failed so haplessly in "Puttermesser and Xanthippe," or perhaps in response to the conservatism of the 1980s, the heroine of "Puttermesser Paired" (in the *New Yorker* of 8 October 1990) displays some strong contrasts with her earlier manifestation. Most notably, she now withdraws totally from the larger community to pursue an exclusive interest in her interior life. New York, in turn, lapses from an object of Puttermesser's reformist zeal to a setting—both stimulating and suffocating, culturally rich and socially sordid—for her private fantasy of perfect love and friendship. And there are other contrasts: as a strict "rationalist," Puttermesser no longer practices golem magic; as a fiftyish bride, she no longer eschews marriage; and as an impersonator of George Eliot, she no longer evinces a paramount interest in Jewish identity. Instead, mindful of George Eliot the artist-hero, the story develops Ozick's long-standing theme of impersonation in terms of artistic identity.

The idea of Puttermesser reliving the life of George Eliot apparently carried over from the title story in *Levitation*, where a husband and wife, both novelists, achieved an ideal intimacy: "Sometimes, closing up their notebooks for the night [from which they read aloud to one another], it seemed to them that they were literary friends and lovers, like George Eliot and George Henry Lewes" (LE 4). On numerous grounds it is natural that Cynthia Ozick would feel strong affinities with George Eliot. As women artists, each had to fight her way into a male-dominated principality of prestigious achievement; each tasted major success only when nearing the age of forty. As inheritors of a powerful religious heritage, each had to subordinate that heritage to the artist's calling, with Ozick agonizing over her "Jewish writer oxymoron" and Eliot finally sloughing off her Christian evangelism in favor of a freethinker's credo.[18] And, although Eliot was far more prolific than Ozick, each achieved excellence in a broad variety of forms and genres—poetry, plays, essays, stories, and novels. Uniquely among Gentile writers, Eliot also portrayed Jewish characters not merely with sympathy but with an uncomplicated admiration that some critics found propagandishly sentimental, a charge notably laid against *Daniel Deronda*.[19] Most important of all, Ozick found in Eliot and her contemporaries the convergence of the Judaic ethos with the art of fiction:

> The novel at its nineteenth-century pinnacle was a Judaized novel: George Eliot and Dickens and Tolstoy were all touched by the Jewish covenant: they wrote of conduct and of the consequences of conduct: they were concerned with a society of will and commandment. At bottom it is . . . the novel as a Jewish force. ("Toward a New Yiddish," AA 164)

In her essay on Edith Wharton, Ozick remarked that we "have always known (Freud taught us only how to reinforce this knowledge), that the secret self is the true self, that obsession is confession" (AA 25). Her own obsession, here and in many other tales, focuses on the idea of the impersonator. In "Puttermesser Paired," the most fundamental difference between Ozick/Puttermesser and George Eliot is precisely the theme of impersonation, which is Ozick's obsession but not Eliot's. That difference is also, obviously enough, the measure of change that marks off the Victorian novel from the postmodern sensibility. The idea of a real, stable, and unitary self would have seemed as natural to Eliot as to her contemporary Charles Darwin; in the late twentieth century, impersonation would seem equally natural for many writers for whom selfhood is a dubious construct—one thinks of Philip Roth, John Barth, and Thomas Pynchon as engaging impersonaters.

Another difference between Ozick and Eliot is the sharp-edged humor with which Ozick renders her subject, both Puttermesser and New York City being subject to an ongoing satire that varies between acerbic and gentle. The high-toned seriousness of George Eliot's Mordecai in *Daniel Deronda* has no counterpart here, primarily because Puttermesser, unlike her maker, has no religious seriousness. For her, being Jewish means having a mother who, between complaints about the heat in Miami, nags her daughter to get married; it means scanning the ads in the *New York Review of Books* in search of a love partner; it means enduring the Age of the Slob in contemporary courtship manners (Puttermesser counts two pairs of corduroy trousers and one of denim on the couch during a singles party); it means soliciting strangers to make up the minimal number of witnesses necessary for a Judaic Reform wedding.

But these cultural deficiencies argue all the more ardently in favor of Puttermesser's obsessive project, to impersonate George Eliot and thereby "to leave New York behind, to be restored to glad, golden Victoria." All she needs is the right man to impersonate Eliot's ideal love mate, George Lewes, so as to emulate their original "marriage of true minds, admitting no impediment." When the right man appears, the copyist-painter Rupert Rabeeno, the metamorphosis seems complete. Like one of Henry James's confidantes, Rabeeno readily agrees to the role assigned to him, to the extent of immersing the two of them in readings about the Eliot-Lewes honeymoon. But it turns out that he has a more subtle role in mind. In his vocation as a professional copyist—a task that he insists on defining as original creativity—his eye falls not on Lewes but on a copyist of Lewes: the man named John Cross who married George Eliot after Lewes' death and then retraced for their honeymoon the exact itinerary of the Eliot-Lewes honeymoon almost three decades earlier. What broke the spell for the Cross-Eliot union was the humiliating fiasco of his sexual nonperformance (as Ozick renders it), which may have hastened George Eliot's death just nine months after the wedding. For Puttermesser, too, her wedding ends in disillusionment as her bridegroom, whom she understood to have accepted the role of Lewes, instead reveals himself to be impersonating John Cross: he abandons Puttermesser on their wedding night without fulfilling his amorous duties.

Beginning with the title, "Puttermesser Paired," and extending through a broad web of details, the story expounds its theme of duplication and duplicity. Puttermesser's first conversation with Rupert, when she finds him copying Jacques-Louis David's painting of the Death of Socrates in the museum, should have sufficed as a warning. The cultural thrust behind David's original painting was yet another copyist's impersonation: the attempt of the French Enlightenment to emulate the classical age of Greece and Rome. Later, ironically, David lived on to serve a similar function as the grand artist of the French Revolution when it—renouncing the Roman

Empire as an undemocratic model—merely substituted another impersonation, emulating the Roman Republic.

The fact that Socrates is Rabeeno's subject casts an ironic light on Ozick's ground theme of pagan enticement, which has shifted its ground from the erotic to the intellectual not through any decline in Puttermesser's libido but because of the weakness of the postmodern male.[20] In this novella about imposture, a wry mimicry of *Death in Venice* seems to unfold, with the role of Aschenbach given over to the younger man who comes unglued at the prospect of sexual nexus. (In the mid-1950s, Ozick had urged *Death in Venice* upon her friend Alfred Chester, who wrote back to her, she says, "exalted. It was, he said, among the great works of literature.")[21] Romantically ensconced above the Grand Canal, the youthful bridegroom has eyes with "lids as raw and bloody as meat, stretched apart like an animal's freshly slaughtered throat. . . . The eyeballs had rolled off under the skin."

Even Mann's unhealthy atmosphere infects George Eliot's Venice—"The bitter, putrid wind, the drains, the polluted canal . . ." (69). Eliot herself initially appears rejuvenated by the May-December honeymoon—"It all at once struck her that, with her pleasant figure and loosened hair, she had, in the looking-glass, the sweetness of a bride of twenty-two: she did not feel old at all." Unfortunately her groom's potency fell off with his clothing: "He had discarded his cravat—it was a thick serpent on the floor" (68). Meanwhile, as in Mann, a "raucous party" happens by with the gondoliers releasing paganlike "blasts of laughter, . . . and singing, and this time a tremulous guitar" (69). Though her death did not occur in Venice, George Eliot's demise a few months after the honeymoon fiasco seems comparable to that of Mann's pathetic victim of Eros-out-of-season.

In their total effect, the Puttermesser stories accomplish for Cynthia Ozick something comparable to what the Rabbit novels have done for John Updike, permitting the author to respond to personal and social change over a long-term period. The affinity for alliteration in *Rabbit, Run* (*Redux, At Rest,* etc.) and "Puttermesser Paired" hints at a deliberate echo, but there is more to it than that. Near contemporaries, the two writers began their careers at nearly the same time, espousing a curiously similar cultural focus, with Updike's modern/Greek synthesis in *The Centaur* (1962) giving Ozick a terrific case of "Writer's Envy" midway through her fling with the pagan gods in *Trust* (1966).[22] Their obvious differences—man/woman, Christian/Jew, suburbanite/New Yorker—produce in this case a pleasant sense of complementarity as opposed to the often embittered "differance" of race/class/gender theory. ("I love John Updike" was Ozick's opening line of her review of *Bech,* AA 114.) With Puttermesser now nearing retirement age, perhaps we can look forward to a "Ruth at Rest" segment in the midterm future, hopefully of a more benign character than Rabbit's pathetic exit from the Updike tetralogy.

"At Fumicaro"

Levitation (1982) appeared to unblock a fresh stream of creativity for Ozick during the 1980s, as she followed that book with two novels, *The Cannibal Galaxy* (1983) and *The Messiah of Stockholm* (1987), the novella "The Shawl" (1983, 1989), and two essay collections, *Art & Ardor* (1983) and *Metaphor & Memory* (1989). Before we pass on to those works in subsequent chapters, however, one other work of the 1980s deserves a brief commentary, partly for its unique character among Ozick's writings.

In the *New Yorker* of 6 August 1984, Cynthia Ozick published a novella, "At Fumicaro," that tried a hitherto unattempted narrative strategy. Going beyond *Trust,* with its narrator's mutedly Gentile sensibility, "At Fumicaro" posits an avidly Christian central character, so devoutly Roman Catholic as to have "few Protestant and no Jewish friends" (32), and so bent on Christlike sacrifice that he marries his three-months-pregnant peasant chambermaid three days after meeting her. (More subtly, however, by this marriage he reenacts Joseph Brill's avoidance, in *The Cannibal Galaxy,* of union with an intellectually equal female.) The story is also unique in having no Jewish characters, apart from passing mention of a priest named Father Robin ("Né Rabinowitz"), as though to belie thereby its setting in the Italy of the Mussolini-Hitler prewar alliance. In short, she attempted to bring off an act of cultural impersonation such as she castigated Updike for undertaking in his *Bech* novels—an act that she insisted could not succeed beyond the strict limits of light satire.

Possibly her satire on the Catholic tradition is light enough to touch an occasional nerve without stirring resentment. Her protagonist, Frank Castle, has a name that evokes the medieval past of the Church without specifying the Crusader/Inquisition horrors that drove Feingold mad in "Levitation." Attending a conference entitled "The Church and How It Is Known" (presumably omitting how Jews have known it), Castle should be well pleased with the social climate of the affair, directed as it is by an American whose name is allegorically WASPish—"Mr. Wellborn." And the religious conference itself is broadly satirized, with topics ranging from the imperative of sexual purity (an idea that further inflames Castle's lust for his teenage sex partner) to varieties of terminal dullness ("The Dioceses of Savannah and Denver Compared"; *"Parish or Perish"*).

Behind this pseudo-Catholic facade, however, familiar outlines of the old pagan enticement soon appear, transposing Ozick's Pan versus Moses theme into Pan versus Christ. A telling sign is the response of Castle's audience to his paper depicting the reality of evil as the "corridor to Christ." By the time he finishes, his listeners—including the priests—have drifted outdoors in pursuit of their true religion, the worship of nature. With its majestic vista overlooking Lake Como—and beyond it, "like distant ice-cream cones, the Alps"—the village of Fumicaro can obliterate at a glance the two Christian millennia since the gods of nature possessed this land: "Glorious disc of a lake! . . . It summoned eternally. The bliss of its flat sun-shot surface. . . ." We are reminded that Frank's name-saint—and San Francesco is an important reference in this story—was a near-heretical figure for his immersion in nature. (The other saint that Ozick cites importantly, Augustine, also suits her neopagan theme because of his illicit fathering of a son named Deodatus—"Given by God").[23]

As always, the essence of the pagan enticement is illicit sex, which here binds the three main characters in an odd triad. The main character, Frank Castle, is reminiscent of the Pagan Rabbi in his sudden lapse from Catholic monasticism—his initial intention "to be strong and transcendent above the body"—to ardent erotic carnality. The Tilbeck figure of the tale is another conference participant whose name, Percy Nightingale, bears the pantheistic overtones associated with two Romantic poets. With—belying his name— "the pouncing syllables of a hawk," Nightingale evokes the image of sexual predation both in his habit of appearing minus his trousers and in his rabbitlike appearance, which is suspiciously like that of Updike's favorite practitioner of free love: "his eyes, blue overrinsed to transparency, were humps in a face flat as zinc. . . . His shirt was white, his [naked] thighs were white, his shoes the same." A defender of (the prewar) Hitler—"At least he holds off against the Commies"—Nightingale clearly favors Nazi-Fascist culture, a truly neopagan resurgency, over the Christian heritage that he nominally serves. To the charge that "you are forgetting Christ" Nightingale replies: "Oh Jesus God. I never forget Christ. Why else would I end up in this goddam shack in this godforsaken country? Maybe the Fascists'll make something out of these Wops yet. Put some spine in 'em."

If Nightingale is a more engaging version of the evangelist in "Envy; or, Yiddish in America"—the Christian as intellectual huckster—the third member of the triad is the serious exponent of pagan affinities. Repeatedly crying "No belief! No belief!" she has compelling reason for her renunciation of the Christian ethos that, in this seat of Catholic power, failed to protect her from incestuous rape; and compelling reason, also, to doubt the Christian God Who failed to forestall the pregnancy that resulted from her forced sexual encounter. Initially, the girl's words touch a secret nerve in Frank

Castle's religious psychology, "because every day of his life he had had to make this same pilgrimage to belief all over again, starting out each dawn with the hard crow's call of no belief." But soon he sees her as a divinely ordained subject of conversion (his academic specialty), which he can accomplish by marrying her and thus restoring her capacity for Christian belief: "He had, he saw, been led to Fumicaro . . . for the explicit salvation of one needful soul."

Predictably, the needful soul turns out to be his own, and it is his fiancée who meets the need by bringing him to her ancient but vital rites of idolatry. Viviana's favorite idol—a statue of San Francesco—has a pedigree of probable classical vintage: "The torso had crumbled. It hardly looked holy. . . . [It] might have been as old as a hundred years, or a thousand; two thousand. Only an archeologist could say." It does not require an archeologist, however, to link this crumbling graven image with two authentic icons of the Christian faith, Leonardo's *Last Supper* and the *Pietà*, which are badly deteriorating—and further corrupted by renovators—when Castle goes to view them.

In this setting of Fascist Italy, that physical deterioration bears obvious symbolic implications for Frank Castle. They begin with the irrelevance of the religious conference at Fumicaro, with its high-minded and unlistened-to papers on Churchly idealism. For all his crude vulgarity, Nightingale is right to wonder why "*anyone* shows up for these things," and Castle himself comes to think of its participants as fostering "a sham—mountebanks all." But the unreality of Christian idealism leaves Christian idolatry exposed more clearly as something real and terrifying. As figured in a peasant girl, Viviana, idolatry may seem little more than a harmless throwback to primitive times: "She gave God a home everywhere—in old Roman tubs, in painted wooden dolls: it did not matter. Sticks and stones." But Frank Castle's encounter with a lifesize crucifix—"a medieval man of wood"—makes him wonder about the cruelty behind the central icon of the Christian religion. "Red paint, dry for seven centuries, spilled from the nail holes," he muses, moving him to "reflect on their [the nails'] cruelty—a religion with a human corpse at the center, what could that mean?"

At best, what the corpse at the center will mean is an otherworldly fixation contrary to the L'Chaim! principle. At worst, the corpse at the center prophesies what idolatry always predicates in Ozick's writing: a bloody lapse into the inhuman, the uncivilized, the ungodly. Immediately following this paragraph about the religion with a corpse at its center, Ozick portrays a sudden appearance of Fascist propaganda: "In the streets there were all at once flags, and everywhere big cloth posters of Il Duce flapping on the sides of buildings." During the next half decade, the new idolatry would claim fifty million dead, including the six million Jews. Ozick's excursion into a Catholic/Christian consciousness thereby effects in the end a connection to Jewish history: fresh blood flowing from those medieval nails.

Because "At Fumicaro" is an excerpt from a novel-in-progress, Ozick has recently stated misgivings about its potential for misleading her readers. In the finished novel, she says, Frank Castle will turn out to be a converted Jew, and his child will bear the brunt of the theme, which will question how a child of mixed parentage handles the contradictions of Jewish-Christian ancestry. As it happens, several years after publishing "At Fumicaro," Ozick developed a close relationship with just such a young person, an extremely bright and engaging thirtyish daughter of a German-Jewish father and German-Catholic mother. Whether the novel will trace the life pattern of this person (who as an adult chose to change from Catholic to Jew) remains to be seen, but it seems plausible that the young woman's story may have affected Ozick's original plans for "At Fumicaro." The completed book, if and when it appears, figures to extend Ozick's range into a new and very important permutation of her master theme, the quandaries of Jewish identity. Meanwhile, Ozick's exposition of that theme in her three novels of the 1980s will complete our set of readings.

The Cannibal Galaxy: Curriculum Duel

There is no Jew alive today who is not also resonantly Greek.

"Bialik's Hint"

In approaching *The Cannibal Galaxy*, we shall begin with the standard formulation that Western civilization has a Greek mind, a Roman body, and a Jewish soul.[24] As propagated by the majority culture in Europe and the Americas, this formulation generally accredits both the civilization as it now stands and its three ancient tributaries for their admirable achievements. Away back in her first novel, however, Cynthia Ozick was writing—according to her later recollection—out of a violent hatred of the whole of Western civilization: "all of it."[25] The reason for this hatred is of course "Jewish history," in so far as that history comprises a record of interaction between Jews and Gentiles.

From the perspective of Jewish history, the Greek mind and Roman body have had little relevance to the Jewish soul. Matthew Arnold to the contrary, in Ozick's view Hellenism and Hebraism have more typically proved incompatible adversaries than complementary pillars of modern culture. With respect to Ozick's writing, the Greek mind presents itself mainly by way of subverting the Law and the Prophets in *Trust, The Pagan Rabbi,* "Usurpation (Other People's Stories)" in *Bloodshed,* and the Puttermesser-Xanthippe episodes of *Levitation.* Hellenic-Hebraic incompatibility does not suffice, however, as grounds for the hatred to which Ozick confesses. It is the third part of the Jewish/Greek/Roman triad that must claim this distinction: the Roman body which has presented something more serious than enticement and subversion for Judaic culture to contend with. From the Emperor Titus through the Inquisition, from the pogroms to the Holocaust, the "Roman body" of Western civilization—that is, the expanse of Europe bequeathed by Rome to Christendom—has repeatedly undertaken the physical annihilation of the Jewish people and their culture. This fact is the groundwork of *The Cannibal Galaxy;* and Principal Brill's failure to acknowledge it contributes largely to the failure of his experiment in Jewish/Western education.

This is not to deny the role of mediocrity in Brill's failure. The sign of mediocrity—"you stopped too soon"—applies to many of Brill's actions, most notably those involving his relationship with Hester Brill's apparently unremarkable daughter Beulah. But his most egregious instance of stopping too soon is his excision from the Dual Curriculum of the Jewish history which he himself lived through in Vichy France, suffering the loss of his parents and several siblings as well as traumatic concealment in a convent basement and a farmer's hayloft. Because he falsifies both Jewish history and Western civilization by this excision of truth, his Dual Curriculum cannot effectively sustain Jewish identity, which is thereby subject to the two leading implications of the book's title: the *Judenrein* effects of the Holocaust in Europe (a continent that she considers "one vast Jewish graveyard");[26] and the likelihood of assimilation in America.

Ironically, Principal Brill persists in his autolobotomy concerning Jewish history even though his dwelling place throughout his career as principal (a converted hayloft) is a daily reminder of his Holocaust experience—as is the stable downstairs through which he must pass, a virtual replica of the convent basement in which he was hidden. Those two hiding places represent a sort of Dual Curriculum in themselves, revealing the two extremes by which Europe has threatened for centuries to extinguish the Jewish heritage. Brill's experience of the hayloft, where he was starved and frozen and at one point clubbed senseless by his host farmer (for bathing himself in the nearby brook), typifies Jewish life vis-à-vis the lower classes of Europe since the Dark Ages, particularly in the shtetls of Eastern Europe. The hayloft episode stands for the agony of Jewish survival through a millennium of persecution by peasants, soldiers, and urban mobs who killed, burned, and ghettoized

Jews in random spasms of cruelty and ignorance. The animal imagery of the episode—Brill sleeping between two cows for warmth, defecating "side by side with oxen," his "palms as hard and dented as goat horns," he himself "more and more turning into a beast of the field," having lost his will to read (32, 33)—underscores the thinness of "civilization" on this side of Europe.

The convent basement represents the opposite extreme of Europe: the best fruit—within the strictures of the Holocaust years—of Western and Christian civilization. The brave, kindly nuns who risk their own lives to protect Brill are not merely preferable to the peasant farmer; without irony we may say that they exemplify the supreme Christian values of humanitarian love, sacrifice, and fidelity. Moreover, the basement itself, though it is dark and confined, contrasts with the hayloft by nourishing the life of the mind after the fashion of Europe's grand intellectual tradition. Here Brill enters the exaltation of high learning while devouring the old priest's superb library. It is true that Brill's monastic regimen requires him to shut off the radio, an act that insulates him from the ranting against Jews broadcast throughout Nazified Europe, but that seems a small price to pay for what he imbibes of traditional Europe in his hideout. (This gesture, however, portends his later excision of the Holocaust from his Dual Curriculum.) In his involuntary cloister Brill develops a passion for certain Enlightenment writers and their Romantic-modern successors: Corneille, Racine, Rousseau, Heine, Proust, and the mysterious Edmond Fleg.

Like the kindly nuns, the French priest who owned these books exemplified Christianity at its best—"he had had a dangerous reputation for liberalism" (20)—but with the added grace of a probing, independent intellect. When, gradually, Brill realizes "that the old priest had loved thought more than Jesus" (21), he recognizes a Gentile version of the Jewish mind, a judgment borne out by the priest's partiality for an obscure Jewish writer named Edmond Fleg (originally Edmond Flegenheimer, 22). It is through the writings of Fleg that Brill becomes enthralled to the Dual Curriculum, for it is Fleg who formulates for Brill the synthesis between Jewish and European cultures. In his books about the Judeo-Christian tradition—*Jésus, raconté par le Juif Errant (Jesus, as told by the Wandering Jew), Le Juif de Pape (The Pope's Jew), L'Enfant Propheté (The Prophesied Child*, 21–22)— Fleg has accomplished a fusion that the old priest, in a marginal comment, found irresistible. (The priest's statement incidentally reflects a view that Cynthia Ozick has often stated in her own right about Western civilization at large—in her oral interview with Kay Bonetti, for example, recorded in April 1986 by the American Audio Prose Library.) This is the priest's comment:

The Israelitish divinely unifying principle and the Israelitish ethical inspiration
are the foundations of our French genius. . . . [Edmond Fleg] harmonizes the
rosette of the Légion d'Honneur in his lapel with the frontlets of the Covenant
on his brow. (22)

From Fleg's example Brill derives his vision of his life's mission: "The fusion
of scholarly Europe and burnished Jerusalem. . . . Corneille and Racine set
beside Jonah and Koheleth. . . . the civilization that invented the telescope
side by side with the civilization that invented conscience—astronomers and
God-praisers uniting in a majestic dream of peace" (27).

In time, the brutality of the hayloft episode cancels Europe from Brill's
dream; afterward, "[he] never once meditated on the intellectual union of
Paris and Jerusalem" (34). Dreaming instead "of razing Paris to the ground"
(34), he has learned the lesson of the Holocaust—"Europe the cannibal
galaxy. Edmond Fleg's Parisian Jerusalem a smoky ruin. He saw how France
was Egypt" (83). In taking his dream to America, however, Brill fails to
absorb the lesson from the other Europe, the high civilization of Christian
goodness and intellectual achievement experienced by him in the nuns'
cellar. That lesson is the danger that the majority culture, in its most appeal-
ing dress, will cannibalize the Judaic heritage through assimilation. The
transmitter of enlightenment in this case is not Edmond Fleg but the fifteen-
year-old girl who discovers Brill in the basement and who turns out to be
another Jewish refugee in hiding.

This girl epitomizes both meanings of the book's title: assimilation and
Holocaust. By Nazi calculation there is no question that she is a Jew, and the
fact that she is in hiding confirms beyond question Brill's repeated remark
that "You're a Jew" (29). But though she would certainly have died in the
Holocaust were it not for the grace of the nuns who shelter her, she insists
that she is not a Jew but a third-generation Catholic. ("My grandfather on
my father's side was the first," 29). The girl's name, Renée, clearly suggests
the assimilationist status in which thousands of Jews expected to find refuge
from persecution; her reply to being called a Jew—"I don't care. I'm not
afraid" (30)—likewise duplicates the tragically misplaced confidence of
those countless victims of the Cannibal Galaxy.

It is not Nazis but the kindly, courageous nuns who disclose the great
danger that Renée's assimilationist experience engenders:

> "Is she a Jew?" [Brill asks the nun]
> "She is of the same family as Our Lord."
> "She said she's a third-generation Catholic."

"She is already beautiful in the faith. She wishes to be as we are, and we thank Our Lord for the gift of His blood through His seed of the flesh. Monsieur Brill, be calm." (31)

Even the girl's punishment for sneaking into the basement discloses this more benign form of the Cannibal Galaxy at work. Her translation of *Julius Caesar* into English is a bridge from the classical past of Western civilization to its imminent future, with no niche provided for the Judaic heritage other than whatever a Catholic education might make of it.

Brill's education is of course the main subject of Ozick's narrative, and his departure from the convent in a nun's habit implies the cultural overlay that might have superseded his Jewish heritage had he remained subject to the good sisters' teachings like Renée of the "born again" nomenclature. The subsequent hayloft episode, by proving a timely reminder of the Europe that most Jews have immemorially had to cope with, effectively relieves Brill of any delusions he might have nourished about Christian goodness as a basis for future Jewish life in Europe. Christian evangelism, however, even in so godly a countenance as that of the good nuns, is never for Brill the most dangerous attraction of non-Holocaust Europe. That distinction goes instead to the pagan enticement of idolatry—an infallible sign in Ozick's work of the cannibal propensities in any civilization.

During his upbringing in Paris, preeminently Europe's City of Light and of the Enlightenment, Brill's education veered off early toward the pagan enticement in a minor emanation of the book's title. The Dual Curriculum that he frames in the convent basement had its long foreground in these Paris years, in the tension between Brill's life as an immigrant Jew and the pleasure he experienced while "drinking in Western Civilization at the University" (11). Originally there was no tension, but rather gratitude toward Paris for its Vieille du Temple boulevard: "such a noble name, such reverence for the pieties and principles of an ancient people—a street called after the overrun and rubbled lost Temple of Jerusalem!" (7). But when told by a classmate about Jonathan le Juif, a medieval violator of the Eucharist who brought punishment on all the Jews of Paris, Brill realized that "he lived in a place where there had once been a pogrom no different from the pogrom in the savage Czarist village his parents had fled" (7). Even so, despite the role of the Eucharist (or Host) in this tale of medieval cruelty, the Jewish youth was torn in two by its blandishments: "After that Joseph kept secret from his father and from Rabbi Pult everything he was savoring about damsels and chivalry and—he hardly let his eyes pluck at the words—the Holy Grail.

They would have judged these enchantments and glorious histories to be frivolity, idolatry" (7).

From this time forward, the battle goes badly for the Jewish component of Brill's personal Dual Curriculum. On the Jewish side are the constraints of his father's fish market, situated among "fruit hawkers and drygoods peddlers, vegetable carts and street criers, all in the dialects of the immigrants from Kiev and Minsk and Lithuania" (6). (Brill's ancestral ties to Minsk—also Ozick's ancestral city—suggest not only the pogroms that drove his parents to Paris but also the geographic span of the coming Holocaust, from France across Germany and Poland to deep inside European Russia.) So Brill's foremost concern is to conceal the signs of his origins: "The University inspired him to alter his diction. . . . It was humiliating to be an immigrant's child and fill one's mouth with the wrong noise. Every night Joseph scrubbed the fish smell off his hands with an abrasive soap that skinned his knuckles mercilessly" (12). This class snobbery, so typical of Ozick's "Europe," would contribute later to Brill's ruin, bringing his "scheme of learning luminous enough for a royal prince or princess" to an incongruous end: "Instead he was educating commoners, weeds, the children of plumbers" (57).

The formal education of Joseph Brill proceeds in a fashion analogous to these surface manners of speech and grooming. Despite Rabbi Pult's teachings from Hillel and Akiva—Enlightenment figures eighteen centuries ahead of their time, he tells Joseph (7)—it is Gentile idolatry that takes the youth's imagination, particularly as exhibited in the museum just two blocks away from the Vieille du Temple. Here the stone images, set in "a secret flowery courtyard emblazoned with statuary" (8), merely epitomize the true meaning of idolatry: the worship of anything instead of God. The chief instance of idolatry by this standard is a woman of the French Enlightenment period, Madame de Sévigné, whose portrait hangs in the museum (which was once her home) and whose daughter comprised the idolatrous object: "she loved her daughter obsessively, pathologically, so much so that she spent her life penning her longing in letter after letter" (10). For Joseph, the enticement of her idolatry lies in the correlation between art and passion. The mother's "unreasonable passion for her undistinguished daughter had turned the mother's prose into high culture and historic treasure," creating "the purest and most perfect French hitherto written in the land," which in turn "had molded the literature of France" (10–11).

From Brill's (and Ozick's) point of view, Madame de Sévigné's grand achievement—converting passion into art—has in time become the hallmark of the Gentile culture that entices him, a culture that could go under the name of European modernism. Aesthetics, a Greek legacy, prevails over ethics, the Jewish legacy, in this view of the Dual Curriculum. Brill's tutor in the Aesthetics of European Modernism is Claude, his supersophisticated college friend and mentor. "Claude was an aesthete," we are told, whose "worship of beautiful things and beautiful words" soon enlists Brill's ardent devotion (12, 14).

Claude's impeccable taste shortly throws open to Brill the art works of the Louvre, the writings of modern neopagans (Pierre Louÿs' *Aphrodite* and Paul Valéry's response to "Leonardo's naked sketches," 13), and a personal encounter with Cynthia Ozick's favorite modern neopagan, E. M. Forster, who reads to a group of young intimates from his secret homosexual novel *Maurice* (14–15). Although Ozick had once immersed herself in Forster, reading *The Longest Journey* every year and drawing upon his "Greeky heroes" for her portrayal of Tilbeck in *Trust* (Ltr 1/14/82), she later found him ethically deficient (for preferring "situational ethics" to the universal decrees of the Covenant) and intellectually conflicted (for worshiping Demeter, the goddess of fertility, while affecting a defense of homosexuality. In *The Cannibal Galaxy* Forster associates Demeter with Brill's future, 15).[27]

Though nearly submerged by these neopagan aesthetic temptations, the Jewish half of Brill's personal curriculum at last makes a comeback of sorts when Claude moves too strongly toward homosexual seduction. His sexual kiss—"not as two bold friends kiss"—awakens the old Jewish revulsion: "it frightened him terribly; it made him think of Leviticus" (15). It also makes him question somewhat the whole concept of the Enlightenment, whose chief luminary, Voltaire, "could not be trusted; even Voltaire had contempt for Leviticus" (15). And most important, the incident soon reveals what the primacy of aesthetics over ethics really implies about European modernism in the last prewar decade:

> After that he kept away from Claude. Claude was scornful, and called him Dreyfus, and inveigled his friends into calling him Dreyfus too. Joseph was again isolated. . . . Reluctantly, Joseph brought this news to Rabbi Pult . . . [who said:] "Joseph, the Enlightenment engendered a new slogan: 'There is no God, and the Jews killed him.' Joseph, this is the legacy of your Enlightenment." So Joseph abandoned literature and history, the side of the mind that . . . was like a cave teeming with bestial forms; he looked for a place without a taint. He . . . thought of the stars. (16)

Herewith, Joseph Brill has reached a moment of unpleasant awareness familiar to other Ozick protagonists. Reminiscent of what happened to Lushinski in "A Mercenary" ("Morris had called him Jew") and Tchernikhovsky in "Usurpation" (called "kike" by the Canaanite idols he had begun to worship), Brill's strong effort to assimilate has met bedrock rejection. In the end the goys call him Jew: "He had felt an unknowable warmth and feared it. It had betrayed him and called him Dreyfus" (16). Rather than revert to the Jewish ethos, however, Brill tries to pursue his Dual Curriculum in a new direction. Being "sick of human adventure," he will give up the Aesthetics of Western Civilization in favor of its science: "He . . . set out to learn the cold, cold skies" (16). And he will take his vision to a New World untainted by blood and ash of pogrom and Holocaust—a place, that is to say, without "Jewish history."

The new place, however, reminds him on every side of Jewish history, not only via the hayloft where his school's benefactress insists he must live, but in the very shape of the school buildings: "The Edmond Fleg Primary School had the forthright design of a freight train on the move: three hapless boxcars" (17). The lake by which the school sits, likewise, is "an inside ocean" reminiscent of "the Mediterranean, Europe's old puddle" (17); and even the chairs bequeathed to the school by the defunctive factory bear disturbingly idollike imagery: legs, arms, a gigantic hand in which to sit, and a replica of a globe topped by a cross. Perhaps America is, as Hawthorne might have phrased it, the Old World yet, at least in so far as it has inherited Western civilization. But rather than acknowledge the Jewish history implicit in these reminders, Principal Brill turns away from this vital subject just as he earlier turned away from "human adventure" so as to study the "cold, cold stars."

As a result, the Jewish component of his Dual Curriculum will once again fall victim to the Gentile enticement, with no Renée or hayloft episode to correct the balance in the American Eden. Absent the tough-mindedness of Jewish history, Brill's Dual Curriculum is a bowl of mush.[28] Instead of creating "a children's Sorbonne dense with Hebrew melodies" (36), Brill lowers himself to the American level of mediocrity, sanitizing both halves of his Dual Curriculum with his tale of Two Tantes:

> "Two aunties nurtured me," he often explained, "my Torah TANTE and my Paris TANTE, each the heiress of an ancient line." And then he would weave the "atmosphere" of each, the Talmud auntie analytical, exegetical, an extraordinary cogitator . . . at the same time a softie, merciful, her bundles tumbling and tears often in her eyes; the Paris auntie, though herself very old, nevertheless aeons younger than the Talmud auntie, and rather more callous, a bit cold, . . . her gaze an ascent of gargoyled spires and her lips overflowing with Baudelaire. "From these two TANTES," he would say (using the French intonation) . . . "I derived my inspiration for the Dual Curriculum." (61–62)

The Paris auntie was "rather more callous" than the Talmud auntie, "a bit cold." So much for the Inquisition, the pogroms, the Holocaust, and Brill's life in the hayloft and basement of Western civilization. He does not tell them—his audience of students' mothers—about Edmond Fleg, nor about the nuns, nor about his "hidden life" (62). To cite the book's major leitmotif, he "stopped too soon" (63). Instead he retreats into his astronomer's persona ("I am still in pursuit of the stars," 62), thereby turning his school's motto, *Ad Astra,* into a slogan of evasion.

The central relationship of the novel is Brill's encounter with the one person who sees through his evasion, Hester Lilt, a European intellectual of his own age, temper, and refugee background. Among the multiple purposes served by this character, Ozick uses Hester Lilt to satirize two contrasting adversaries of American feminism. On one side, Hester's cool dispassion about her daughter mocks the maternal frenzies of the "Jewish mother" syndrome, evident in virtually all the mothers Brill deals with. "Encirclement, preservation, defense, protection. . . . That was why they lived, and how: to make a roiling moat around their offspring" (64). On the other side, Hester's absolute self-reliance—her state of manless emotional and intellectual independence—unsettles Principal Brill's easy assumption of male superiority. Up to now, he had been the mothers' "ruler; . . . their god; their gleaming seated Buddha" (40), but Hester is so different that "it was hard for him to think of her as a woman" (50). With her "mannish signature," her "man's voice: full and low," and her discomfiting manner of "speaking so directly" to him (51), Hester embodies the feminist truism that equality with men requires a woman to adopt the male code of manners.

Hester's most crucial role, however, relates not to feminism but to parenting, and in this respect the judgment upon Hester is a mixed one. To her credit, perhaps, her daughter does in the end—possibly in emulation of the totally self-reliant mother—develop her innate genius so as to become an internationally celebrated, prize-winning painter. Or possibly this success occurred in spite of Hester's failure as a mother, which imposed a scandalous waste of hope and youth on the hapless child by giving her over to Principal Brill's unworthy institution. Certainly the endless humiliation and sense of inferiority bred into the child under Brill's tutelage call to mind the "Old School Hurts" so vividly recounted in Ozick's own reminiscences of Public School 71.[29] (In her audiotape interview with Kay Bonetti, Ozick indicated her judgment that Hester had failed her daughter by putting her through such a miserable grade school experience.)

The key issue, in any case, is Principal Brill's "parenting" of his charges, particularly with respect to this one and only wunderkind to have passed through his domain of power. Beulah's lack of a biological father makes Brill's "fathering" all the more potentially significant, both with regard to transmitting the Judaic tradition to the child (a prime obligation of any

Jewish father) and with respect to any young artist's need for an appropriate patronlike figure. With respect to transmitting the Judaic tradition, Brill shuffles his eighth-grade teachers so as to make Rabbi Sheskin Beulah's instructor, a man "who appeared to believe in sacred texts" and seemed capable of "turning Scripture into story." But Sheskin's story, instead of inculcating ethical conscience, purveys mere entertainment—"Old King David was dying. He was dying in this very room" (97–98). Among the doodles with which Sheskin's class escapes its boredom—"balloons, eggs, dogs' ears, women's lips and breasts"—Brill notices something different about Beulah's drawing, a reminder of the subject matter he has excised from Jewish history: "Brill glimpsed a drawing of a house. . . . He looked again: the whole house was on fire, and the trees all around it, even the sky behind—a conflagration" (97–98).

Beulah's other fathering need, for an adult male's inspiration and confidence in her budding talent, also elicits an inadequate response on Brill's part. Assuring her that "you are not a genius, and neither am I," he centers her attention on the three Jewish faces pictured on his wall—Freud, Spinoza, and Einstein. Although they are indeed figures of genius, "very intelligent men [who] never stopped too soon" (85), Brill himself does stop too soon by failing to include any artists or women among his exemplary models. The chauvinist purpose of this gesture, moreover, becomes inescapable when he stations those three male faces against the "would-be gynecocracy" (94) of hostile mothers in his office.

To suit Beulah's needs, Hester is a better educator than Brill not only as a model of feminist freedom but also in her capacity for the arts. Her professional status as an "imagistic linguistic logician" (47), for example, occasions an Ozick-style definition of the image: "Every image, she said, has its logic: every story, every tale, every metaphor . . . is inhabited by a language of just deserts" (88). And it is Hester's lecture at midpoint in the novel that disseminates the book's most crucial images: the fox whom the four rabbis saw running across the ruined Temple; the laughter of Akiva, the rabbi who inferred the Temple's resurrection from seeing the fox while the others wept over its ruin; and the cannibal galaxy metaphor (67–70). ("The Laughter of Akiva" was the title Ozick used for the portion of this book she published in the *New Yorker* of 10 November 1980.)

From her fables of Akiva and the fox, Hester derives the book's chief motif of failure: "we have stopped too soon" (69). Because her lecture concerns "the hoax of pedagogy" ("The hoax is when the pedagogue stops too soon," 66,68), there is a special irony in Brill's pedantic response to her imagery: "From all these—the bee, the little fox, the laughter of Akiva, especially the cannibal galaxy—Brill did not feel estranged. He suspected, in fact, that the lecturer's familiarity with the midrash was secondhand, and not out of the original text or tongue" (70). But he is "estranged" from Hester's primal meaning, that her daughter has been victimized by Brill's low estimate of her. His error, based on "the judgment from early performance" that victimized Ozick's own childhood, was Hester's central instance of "the hoax of pedagogy" (66). Her chief contribution to her child's well-being occurs after Beulah's miseducation at Brill's hands has run its course, and the mother at last places her daughter in an environment suitable for burgeoning young talent. So the narrative curve circles back to Paris, City of Light, world mecca for painters, and site of Brill's education in the Holocaust and the Aesthetics of European Modernism.

Because Paris signifies merely European aestheticism for his former student, Beulah's success via Paris signifies bitter failure for Brill's grand educational project. Although he had sold the rich benefactress on bringing "a shadow of the Sorbonne into being in the middle of America" (36), Paris in his memory was greatly removed from "the high muse of Europe she meant to snare" (36). Instead of "the waters of Shiloh springing from the head of Western Civilization" (36), what he had seen was how "fire and steam had transformed the world" (23): Rabbi Pult's books turning to ash in a bonfire, while "creatures like centaurs" roamed the streets with clubs and rocks and his family were jammed like stockyard cattle in a sports stadium awaiting their transport to a death camp. For Beulah to redeem her talent in this place without knowledge of its Jewish history gives special meaning to her mother's essay, "On Structure and Silence"—first read by Brill fifteen years after Beulah brought it to his office. Too late (he stopped reading too soon), Brill encounters its central idea, "Silence is not random but shaping" (101), which describes the effect of his own silence in shaping the de-Judaized art of Beulah Lilt.

Especially appalling is the postwar extirpation of Judaic culture even within the tiny Jewish population that still lives in Paris. Brill's own sisters deny Jewish history to the extent that they "resisted memory" and "would not let him speak of loss" (133). Meanwhile, their sightseeing with Brill's stepson Albert comprises a wholly de-Judaized list of tourist attractions— the Eiffel Tower, the Bastille, Notre Dame, the Arc de Triomphe, Montmartre, the Elysée Palace, Versailles (127). Worse yet are the vacuous American pastimes that have taken root in this ancient center of high culture: the circus and a Disney movie for Albert, a shopping spree for Brill's wife, Iris, at "some really decent stores, the sort of places you'd almost expect to see back home" (133).

The culmination of this *Judenrein* effect occurs during Brill's visit to that grand repository of Western civilization, the Louvre, where he glimpses the fourteen-year-old Beulah Lilt going through the halls with her classmates to gaze "with vivid eyes at old Greek wine jugs" (131). In these halls displaying the artifacts of five millennia there will be no semblance of a Dual Curriculum. Guarded at its entrance by the Winged Victory, the building's classical galleries seem entirely given over to pagan antiquity, "as if there had never been a Hebrew people, no Abraham or Joseph or Moses. Not a trace of holy Israel" (131). Instead, Beulah's tour moves past "a glowing torso of Apollo . . . a Spartan horseman . . . the Venus de Milo . . . Isis on a throne of gold" (131). In the end the Jewish heritage disappears from Beulah's mind as completely as holy Israel vanishes from sight among these pagan idols. As a young artist interested only in "the colors, the glow, . . . above all the forms of things" (156), she will make her mark as a disciple of European modern aesthetics and neopaganism. Appropriately, she names her career-making series of paintings after ancient Greek statuary, the Caryatids (145). Beulah's credentials in European modern aesthetics are approved and certified by none other than Brill's aging anti-Semitic schoolmate Claude, who reappears now as a pseudo-British, quasi-aristocratic critic to endorse the art work of the ex-Jewish expatriate Beulah Lilt.

In Beulah's success—both the earliness of her breakthrough, as opposed to Ozick's despairing decades of oblivion, and its triumph over "Old School Hurts"—Cynthia Ozick's dream self is vindicated. Ozick's interview with Elaine Kauvar makes the connection explicit. "The story of Beulah is me, the sense of having been written off," she says; "I'm Beulah in school. Absolutely, Beulah is P.S. 71 for me, there's no question about that." Ozick likewise admits that the book's "protest against 'the prediction from earliness'" embodies her "arguments with Freudian [deterministic] thought" (389). Because of her conflicted concept of art, however, Beulah also represents Ozick's nightmare self, the de-Judaized art-for-art's-sake practitioner she would likely have become if her own education had resembled Brill's eviscerated curriculum. "I'm not Beulah at the end," she says, because

> she repudiated the Jewish cultural side of her education. She said she forgot it, and she escaped and ascended into the nimbus. She left obligation, the idea of duty, perhaps. She left a sense of a moral civilization. She became an aesthete. (Kauvar 381)

What remains for Brill's later years is the total de-Judaization of his own family as the House of Brill gradually becomes altogether consumed by the cannibal galaxy of Jewish-American assimilation. Although he "wore his Yarmulke always" and took care to have his infant son circumcised (67, 136), on all sides the pagan incursion predominates. Brill's graduation ceremonies feature songs about the Knights of the Round Table and the March from *Aida* (118–19), his de-Judaized bride bears the unbiblical name of a flower, Iris (sometimes confused with Daisy), his downstairs neighbors are uproarious Greeks reminiscent of the Purses in *Trust,* and his wunderkind son disdains things Jewish. Just as Beulah Lilt becomes a totally Europeanized artist, so as to earn Claude's aestheticist approval, Brill's son becomes a totally Americanized business student, fluent in French but not Yiddish, and his stepson Albert abandons both Judaism and America by moving to Canada.

The closing sentence of the novel, describing how "Beulah Lilt's language assailed him endlessly, endlessly," focuses on a "flaming nimbus" that "sometimes spread" out of the "calculated and enamel forms" of her art work. It is a subliminal image, to be sure, and it would likely mean different things to different observers; but the reason for Brill's fixation on the flaming nimbus most plausibly relates to the Holocaust—that crucial life experience which he has suppressed and denied through a lifetime. In this respect, the scene compares with the end of "A Mercenary," where Lushinski's simple act of smoking a cigarette evokes first the blue and white colors of the Israeli flag, and then the Jewish self that he killed and buried in Holocaust Poland.

For Brill the coup de grace to his life's work is his successor's renaming of the school as the Lakeside Grade School—a fully Americanized and de-Judaized construction. But the disappearance of Edmond Fleg's name gives us one last instance of the "stopped too soon" motif. Although the Holocaust galvanized Jewish identity around the world for people of Ozick's generation, Jewish identity has also rested with equal weight on the miracle engendered by the aftermath of the Holocaust, the restoration of Israel. That motif is the other subject toward which Principal Brill displays an indifference that proves fatal for his Dual Curriculum. Decades before Gorchak changed the name of the Edmond Fleg School, Brill had himself betrayed the name by failing to fully emulate Fleg's example. When he had first read Fleg's work back in the nuns' cellar, he had observed the final terminus of Fleg's odyssey as follows: "In a decade or so Edmond Fleg, né Flegenheimer, had gone from a skeptical playwright and (Joseph imagined) stylish Parisian boulevardier to a Jew panting for Jerusalem" (22). Those last five words, set off against Brill's other failure to acknowledge Jewish history, summarize the full measure of Brill's inadequacy. His grand experiment in Dual Education failed, at the last, because with respect to both Israel and the Holocaust, he—in the book's most significant instance of the theme—stopped too soon.

The Messiah of Stockholm: Gift of the Magi

Oh, why can we not have a magic God like other peoples?

"Usurpation"

In *The Messiah of Stockholm* Cynthia Ozick managed the unlikely feat of synthesizing within one shadowy figure her three disparate master themes— Jewish identity, the pagan enticement, and the dangerous efficacy of art. Her agency for achieving this effect was the figure of Bruno Schulz, a Jewish writer of magic stories who in 1942 was shot dead in the street of his Polish village by a Nazi officer. In the style of a classic quest novel—one could cite forebears from Don Quixote to Thomas Pynchon's V.—the main character of this story, Lars Andemening (who believes he is Bruno Schulz's son), hunts the lost masterpiece by Schulz called *The Messiah*. Because Schulz was an actual historical figure, Ozick incidentally uses her opportunity to deliver a sly critique of the postmodern "metafictional" approach to literature which Philip Roth—to whom she dedicates this novel—brought to a consummation a year earlier (1986) in *The Counterlife*. (Her dedication, however, is also a tribute to Roth for getting Schulz published in English.)

The three main strands of her novel come into view very quickly, even before we get to her opening sentence. Opposite the title page, the self-portrait sketched by Schulz is a haunting image of this tragic-mysterious figure, a face whose willful strength is at once evocative of both waste and triumph. Shot in the street by an SS man when he ventured into a forbidden, "Aryan" section of town, Schulz stares from this page like an icon of Miltonic prophecy from *Areopagitica:* "Who kills a man kills a reasonable creature, . . . but a good book is the precious life-blood of a master spirit, embalmed and treasured up on purpose to a life beyond life." But yet, we cannot help but understand that when Schulz was murdered, his book *The Messiah* met its un-Miltonic demise as his co-victim of Jewish identity. Despite his Catholic fiancée and his paganized fiction, written in Polish not Yiddish, the life and work of Bruno Schulz were cut off in midcareer solely because he was a Jew.

The pagan enticement in this novel, which ramifies into manifestations ranging from a fairy-tale format to the Messiah of the Gospels (Christianity here being a pagan religion), also asserts its power before we reach the opening sentence of the novel proper. Ozick's choice of an epigraph, cited from Schulz's own *The Street of Crocodiles,*[30] brings this theme to the fore with a Spinozan force reminiscent of *The Pagan Rabbi:*

My father never tired of glorifying this extraordinary element—matter.
    "There is no dead matter," he taught us, "lifelessness is only a disguise

behind which hide unknown forms of life. . . . The Demiurge was in possession
of important and interesting creative recipes. Thanks to them, he created a
multiplicity of species which renew themselves by their own devices. . . .
[Even] if classical methods of creation should prove inaccessible for evermore,
there still remain some illegal methods, an infinity of heretical and criminal
methods."[31]

Ozick has presented this Demiurge in many earlier guises: as Tilbeck pro-
creating "illegitimate issue" in *Trust;* as the dryad seductress of "The Pagan
Rabbi" and the Phoenician sea goddess in "The Dock-Witch"; as the dai-
mon of artistic fecundity in "Usurpation"; and as the idolatrous imagination
flouting the Second Commandment across the whole range of her writings.
In this novel the Demiurge ("Dr. Eklund") assumes the sophisticated guise
that we often see in a Henry James novel—the duplicitous European who
perpetrates a scheme of exploitation while affecting the role of a confidant
to the book's protagonist.

Besides Schulz's self-portrait and his paragraph from *The Street of Crocodiles,* one further intervention detains the reader from Ozick's opening sentence of *The Messiah of Stockholm.* This prefatory citation consists of two
brief lines from the popular Swedish writer Par Lagerkvist, which are rendered both in Swedish and in English translation: "I am the star that mirrors
itself in you"; and "Your soul is my home. I have no other." In both of these
quotations, which together constitute an imagistic account of the efficacy of
art, the "I" and "you" stand in for the artist and audience respectively. The
latter statement—"Your soul is my home. I have no other"—is a version of
Milton's "life beyond life" that art makes possible via the artist's mirror/
reader of the first statement. In Ozick's novel, Lars Andemening is that ideal
reader with respect to Bruno Schulz, having by his obsession made himself
Schulz's "son" in a deeper way than mere biological paternity would have
predicated. Behind Andemening, however, Cynthia Ozick is the actual
reader-conjurer of Schulz who uses her art to summon his ghost from the
Nazi killing field. Finally we, as Ozick's readers, in turn perform the metafictional magic of "redeeming" (she favors that word) both her art and
Schulz's through our assumption of the mirroring function.

It is a precept as old as Aristotle that conflict is the essence of drama, and
a precept as recent as Faulkner that the most meaningful form of conflict is
"the heart in conflict with itself," which is "the only thing worth writing
about" in Faulkner's Nobel formulation. For Ozick, the heart in conflict
traces back to her earliest formative years: to her love of fairy tales as a
girl—pagan, magical, forbidden, irresistible—versus her favorite writer in
the "Judaic" mode of nineteenth-century fiction, Henry James, a reality-

centered apostle of the ethical imagination. The most crucial Jamesian motif in *The Messiah of Stockholm* is the format of a highbrow detective story, like *The Portrait of a Lady* or *The Wings of the Dove,* in which the protagonist-detective gradually sheds comforting illusions in favor of an enhanced but tragically sordid perception of reality. The opening sentence of *The Messiah of Stockholm*—now that we have finally reached it—is a notable amalgam of the two voices. In an unmistakably Jamesian style—seventy-two words that herd three "when" clauses toward a periodic main statement—the sentence pits its subordinate clauses, brimming with the world's vitality ("when the literary stewpot boils over," "when gossip . . . is most untamed and swarming"), against its main statement: "[now] Lars Andemening could be found in bed, napping." That final word, "napping," combines with the earlier "stewpot" to form the dramatic crux of the work, indicating the counterpoint of opposites that comprises the overall design of the novel. Throughout the book we can measure Andemening's relation to the reality principle by his distance from the stewpot, the daily three o'clock gathering point of his worldly-wise peers in the book reviewing trade.

At the outset Lars's daily naps during the stewpot hour signify his total withdrawal into his private domain of illusion. This would not be an Ozick novel, however, if the "napping" signified mere illusion. The whole great realm of imaginative creativity falls within its realm: the creation of art, of value, of sustaining (if illusory) relationships, of a world more answerable to the needs of the psyche than anything the external setting—the dark, cold onset of a Stockholm winter—can emulate. Those needs are of course the original reason for the existence of fairy tales, which on a higher level of imagination evolved into myths like the concept of the Messiah. Given the incompatibility between his interior life and the reality principle, Lars's daily nap during the stewpot hour, along with the solitude of his late-night work schedule and his refusal to have a telephone, is more a protective tactic than a mind-dead hibernation—though it resembles hibernation in its calendar span from November to early March (3).

Prior to his waking "in the kitchen of Sleeping Beauty's castle, when the trance is broken and all the pots begin to boil again" (112), the dream life of Lars Andemening is irradiated with the world's inherent passion and meaning, much as in the epigraph from *The Street of Crocodiles:* "There is no dead matter. . . . The range of these forms [of life] is infinite and their shades and nuances limitless." Because he had "long ago thrown himself on the altar of literature" (7), the pagan gods have rewarded him with their living presence. His workplace, an ancient building in Stockholm's Gamla Stan (Old City) that "hints at ancient festivities lasting till dawn" (10), seems possessed by poltergeists—a place "subject to spectral mutterings, . . . growling, or . . . even whistling under their feet" (10). Nearby, in another "old, old" building that seemed like "a benign dungeon, scalloped with monastic arches," the Library of the Swedish Academy offered a rich repast of pagan lore—"many-stanzaed Eddas," "old Norse twilights," the "cold gods with their winking breastplates and their hot whims. Hammer of the terrible Thor. Odin and Freya" (16). Even the churches disclose their pagan origins as the twisting snowflakes give their steeples "the look of whirling Merlin hats" (18).

At the center of this medieval township is the antique bookshop operated by Heidi, the sole confidante of Lars and herself a creature out of a medieval storybook—"a thick globular dwarf of a woman" (19) who looks "as if she were a forest gnome" (20). Enhancing this effect is her display window, given over chiefly to the pure theater of royalty in a quasi-fairy-tale mode: "a formidable edition . . . with color pictures of the Royal Family: the wavy-haired King tall and fair and unperturbed, the two little Princesses charming in a garden, the diffident little Prince in a sailor suit . . ., and the shiveringly beautiful Queen" (19). And when Lars asks her help in finding a tutor in Polish, Heidi produces a refugee "Princess," a "Radziwell actually," to keep the quasi fairy tale going a little longer (26).

Like a Jamesian protagonist, then—like Isabel Archer with Madame Merle, or Milly Theale with Kate Croy—Lars gratefully accepts Heidi's gift of intimacy: "He was grateful: Heidi had fallen into his condition alongside him, a companion, a fellow collector of his father's fate, a kind of partner" (32). And like those Jamesian heroines, he seems not to notice certain warning signs that the intimacy is spurious. Despite the fantasy theater of royalty in her display window, for example, the fiction section in her shop heavily favors the "Jewish" reality principle—"the newest Americans, North and South, the oldest Russians, that large and steady company of nineteenth-century Englishmen and Englishwomen [Ozick's favorite, "Judaic" mode of realism in fiction], a whole forest of Balzac; and then the dictionaries and encyclopedias" (19).

Most crucially, Heidi's reality principle extends to the figure of Bruno Schulz, whose death as a Jew outweighs (for her) all the magic of his pagan artistry. Because of its portrayal of direct contradiction between Schulz's Jewish identity and his pagan enticement, this scene is one of the most important in *The Messiah of Stockholm*, reminiscent of Bleilip's despair in "Bloodshed," of Lushinski's buried self in "A Mercenary," of Feingold's crazed storytelling about atrocities in "Levitation," of the map (of Europe) made of vomit in *Trust*. Lars's relation with his "companion," his "partner," his "fellow collector of his father's fate" begins its gradual unraveling with this moment of realization of their difference:

It was the shooting that drew her. The shooting; the murder. Shot in the streets! Lars suspected that Heidi cared more for his father's death than for his father's tales, where savagely crafty nouns and verbs were set on a crooked road to take on engorgements and transmogrifications: a bicycle ascends into the zodiac, rooms in houses are misplaced, wallpaper hisses, the calendar acquires a thirteenth month. Losses, metamorphoses, degradations. In one of the stories the father turns into a pincered crab; the mother boils it and serves it to the family on a dish. Heidi shouldered all that aside: it was the catastrophe of fact she wanted, Lars's father gunned down in the gutters of Drohobycz along with two hundred and thirty other Jews. A Thursday in 1942, as it happened: the nineteenth of November. Lars's father was bringing home a loaf of bread. (32–33).

Clearly, Heidi's passionate fidelity to fact—naming the exact date of the killing, the number of other victims, the loaf of bread in transit—bespeaks the "Jewish history" side of Cynthia Ozick's literary imagination, while Lars's affinity for Schulz's magic transformations of his world reflects the longings Ozick confessed to in works like "Usurpation": "The Jews have no magic. . . . oh, why can we not have a magic God like other peoples?" (BL 134–35). In effect, the disparity between Heidi's and Lars's views defines the conflict at the heart of *The Messiah of Stockholm*. From this point in the novel, the conflict between "Jewish history" and the pagan imagination governs the remaining dozen chapters, as Lars moves gradually toward his simultaneous waking and disillusionment—from his nap of imagination to his place around the stewpot.

Complicating the issue is the role reversal that Lars and Heidi play out concerning her own "Jewish history." Although she judges Lars "a master of the insubstantial: a fantasist" (32), her own obsession with Schulz's death displays a core of self-protective fantasy. If Lars's fantasy is his appropriation of Schulz as his father, Heidi's is her appropriation of Schulz as a surrogate for her own life memories. Whereas Lars has assimilated Schulz's pagan fictions, Heidi has fed like a vampire on Schultz's real-life biography— the "wild action" surrounding his death (38–39), his abandonment of "the world of the Jews" for the sake of his Catholic fiancée (35), his craving for intimacy in a letter: *"I need a companion. I need a kindred spirit close by me. I long for an acknowledgement of the inner world whose existence I postulate. . . . I need a partner in discovery"* (36, emphasis Schulz).

In her appropriation of Schulz's life instead of his art, Heidi fastens most crucially on the shooting as a surrogate for her own Holocaust memories. With the shooting, her own Jewish history ceased, along with her Jewish identity. She has assumed instead a German identity, totemized in "that funny old German lamp" that "was all she thought worth bringing with her from Germany," with its lampshade shaped like an innocent flower (a daisy) supplanting the infamous Jew's-skin lampshade of the Holocaust years (20, 19). Most important, she has revised her role in the Holocaust from that of a death camp inmate to that of a Gentile sympathizer who threw food at night over the camp fence (42–43). But Heidi's fixation on death—like that of Enoch Vand in *Trust*—betrays her identity as a Jewish survivor: only a survivor "could see straight through to the skeleton" so as to see "the xylophone of the ribs" in her husband, or see "no more than a clean skull" in looking at Lars (40). Now it is Lars who is the reality-centered skeptic— "I saw what your name used to be"—and Heidi who retreats into a new realm of concealment: "There are plenty of Bavarian burghers called Simon. They're all Catholic" (44).

Despite her claim to the reality principle, then, Heidi seems as subject as Lars to the Schulzian precept that Lars is most fond of citing to her: *"Reality is as thin as paper"* (37, 59).[32] Her apostasy toward the reality principle in turn undermines her attack on Lars's idolatry—that is, her condemnation (itself a telltale sign of her Jewish culture) of his "ceremonial mystification" of Schulz and the "smoldering cultishness in all of it" (33). So he will carry on as a "priest, a holy man" of his pagan ancestor worship (29), yielding more deeply to the "sorcery in it" (31) as he seeks alignment of his own vision with his father's magic eye. Still spurning conventional realism, just as "his father too had shunned the stewpot" (64), he juxtaposes its thin gruel and the transcending power of the Schulzian imagination:

> There was . . . in all of them, the whole three-o'clock crew—the weak honey of reverence. Literary creatures who served, sidestepped, and sometimes sold out the Muses. Their so-called scandals, their scramblings, their feuds, their poly-morphous life in the stewpot: how innocent, how distant from the palaces of live thunder, how weak they were before the altar of Lars's father's unmoving eye. (64)

With that transforming eye freed now from Heidi's skepticism, Lars finds the auxiliaries in Heidi's circle easily amenable to his magic narrative. The mysterious Dr. Eklund, for example, resembles (when he finally appears) a sea captain, with a "seaweedy merman's odor" (89), thereby evoking earlier pagan sea gods in Ozick's work such as Tilbeck in *Trust* and the title character of "The Dock-Witch." Lars's filial counterpart, Adela—Schultz's putative daughter—appears carrying the lost manuscript of *The Messiah* like "a witch with a rattle" (70), evoking "old fables: buried vessels, spells, incantations, magical instant dyings" (78). Adela's putative mother, Schulz's teenaged mistress, exhibits the protean guises of a fairy tale, recurring an-drogynously in the artist's illustrations as "A little man in a top hat. . . . A boy with big buttons. A fellow in riding boots. A woman in high heels wearing a coat with a fur collar. All of those. Sometimes she's naked" (81). And the magic talismans of fairy lore abound throughout Lars's narrative, offering the private supernatural empowerment that makes such totems immemorially seductive. Several of these magic totems are personal, like the ancient "fabled chair" in Lars's hallway associated with "magical deliveries" (69), the white beret that Adela leaves behind in lieu of *The Messiah* manuscript (87), and the key to Heidi's shop. But the central totem of magic power is the "amphora" bearing the lost manuscript, which touches on traditional myths that range from Hebe's cup in Greek antiquity, to Ali Baba's jar of Arabic legend, to the chalice of early Christian genesis (101).

As a symbol of cultural appropriation, this motif of originally Jewish creation—*The Messiah*—ensconced within a pagan/Christian vessel carries significant implications. In terms of the Second Commandment, it may be a wholesome sign of Lars's waking when he burns the false *Messiah* in its pagan jar—a *Messiah* made doubly false by the latter-day forgery added to its original author's apostasy. Through this act Lars may expiate his Schulzian heresy of reducing reality to the thinness of a sheaf of paper and then committing idolatry toward this manmade artifact: "[*The Messiah*] had possessed, for one holy hour, his house; his bed; his quilt. He ought to have been on his knees to it. . . . He might have knelt there—gazing—before the caves and grottoes of his quilt" (82). The flames in the jar may also, however, portend the Holocaust writ small, the token of a whole culture—apostate and Orthodox alike—that was turned into ash along with six million bodies. Certainly the "roasting" smell that assails Lars everywhere in the city, along with his sense of ever-present "chimneys" (17), hints at the historic calamity that swallowed up Bruno Schulz and his handiwork.

But then again, the inconceivable atrocity of the Holocaust, like the onset of the Swedish winter, may be all the more reason for turning away from the stewpot, the world out there, the Judaic reality principle, in favor of the inviolable realm of imagination, the magic sustenance of myths and idols, the secret warmth of the quilt. And at this dark, cold time of year, from which half the world seeks refuge in the Advent story, what myth could be more relevant than the dream of the Messiah, divine purveyor of world redemption? Given her memories of P.S. 71, when she was accused of deicide and ostracized for not singing Christmas carols, Cynthia Ozick could not be expected to produce an orthodox Messiah from a Christian point of view; and given her respect for the Orthodox Jewish heritage, neither would she be likely to apply artistic license to the Messiah of the prophets (Isaiah most notably)—a Messiah who in fact has no part in this novel. Instead she frames her own parable around the Christmas story, with Schulz's *Messiah* its sacred text, brought forward by Adela as "angel" of Annunciation (83); with Dr. Eklund, Heidi, and Adela later appearing as three Magi bearing gifts, the paper-filled amphora (appropriately, the word *Magi* is a cognate of *Magic*); and with Lars subserving the Magic Narrative as Advent child.

As a master image dominating the text, Ozick's child imagery serves contrary purposes regarding the theme of myth and idolatry. Its negative meaning is arrested development, the stunting of spiritual growth that characterizes Romantic religion as opposed to the Judaic encounter with time and history. From the outset Ozick stresses this facet of Lars's character. At age forty-two, he "looked much younger," like "a messenger boy," with his face revealing "unripeness," "something irregular—undigested—in his spirit," the stance of "an arrested soul" (3, 4, 6). But the positive meaning of the child image is rejuvenation, an antidote to the soul-snuffing despair that time and history have too often visited upon the psyche, especially the Jewish psyche aware of Holocaust horrors. Rejuvenation is the leading effect of the child motif, with self-purification a secondary effect of Ozick's recurring birth imagery.

Having cut his links with the stewpot by ridding himself of telephone and typewriter, Lars reverts to the pure, unborn state and moves in phases from there. Beginning with "the face of a foetus" (6), he seemed "almost new-born" (9) until his "bed of rebirth" (73) brings on a Blakean state of innocence: "What a baby you are, Lars. Naive" (93). The innocence in turn makes belief possible, most notably belief in the efficacy of the text he craves to idolize—a text that Ozick swathes in its own Christological ambience: "That cradling of *The Messiah:* good God, hadn't he held it in his arms?" (82). Between this "cradling" of *The Messiah* (itself "a round baby," 115) and the "swaddling clothes" of Lars's own infancy (92), Ozick echoes enough of the Gospels to underscore the danger of the pagan enticement. Lars's rebirth via pagan/Christian myth can come about only by the extirpation in him of Jewish history, which is to say, Jewish identity. The Jew in Lars Andemening has thereby been superseded.

Lars's condition thus signifies the split identity of Jewish modernity. Like Lushinski in "A Mercenary," he has buried his Jewish self, the cave of his quilt serving as both burial crypt for Lazarus Baruch (his secret Jewish name, 101) and as womb for his pagan self fathered by Bruno Schulz. To achieve the new birth there must first be a burial, right here in his bed-site: "On account of this father [Bruno Schulz] Lars shrank himself. He felt he resembled his father: all the tales were about men shrinking more and more into the phantasmagoria of the mind. One of them was about a man in his sleep, his fall into the bedclothes. . . . like the captive of a great bowl of dough" (5). So long as the Jew is dead, napping through the stewpot hour, the pagan can live, on fire with the power of his magic narrative and its transcendent vision.

Throughout the magic narrative, vision is a prevalent issue. Described early on as "probably on the brink of needing glasses" (6), Lars peers "into the thickest dark through a lens of snow" on his midnight walk to Heidi's shop (17). In his work as a reviewer, he is already possessed of subliminal powers of seeing that somehow relate to his father:

> Something happened in him while he slept. . . . [His] lids clicked open . . . and he *saw*: what he saw, before he had even formulated a word of it, was his finished work. He saw it as a kind of vessel. . . . In its cup lay . . . [an] eye. A human eye: his own; and then not his own. His father's murdered eye. (8)

So long as the magic narrative lasts, its sign is the eye bequeathed him by his artist father, the transformative eye of pagan imagination: "I can see my father's eye. It seems to be my eye, but it's his. As if he lets me have his own eye to look through" (41). Under its gaze, reality appears to reverse itself: the people of the stewpot appear unreal—"wax faces, wax eyes with (this was odd) wax tears of pain or reproach or deprivation: Gunnar and Anders and . . . even Nilsson, all of them wax exhibits . . . invisibly controlled by distant wireless computers"—while to the contrary "his father's eye, . . . a violent white ray, was spilling out the wilderness of God. A vivid bestiary strangely abundant, discharging the white light of plenitude" (68).

In reducing the real people of the stewpot to wax effigies, the eye reveals the menace of its heresies: the idolatry that here turns people into wax might elsewhere turn millions more into ash. When that measure of idolatry does occur in chapter 13, swallowing up the Jews of Drohobycz, that would be for Lars his waking moment. But meanwhile, the visionary powers of the pagan dispensation are too intoxicating to give over, as they enlarge to assume religious dimensions. Writing "reviews [that] are practically theology" (66), Lars echoes the glad tidings of the Gospels in a sort of Annunciation: "He had proclaimed [to the stewpot] the return of his father's lost book. . . . And the daughter! . . . [He] had proclaimed her, in order to proclaim the risen *Messiah*" (67). And his Ascension into the otherworldly, which happens when his magic eye holds in view the original *Messiah*— "The original! Recovered; resurrected; redeemed"—nearly consumes the eye itself in a daimonic seizure: "Lars, looking with all his strength, felt his own pupil consumed by a conflagration in its socket. As if copulating with an angel whose wings were on fire" (104).

Lars's reading of the *Messiah* manuscript is of course his paramount experience of the radiant eye doing its work. After it is authenticated by a forgery expert—Dr. Eklund the "holographic authority" who scans the pages with "the great [magnifying glass] lens circling" (102–3)—Lars finds in Bruno Schulz's lost masterpiece a geyser of creativity reminiscent of the Demiurge in the book's opening epigraph. Once again the illicit creative powers in this scene are associated—like the pagan gods in *Trust* and *The Pagan Rabbi*—with the sea:

> Lars thought of those mountain ranges growing out of the chasm of the world, along the bottommost spine of the sea, so platonically dark and deep that even the scuttling blindfish swim away, toward higher water—but within this . . . abyss are crisscrossing rivers, whirlpools twisting their foaming necks, multiple streams braiding upward, cascades sprouting rivulets like hairs, and a thousand shoots and sprays bombarding the oceanscape's peaks. (106)

Impressive as it seems, it is notable that nothing in this welter of primal energy is alive, and what was alive is now dead. That is to say, the Adela of Schulz's earlier books (after whom Lars's "sister" was presumably named)— "the servant girl . . . in *Cinnamon Shops* and *Sanatorium*" (106)—is here reduced by "the preternaturally cornucopian eye of the genie" to inanimate matter. The Adela of *The Messiah* first appears as "a bald rag doll left on a shelf" with scalp made of porcelain, then transmutes into "a tailor's dummy, canvas over bent wires," and finally emerges as the object of Lars's (and Ozick's) metaphysical revulsion, the inhuman endpoint of Magic Narrative (in her essay on Schulz, Ozick called *his* Adela "a kind of proto-Nazi," AA 226):

> she had become one of those Mesopotamian priestly statues carved out of stone only for the sake of their terrifying smiles. Finally Lars took in that she had turned . . . into an idol. Her eyes were conventional green jewels. This idol, made of some artificial dead matter, was never called Adela . . . [but] he recognized her all the same. (107)

In sum, the world of *The Messiah,* which is set in Schulz's hometown of Drohobycz, has become "peopled (but that word was unsuitable) by idols," covering the whole range of pagan antiquity—"plump Buddhas," "Egyptian figurines," "mammoth Easter Island heads," and numerous shapes of "large stone birds—falcons, eagles, vultures, hawks, oversized crows hewn out of black marble. Each of these idols was considered to be a great and powerful god or goddess" (107). Irresistibly, as *The Messiah*'s story line moves from pagan antiquity toward the present, idolatry and dehumanization move apace toward that which Lars's napping, his new childlike identity, and his Magic Narrative were designed to evade. The story line moves, drawing Lars with it, back toward reality, toward Jewish history, toward the Holocaust. When "no human beings remained in Drohobycz, only hundreds and hundreds of idols," they include some beautifully crafted specimens made by "ingenious artisans," a "handful of masterpieces," but a familiar and sinister turn develops when "sacrificial bonfires" begin to spring up all over town, in which the smaller idols are seized by the stronger ones and flung into the flames (109). Behind the whole scene we discern at last the cannibal feast of old Canaanite times, "the iron maw of some huge lazy Moloch" insatiably devouring its burnt offerings.[33] Its apocalyptically consummate offering, as the Magic Narrative reaches its climax, is *The Messiah* itself, which comes on first as a living image of vivisection (as if a "spleen . . . or a pancreas, or a bowel, or a brain" had "set out to live on its own"), but shortly mutates into The Book which it is, covered with "inky markings [that] showed themselves to be infinitely tiny and brilliantly worked drawings of those same idols that had taken hold of the town of Drohobycz" (109–10). These printed characters—"peculiar tattoos," "a type of cuneiform," "an unknown alphabet" (110)—suggest both the Holocaust ("tattoos") and pagan antiquity, but they also correlate with Ozick's lines in her preface to *Bloodshed:* "As if ink were blood" (BL 12).

Thus exposed as death-worshiping idolatry, *The Messiah* of Bruno Schulz collapses "with the noise of vast crashings and crushings," taking the other idols with it into its grand dissolution, but yielding up "out of the caldron of that great wind" a small bird, carrying in its beak a single strand of dried hay. The bird brings to mind as its paramount reference the dove that returned to Noah's Ark (the prototype of the Ark of the Covenant, sacred to four thousand years of Judaism) bearing a redeeming sprig of green olive to show that the Flood was abating. Just as Schulz's *Messiah* proves an anti-Messiah, bringing the fires of Moloch instead of redemption, the bird it releases has the opposite function of that of Noah's dove, its piece of dried hay bringing death as its touch dissolves each idol "into flecks of sparks fading to ash" (111). A secondary reference for the bird of death could be the conclusion of *Moby-Dick* (an Ozick favorite), whose Promethean-Satanic protagonist sought blasphemous vengeance against the cosmic powers that had maimed him, but instead of killing the great whale that he saw as the agent of those cosmic powers, he ended up killing only himself and his crew and a solitary bird that Tashtego's hammer nailed to the mast at the last moment of the ship's sinking.

So the apocalypse ends, the napper awakes, and Lars finds himself "in the kitchen of Sleeping Beauty's castle, when the trance is broken and all the pots begin to boil again" (112). As the magic eye fades, Lars cannot suppress regret for his lost visionary powers:

Lamentation remained. . . . That despoiling, withdrawing light, a lightning-explosion. As though—for an inch of time—he had penetrated into the entrails, the inmost anatomy, of that eye. Whoever had dipped into the ink that covered the pages of *The Messiah* had dipped into the vitreous gelatin of that sufficing eye. (115)

But the eye is gone, "over and done with" (124), turned into "a very small mound of ash" (139). And as the napper awakes, "like a man in a coma who has unexpectedly come to, having been declared asleep for life" (132), identity within Lars has shifted. The pagan idolator is superseded now by the Jew who espouses the Second Commandment: "A pack of swindlers. . . . You want to be in competition with God, that's the thing" (128).[34]

With this return to the reality principle, Ozick's narrative technique changes accordingly. From this point on, the Magic Narrative is replaced by a contrary mode of storytelling, the psychological realism of Henry James. As in James's novels, clarity of sight is a continuing motif—Lars even begins wearing glasses (129)—but now it serves to expose reality rather than find an alternate to it. What Lars mainly sees, in Jamesian fashion, is the scam to which he has been subject, and—echoing another Jamesian motif—the metaphor that dominates his thought is that of the theater: actors performing a play. Unaware of the change in their spectator (like Madame Merle in her final performance before Isabel Archer), they continue to ply the Magic Narrative in its full Christological regalia. Dr. Eklund calls for "the heralding," the "annunciation" of the sacred text—"The good news must be given out. That *The Messiah* is here" (115). Heidi presses upon him, Gospel-wise, the necessity for faith: "If it's not believed in, it might as well not exist" (115). And Adela assumes the pose of Madonna and Child, with the jar as holy infant: "Across from him Adela stood, the brass amphora in her arms. It made him think of . . . a round baby" (115). But what he discerns with increasing clarity is a Passion Play, directed by "Dr. Eklund's rawest stage voice" (118), with Lars himself assigned to the role of impassionata ("an impassioned soul!" 120): "You were born to it, Mr. Andemening. . . . You've absorbed it. What we need from you now is some word. A judgment. Is it worthy? Is it beautiful? Will you embrace it?" (118–19).

Knowing now that he "has fallen among players; among plotters" (119), Lars comes into his final Jamesian role, that of detective out to unmask his victimizers and close down their theater of illusions. "How theatrical they were, Dr. and Mrs. Eklund! Two old troupers in rehearsal," he observed among his earlier impressions (92). Now the stage master Dr. Olle Eklund quickly breaks down to "a wheeler-dealer in shady manuscripts" (121) with

the original name of Alter Eckstein. (Its German meaning—"Old Corner-
stone"—is vague, but the pun on "Altar" could combine with his incessant
match lighting to suggest a heathen sacrificial site.) Lars's "sister" Adela
assumes her real name of Elsa Vaz, acknowledges her real paternity as
Eckstein's rather than Bruno Schulz's daughter, and recovers her white
beret—a sort of angel's halo in the Magic Narrative—that Lars flings spiral-
ing down the stairwell after her (142). Heidi, unmasked as a false confidante, sells her shop and leaves the city.

Going over wholly to the stewpot, Lars is its faithful celebrant now,
espoused to all those features of the reality principle that he had formerly
abjured: an upscale new apartment, with not only a telephone but an answering machine, not only a typewriter but a word processor, and a cubicle
of his own at the Morgontorn. His work too reflects his new orientation,
winning an army of avid readers. Instead of writing "reviews that are practically theology," he practices market journalism with popular pieces about
detective novels and star autobiographies; instead of "those indecipherables
that steam up from the stomach-hole of Central Europe"—Kafka, Musil,
Canetti, the exponents of "existential dread"—he gives his readers "the
Swedes and the more companionable Americans" (132).

Like the Morgontorn building with its state-of-the-art renovations, Lars
has modernized himself, casting the quilt-napper out of his being with the
smooth dispassion of the exterminators ousting mice from the broken walls
of the building. All that remains to complete the exorcism is the detective's
terminal confrontation with "Adela," to compel her confession of fraud and
close the case to perfection. At first, that appears an easy task, requiring
only his constant use of the theater metaphor applied with maximum irony—
"part of the scenery," "playacting," "stage fright," "cast of characters,"
"you masqueraded" (137–39). So extorted, the confession is easily come by:
"She lowered her head. 'I came to say you were abused'" (139). But to his
chagrin the case doesn't end there. For one thing, despite her false role she
says true things about his past affinity for Magic Narrative, born of a need
beyond the range of the reality principle: "you still don't know where you
were born. A fairy tale. You picked yourself a make-believe father out of a
book" (138). And the little boy she has brought with her, a feverishly sleepy
napper, presents what Lars cannot help but regard as a déjà-vu situation:
"Tell me, . . . is there a father for this boy somewhere? Or is he going to have
to figure one out for himself?" (139).

"Adela's" unintelligible answer to his question—perhaps "Divorced," or
"It might have been 'Forced,' or 'Lost,' or 'Crushed'" (139)—traces back
thirty years to the opening pages of *Trust,* and its narrator's inexpressibly
mute, deep hunger for the right kind of fathering. It reminds us also of an

even earlier manuscript, Ozick's master's thesis on parable in the later novels of Henry James. What we finally have in *The Messiah of Stockholm* is a parable, never intended as naturalistic realism, in which Ozick has played out with fresh imaginings her familiar dilemma of the Jewish artist. On one hand, the dread of false fathering is real. To revere a Bruno Schulz as the artist-father is to risk the damnation of idol worship, the blasphemy of being in competition with God, the diabolism of serving the inhuman, the deathly, the maw of Moloch. Though this seems an extreme argument, we might consider the relevance to this case of the lessons of "Bloodshed": of the two guns that Bleilip is carrying, "It is the toy we have to fear," just as it was the toy shower head that in the end breathed out the terminal horror of Auschwitz (BL 71).

So the toy—the idea of the thing—hugely matters, because the imagination, if not restricted by some external power (the Second Commandment, Conscience), is inevitably subject to perverse wanderings, to idolatry, to the rationalizing of evil. And yet, in a case like this, the repressed is sure to return, giving voice to the other half of the "Jewish writer" oxymoron. Clearly the ephemeral satisfactions of Lars Andemening's new journalism cannot in the end match the ageless glories of art. His new eyeglasses, designed for stewpot discernments, will never survey the ecstatic heights accessible to the Magic Eye. His state of the art telephone/answering machine in its sleek new quarters will never deliver the "spectral mutterings" of the old building, hinting of "ancient festivities lasting till dawn." And though he has presumably matured, with his waking, beyond the need for such unreal things—"Impossible to mistake him now for anything but a man of middling years" (134)—somewhere inside there may yet reside a little boy who is napping, feverishly sleepy, craving the right kind of fathering, the Magic Narrative. Lars hints as much of himself to "Adela" just before their final parting:

> He said humbly, "I once had a child. She was taken away. I don't have her any more."
> "Platonic. Literary." She didn't believe him, and why should she? It was himself saying it: a father-inventor can just as easily invent a child. (141)

In its closing chapter—a page-long epilogue—it appears that *The Messiah of Stockholm* does give the child in Lars Andemening the last word, in the sense that something in him reverts after all to the Magic Narrative. Despite his commitment to the stewpot, he finds himself subject to "hallucination," most notably in converting "that smell of something roasting—all through Stockholm" into a primal scene of burnt offering: "as if Stockholm, burning, was slowly turning into Africa: the smell, winter or summer, of baking zebra" (143). Since the book makes no previous reference to Africa or its zebras, we are left to surmise that the baking zebra sublimates two scenes from the Magic Narrative. The first is the image of sacred print—Lars has been reading Bruno Schulz's extant novel, *Cinnamon Shops*—as an animal being slaughtered: "He had washed his fingers in that half-familiar dread print like a butcher with a bloody sheep in his grip" (23). With scriptlike lines crossing its body, baking zebra can well stand in for the sheep—and for Schulz's *Messiah*—in the epilogue.

The other scene tells us what the smell over Stockholm actually evokes from the Magic Narrative: not Africa, but Poland; not zebras, but idols being consumed in Moloch's sacrificial flames:

> Bright-torsoed gods, and in particular the little Near Eastern goddesses with their fragile budding breasts and their necklaces, . . . and occasionally even an exquisite miniature Venus-copy no bigger than a finger, were being chopped up or melted down to gratify the iron maw of some huge lazy Moloch. Day and night honeyed swirls of hot incense and the acrid smoky smell of roasting metal circled over Drohobycz. (109)

Although the matured man in Lars forswears idolatry, along with "that perjured eye, thrown like a broken blind coal among the cinders of the brass amphora" (144), the smell evokes a hallucination too precious to abandon, a fantastic hope that perhaps one pagan idol, Schulz's *Messiah,* somehow survived the Moloch flames of the Holocaust. So the epilogue ends with Lars vouchsafed a glimpse, "inside the narrow hallway of his skull," of a paradox and a parable: "the man in the long black coat, hurrying with a metal garter box squeezed under his arm, hurrying and hurrying toward the chimneys" (144). The paradox inheres in the figure dressed in the garb of Orthodox Judaism using the brief span that remains of his doomed life to assure the future life of a heretically blasphemous pagan text. The parable is the deep human need for imaginative art that necessitates the paradox.

Concerning that need, Bruno Schulz will have the last word, directed toward the deficiencies of ordinary reality. "Are we to betray the last secret of that district, the carefully concealed secret of Crocodile Street?" he asks, to which he answers: "Let us say it bluntly: the misfortune of that area is that nothing ever succeeds there, nothing can ever reach a definite conclusion. Gestures hang in the air, movements are prematurely exhausted and cannot overcome a certain point of inertia." So the Street of Crocodiles, which is to say naturalistic realism, is peopled by T. S. Eliot's Hollow Men—"Paralysed force, gesture without motion"—and it terminates in Eliot's "Unreal City," whose victims suffer "a fermentation of desires, prematurely aroused and therefore impotent and empty" in a place of "modernity and metropolitan corruption" (*Street* 103, 105). For Ozick, this unresolved conflict between imagination and reality was to carry over into her next novella, "The Shawl."

The Shawl: Tale of Two Cities

[In my youth] I was slow to "get" social clues—especially about this thing called "class."
(Ltr 7/13/90)

After she wrote "The Shawl" and "Rosa" in 1977, Cynthia Ozick waited four and seven years before publishing them, separately, in the *New Yorker,* and a full twelve years before publishing them together in book form under the title of *The Shawl.* Her reluctance to publish, she says, stemmed from her aversion to making a work of art about the death camps.[35] Given her view that all fiction is idolatry, this point of view regarding the Holocaust is certainly understandable. Even so, there is an additional reason why this book may have been Ozick's most painful writing experience: namely, the annihilation of her protagonist's Jewishness under the pressure of more urgent claims of identity, particularly those of motherhood. In the end, the tensions between cultural, maternal, and class-based modes of identity are as largely responsible for the designation of "Rosa Lublin, a madwoman" (13) as is her trauma in the death camp.

Undergirding Rosa's problems of identity are the contrasting sites of "Jewish geography" that distinguish the unified text of *The Shawl* (1989) from its two components parts, "The Shawl" and "Rosa." In the unified text, two thriving Jewish-American cities, New York and Miami, are juxtaposed with two sites of European-Jewish horror, Warsaw and the death camp (presumably Auschwitz). But along with their obvious contrasts, America and Nazified Poland display some curious resemblances. Though Poland was bitterly cold and Miami intensely hot, they both strike Rosa like settings from hell. "Cold, cold, the coldness of hell," says the opening sentence of "The Shawl," while in Miami, "The streets were a furnace, the sun an executioner. . . . She felt she was in hell" (14). What makes them both hellish is their evisceration of Jewish identity—in the death camp through physical annihilation, and in Miami through displacing traditional Jewish culture in favor of contemporary American hedonism. With New York City likewise unable to sustain Rosa's sense of self, no site outside her imagination serves to answer her need for identity. (Significantly, the one site in the world unarguably capable of sustaining Jewish identity, the State of Israel, gets only one dismissive mention from this Holocaust victim.)

Against her fixed grid of geographical places, Ozick develops her successive modes of identity. The most fundamental, coming first both in human biology and in Ozick's book, is the idea of identity centered in the body. William James maintained a genteel tone toward this depressing precept, noting that "The world experienced—otherwise called 'the field of consciousness'—comes at all times with our body as its center." Characteristically, Jean-Paul Sartre seemed to relish the nausea that he associated with this insight: "A dull and inescapable nausea perpetually reveals my body to my consciousness. . . . [It] is on the basis of this nausea that all concrete and empirical nauseas (nauseas caused by spoiled meat, fresh blood, excrement, etc.) are produced and make us vomit."[36]

In *The Shawl* both the death camp and Miami evoke the nausea that the spirit suffers on finding itself trapped in a decaying cylinder of flesh. In Auschwitz, starvation, disease, and random murder render body consciousness more intense—"On the road they raised one burden of a leg after another" (5)—but eventually they effect an annihilation of the body, so that the death camp inmates increasingly identify themselves with nothingness: "The weight of Rosa was becoming less and less; Rosa and Stella were slowly turning into air" (6), and Magda's starving belly is "fat with air" (5). Miami by contrast is airless—"In her room it was hot, hot all night. In Florida there was no air" (47)—but the same theme of bodily decrepitude prevails, here because of old age: "Everyone had canes, dowager's humps, acrylic teeth, shoes cut out for bunions. Everyone wore an open collar showing mottled skin, ferocious clavicles, the wasted foundations of wasted breasts. . . . If she moved [in her seat] even a little, an odor would fly up: urine, salt . . ." (24).

This alienation from one's body, caused in youth by the death camp horrors and later by the aging process, results in a bifurcation of identity throughout *The Shawl*. On the one hand, the goyish fantasy of angels replaces the human body as the anchor of Rosa's identity during her death camp trauma: "Rosa did not feel hunger; she felt light, . . . like someone in a faint, in trance, . . . someone who is already a floating angel, alert and seeing everything, but in the air, not there, not touching the road" (3–4). So too her infant daughter Magda turns into an angelic creature at her death, hitting the electric fence "like a butterfly touching a silver vine" (9).[37] Decades later, this recourse to fantasy still sustains Rosa, bringing Magda to Miami as an angel/butterfly, filling the room with her "hair . . . as yellow as buttercups" and her "sky-filled eyes" (65).

The opposite side of this bifurcation, with identity subhumanized to a bestial level, threads through the text in a web of animal imagery: Magda is like a squirrel wrapped in the shawl (4) or like a lioness (39); Rosa is like a "led animal" (22), a "ragged old bird with worn feathers" or "sluggish bird" (23, 30), a stork (23), a dog (29, 30, 40), and a wolf (10). Implicitly but very significantly, Dr. Tree compares the Jewish tribal sense to "The Way of the Baboons" (60). Even the insects participate in the general decline as "squads of dying flies" in Miami (13) appear to replace the butterflies of the death camp (8).

From this bifurcation between angel and animal, additional dualities proliferate: the imaginary versus the rational, the ideal versus the real, vitalism versus death consciousness, and—to translate these dualities into the Jewish idiom—L'Chaim! versus Moloch. In every instance throughout *The Shawl*, the decrepitude of the body gives precedence to the latter part of these binary opposites. Between fantasy and the reality principle, the Jewish ethos must choose reality even if that is unarguably where Moloch holds residence.

The sovereignty of death is not a new idea in Ozick's writing, nor does it necessarily derive from the Holocaust. Back in her first novel, *Trust,* she posed the idea as a question: "Who can revere a universe which will take that lovely marvel, man (. . . aeons of fish straining toward the dry, gill into lung, paw into the violinist's and dentist's hand), and turn him into a carbon speck?" (373). And in her essay "The Hole/Birth Catalogue," she asserts that "all the truth any philosophy can really tell us about human life is that each new birth supplies another corpse. . . . What is a baby-machine [a woman's body] if not also a corpse-maker?" (AA 255). But yet, so strong is the L'Chaim! principle in Ozick's consciousness that it pervades death itself in her essay "The Biological Premises of Our Sad Earth-Speck." Here she assents to the natural law that—as John Updike put it in *Rabbit Redux*—to live is to kill. Life on earth, she admits, survives only by feeding on other life, but the resulting expansion of life's kingdom justifies the whole Darwinian process:

> Now the planet whereon we live and die decrees the rule of prey (or, to say it plainly, the ingestion of one creature by another) for the benefit of the planet itself: that it may multiply in all its diversity and teem with ever-renewing plenitudes of kind and of form. (AA 235)

The Holocaust differed from this Darwinian struggle, she says, by killing solely to propagate death rather than to generate new life out of the killing process:

> The Holocaust—the burnt offering of the Jewish people in the furnace of the German Moloch—is an instance of aberration so gargantuan that it cannot

leave wary nature . . . unshaken. Killing for the pangs of hunger, nature always celebrates; but killing . . . on behalf of the adoration of death, nature abhors. (AA 236–37)

Although the Auschwitz episode occupies only seven pages, the intensity of its death consciousness threatens to overwhelm the fifty pages of "Rosa." Nearly starved to death, Stella—"her knees were tumors on sticks, her elbows chicken bones" (3)—is reduced in spirit to pure beastly appetite, hungry beyond the reach of any taboo: "Stella gazed at Magda [her infant niece] like a young cannibal. . . . [Rosa] was sure that Stella was waiting for Magda to die so she could put her teeth into the little thighs" (5). Later, in Miami, Rosa's subconscious would transpose Stella into the role of victim of this ultimate sacrilege: "Sometimes Rosa had cannibal dreams about Stella: she was boiling her tongue, her ears, her right hand, such a fat hand with plump fingers . . ." (15). Magda herself, ostensibly a bundle of new life, has become a death's head, her one tooth resembling "an elfin tombstone of white marble" (4) as the shawl in which she lies "buried away deep" (5) becomes her shroud. As she expires on the electric fence in the "ash-stippled wind" (7), death becomes vocal for the moment, the "sad, grainy voices" in the wires "[going] mad in their growling" during the immolation.

Confirming the sovereignty of death for Rosa is the heartless sarcasm of nature during this scene, figured in the contrast between the horror inside the fence and radiant beauty on the outside:

> The sunheat murmured of another life, of butterflies in summer. . . . On the other side of the steel fence, far away, there were green meadows speckled with dandelions and deep-colored violets; beyond them, even farther, innocent tiger lilies, tall, lifting their orange bonnets. In the barracks, they spoke of "flowers," of "rain": excrement, thick turd-braids, and the slow stinking maroon waterfall that slunk down from the upper bunks. . . . (8–9)

Though it has presumably kept the Jewish ethos alive through centuries of bitter persecution, the L'Chaim! ethos appears overmatched at last, its eternal flame swallowed up in crematoria fires. The theme of *The Shawl* is the question whether Jewish identity, perhaps abetted by Jewish geography (the move from Auschwitz to Miami), can survive this greatest of all historical traumas. Or to rephrase the question: Can the two primary modes of Jewish identity survive their mutual contradiction—L'Chaim! versus the sufferings of Jewish history?

It would appear that the answer is No. Jewish identity in Rosa's case is overwhelmed not only by the fires of Moloch turned on her own body but also, paradoxically, by Moloch's leading adversary: motherhood. The maternal passion that arrests Rosa at the moment her baby is immolated, keeping her traumatized for the next forty years beyond the reach of reality, cancels her Jewish heritage. In the name of her lost motherhood, Rosa violates that most fundamental precept of Jewish law, the taboo against idols. Explicitly, in her letter to Magda, she worships Motherhood "instead of" God: "To have the power to create another human being. . . . To pass on a whole genetic system. I don't believe in God, but I believe, like the Catholics, in mystery" (41). And not only does she worship the image of her daughter instead of God, she further flouts Jewish law by her reliance on magic to conjure up the lost child's reappearance.[38] As a rational religion, Judaism condemns magic and the occult, but such magic is Rosa's only recourse for recovering her beloved daughter. The child's name, Magda (which has the same root as Magic) heightens the impression of heresy.[39] The narrative bears a curious resemblance to Toni Morrison's *Beloved* in this respect, though Morrison appears to favor the recourse to the occult that Ozick finds heretical.

The shawl itself is Rosa's magic totem of motherhood, a direct link spanning forty years to her lost child. Deliberately echoing—it would seem—the Shroud of Turin stories, which were much in the news during the period when Ozick wrote this work, Rosa imparts to the shawl a quasi-Christological ambience: "Magda's shawl! Magda's swaddling cloth. Magda's shroud. The memory of Magda's smell, the holy fragrance of the lost babe" (31). Rosa's gravitation toward Christianity (more specifically, Roman Catholicism) heightens with Stella's warning that Rosa is making a "relic" of her daughter (42) as well as turning the shawl into an "idol" that is broadly comparable to the "True Cross" (31–32). The motif culminates in the reverence for the Virgin and Child whose statue Rosa remembers from her mother's kitchen, even citing her mother's poem to the "Mother of God" (41).

As bad as it is from the Jewish point of view, this affinity for Christian otherworldliness is not the worst instance of Rosa's penchant for escape from reality. The worst comes when, abandoning the reality principle completely, Rosa rests her ideal of perfect Motherhood on two transparent fabrications. The first of these involves Magda's paternity; Rosa cannot abide the idea that Magda's father is a death camp officer:

> Your father was not a German. I was forced by a German, it's true, and more than once, but I was too sick to conceive. Stella has a naturally pornographic mind, she can't resist dreaming up a dirty sire for you, an S.S. man! (43)

But Rosa's claim that her Polish fiancé fathered Magda (43) is belied by the baby's clearly Teutonic features—"not Rosa's bleak complexion, dark like cholera, it was another kind of face altogether, eyes blue as air, smooth feathers of hair nearly as yellow as the Star sewn into Rosa's coat. You could think she was one of *their* babies" (4).

Rosa's other denial of reality is her insistence that Magda is still alive. "To keep [Stella] quiet," Rosa writes to her imagined Magda—now supposedly a grown woman in New York City—"I pretend you died" (42). For all the pathos of the case, a comic tone initially affects Rosa's fantasy in so far as she embodies the parental pride so often lampooned by Jewish comedians in the phrase "My son, the doctor." For Rosa the phrase is amended to "My daughter, the doctor," with her mother's pride amplified by Magda's success in nabbing a successful husband—"Magda, a beautiful young woman of thirty, thirty-one: a doctor married to a doctor; large house in Mamaroneck, New York; two medical offices, one on the first floor, one in the finished basement" (35).

It soon transpires, however, that Rosa's noble ideal of Motherhood masks a class-consciousness that is a deadly enemy of Jewish identity, second only to Nazism itself. This motif of class snobbery, in turn, gradually evolves into the central irony of the book, the real reason for the Jewish geography which undergirds Ozick's portrayal of post-Holocaust betrayals of Jewish identity. In juxtaposing the Old World and the New, *The Shawl* shows the Jewish idea torn by class-based conflict: Poland versus America; Warsaw versus New York/Miami; high-class European culture versus vulgar, low-class American; Rosa versus Persky.

By beginning *The Shawl* with seven searing pages that portray Rosa's suffering in the death camp, culminating in the scene of Nazi infant-murder, Ozick evokes maximum sympathy for her protagonist. But her death camp victim in "Rosa" turns out, in "The Shawl," to be a Jewish anti-Semite. Moreover, Rosa's anti-Semitism is in no way attributable to the trauma that she suffered in the death camp, in the way that Lushinski's anti-Semitism in "A Mercenary" was Holocaust-related. Instead, she was born and raised as a Jew-hater during the glory years of that great center of Jewish culture, Warsaw—"the world capital of Yiddish literature" in the 1920s according to historian Ronald Sanders.[40]

Rosa's last name, Lublin, adds a layer of irony to this characterization by referring to the city in Poland where the Nazis planned in 1939 to establish a Jewish version of an American Indian reservation. (Hitler got his idea of the concentration camp from reading about Indian reservations in Karl May's greatly popular Western novels.)[41] Here some 400,000 Jews were to establish an agricultural commune called Lublinland, where their capacity for self-sufficiency could be experimentally tested. In fact, some 200,000 Jews did get crushed into the Lublin ghetto, where they lived as many as ten to a small room and suffered mass starvation.[42] Lublin soon became, along with Auschwitz, a preeminent killing center with huge gassing facilities.

Despite the common heritage of Jewish suffering implied in her patronym, Rosa insists on her difference from the Jewish rabble around her. Even her daughter the doctor, though originally imagined in the role of medical practitioner, ascends (in Rosa's fantasy) above that typically Jewish mold into the WASPish Ivy League professoriat, so as to pursue a blatantly heathen interest as Professor of Greek Philosophy at Columbia University (39). Her precious daughter, that is to say, is not really a Jew. Rosa herself takes every opportunity to assert her cultural superiority to these crassly vulgar American Jews in Miami. Although they appear to maintain the Jewish tradition of highbrow bookishness—"She saw them walking with Tolstoy under their arms, with Dostoyevsky" (16)—she is not fooled for a moment: "she had nothing in common with them." (As a Pole, she would not in any case be greatly impressed by Russian novels—unlike Ozick, a daughter of Russian Jews who reveres Tolstoy.) And from the moment she meets Persky, her fellow immigrant from Warsaw, her recurring refrain would be "My Warsaw isn't your Warsaw" (18).

Rosa's Warsaw differs from Persky's not only because Persky escaped the city before Hitler became its master, but more important—to Rosa—because of the class system that prevailed in Poland before the war, dividing that nation's Jews into disparate, unrelating segments. Before Hitler "unified" these segments within a single scapegoat category, Rosa's family had belonged to the most perfectly assimilated segment of the Jewish intelligentsia, having totally abandoned its Jewish heritage in favor of the Europe of the Enlightenment. Theirs is the Europe of Allegra Vand in *Trust*—"this fountain of the world (she called it life, she called it Europe) all spectacle, dominion, energy, and honor. And all the while she never smelled death there" (TR 78).

Even now, decades after the Holocaust, Rosa yearns to resurrect that totally de-Judaized ideal of civilization:

The Warsaw of her girlhood: a great light: she switched it on, she wanted to live inside her eyes. . . . the house of her girlhood laden with a thousand books. Polish, German, French; her father's Latin books. . . . Cultivation, old civilization, beauty, history! (20–21)

Notably absent from that bookshelf given over to the languages of the genocide are the Torah, the Talmud, the Jewish philosophers. Nor of course is the vulgate tongue of working-class Jews allowed to defile this aristocratic ambience. Rosa's reverie specifically recalls the triumph within her family heritage of the European high style over the Yiddish low:

Surprising turnings of streets, shapes of venerable cottages, lovely aged eaves, unexpected and gossamer turrets, steeples, the gloss, the antiquity! Gardens. Whoever speaks of Paris has never seen Warsaw. Her father, like her mother, mocked at Yiddish; there was not a particle of ghetto left in him, not a grain of rot. Whoever yearns for an aristocratic sensibility, let him switch on the great light of Warsaw. (21)

Persky, of course, comes from a different Warsaw, that of the peddler-class migrants from the even lower class rural shtetl, and Rosa is chagrined to think that these ignorant Americans would not understand the difference between them:

[Persky was] From Warsaw! Born 1906! She imagined what bitter ancient alley, dense with stalls, cheap clothes strung on outdoor racks, signs in jargoned Yiddish. . . . The Americans couldn't tell her apart from this fellow with his false teeth and his dewlaps and his rakehell reddish toupee bought God knows when or where—Delancey Street, the Lower East Side. A dandy. Warsaw! (20)

The fact that Persky has escaped this poverty through realizing the American Dream does not impress Rosa in the slightest. Instead, Persky's success in the junk-jewelry business—"buttons, belts, notions, knickknacks, costume jewelry" (25)—only confirms his irredeemable vulgarity. But here again Rosa's indifference to Jewish history betrays her stuntedness of spirit. When Jews in medieval Europe were prohibited from economic competition with Christians, virtually every mode of livelihood, from guildhall to farmyard, was closed to them. Only ragpicking and usury, occupations deemed unsuitable for Christians, were left wide open for Jewish development. With great enterprise the Jews of Europe and America eventually used those openings to establish two fabulously successful industries: great banking houses that have helped finance Western commerce and industry since the Renaissance; and the giant garment industry that we associate preeminently with New York City. Rosa simply fails to understand what it means when she notes how, in the laundromat, Persky "handled the clothes like an expert" (19). Nor does she grasp the Jewish triumph over the ragpickers' lot that is on display in the general expertise of the transplanted New Yorkers around her: "They knew good material. Whatever you wore they would feel between their fingers and give a name to: faille, corduroy, herringbone, shantung, jersey, worsted, velour, crepe" (16). If Rosa's Warsaw was not Persky's Warsaw, neither was her New York the working-class city of the garment workers.

In her letters to (the imaginary) Magda, Rosa demonstrates how her class hatred carried right through the Holocaust, as though the true outrage of the thing were her forced proximity to Jews from the lower orders. Of the Warsaw Ghetto, she writes, "most immediately we were furious because we had to be billeted with such a class, with these old Jew peasants worn out from their rituals and superstitions, phylacteries on their foreheads sticking up so stupidly, like unicorn horns, every morning" (67). The Holocaust's dissolving of class boundaries was really quite intolerable:

> Can you imagine a family like us—my father who had been the director-general of the Bank of Warsaw, my sheltered mother, almost Japanese in her shyness and refinement . . . all of us, who had lived in a tall house with four floors and a glorious attic . . . imagine confining *us* with teeming Mockowiczes and Rabinowiczes and Perskys and Finkelsteins, with all their bad-smelling grandfathers and their hordes of feeble children! (66)

Completing this circuit of Jewish anti-Semitism is Rosa's contempt for Israel, presumably by reason of its low-class genesis. "If not for me," she confides to Magda, "they [the Zionist rescue workers] would have shipped Stella with a boatload of orphans to Palestine, to become God knows what. . . . A field worker jabbering Hebrew" (40). With Israel thus dismissed out of hand, and Poland made *Judenrein* by decree of its Nazi and Communist rulers, there remains (for Rosa) only America as a site of contemporary Jewish culture. Here is where Ozick can bring her theme of cultural conflict to its culmination, playing off Rosa's European heritage against Jewish-American mores.

The general depravity of American civilization is implicit in the first words Persky says to her in the laundromat, reading from a Yiddish newspaper about a storekeeper who had managed to survive both Hitler and Stalin ("a camp in Siberia," 17) but succumbed to the savagery of contemporary urban life: "in Westchester, not even the Bronx . . . robbers, muggers, . . . they finish him off. From Siberia he lives for this day!" (18). The specific vulgarity of American Jewry comes across through Persky himself, who publicly picks seeds from his dental plate (26), whose idea of cultural elegance is his kinship to a B-grade movie actress ("Betty Bacall, who Humphrey Bogart the movie star was married to, a Jewish girl," 22), and whose button business Rosa finds crass and pathetic: "Persky's life: how trivial it must always have been: buttons, himself no more significant than a button. . . . All of Miami Beach, a box for useless buttons!" (55).

Unwittingly, however, Persky motivates Rosa's one instance of Jewish mores at work. As a result of her notion that he stole her underpants in the laundromat, Rosa makes a grand tour of sleaze-filled Jewish Miami in search of the missing garment. Here her reflexive embarrassment over her sexuality suggests that the ancient Hebrew taboos still hold sway. "Because of her missing underwear, she had no dignity before him" (55), she thinks when she finds Persky waiting for her; and her revulsion against the two young men having homosexual intercourse on the beach evokes an outright biblical anathema: "'Sodom!' she hissed, and stumbled away" (49).

Beyond vulgarity and sexual corruption there remains for Rosa one last great blemish on American Jewry, and this one is indeed serious. Contradicting the soul of Judaism, these people place no value on Jewish history. Most grievously, as Rosa tells Magda, they have no Holocaust memory, no interest in the way it was:

> When I had my store I used to "meet the public," and I wanted to tell everybody—not only our story, but other stories as well. No one knew anything. This amazed me, that nobody remembered what happened only a little while ago. (66)

Rosa's failure to find an audience for her Holocaust narrative—"I said all this in my store, talking to the deaf" (69)—results in two acts of madness: it is the chief reason why she smashed up her antique store, and also why she writes these letters to her ideal audience, the imaginary Magda. The narrative in the letters, however, contains blazing ironies, especially in this final letter to Magda. The reason Rosa focuses her letter on the tramcar, in which Polish Gentiles rode serenely through the horrors of the Warsaw Ghetto, is that the tram signified her forced change from Polish to Jewish identity, and with it her lapse from high- to low-class status:

> Every day, and several times a day, we had these witnesses. . . . They were all the sort of plain people of the working class with slovenly speech who ride tramcars, but they were considered better than we, because no one regarded us as Poles anymore. . . . And with all this—especially our Polish, the way my parents enunciated Polish in soft calm voices with the most precise articulation, so that every syllable struck its target—people in the tramcar were regarded as Poles . . . and we were not! They, who couldn't read one line of Tuwim, never mind Virgil. . . . (69)

Like Joseph Brill in *The Cannibal Galaxy* and Lushinski's parents in "A Mercenary," Rosa is a child of Europe more than of Israel. To Magda she boasts of the artifacts in her father's house that date back to Europe's genesis, particularly the Greek vases in his collection, most of them replicas but one an archeological find that he personally dug up in Crete, the cradle of Hellenic civilization (68). So too her pride in her father's command of Latin—he knew the "first half of the *Aeneid* by heart" (69)—sets off her Euro-Hellenism against her disdain for all things Jewish: the Yiddish language, the low-class Jews of Miami, and the resurrected State of Israel. As with thousands of other assimilated European Jews, Rosa's Jewish identity thus derives solely from the legal strictures imposed by the Nazi overlords. Because her upbringing as an upper-class Pole left no space for the Judaic ethos, she has no cultural strength to draw upon in the face of her two Holocaust-caused obsessions: her death consciousness, and her propensity to live in fantasy rather than reality. In a word, she has no recourse to the L'Chaim! principle.

This deficiency is the distinguishing feature of Rosa's character. The other two main characters, Stella and Persky, represent two alternatives to Rosa's loss of Jewish identity. Although Stella shared Rosa's experience of Auschwitz, she maintains the L'Chaim! attitude by expunging the past from her consciousness. Calling for "the end of morbidness," Stella tells Rosa, "It's thirty years, forty, who knows, give it a rest. . . . For God's sake, don't be a crazy person! Live your life!" (63, 31, 33). And Persky has no past that needs forgetting; his Warsaw, of pre-Hitler vintage, is not Rosa's. Like American Jews in general, these two Americanized Jews assume the L'Chaim! principle as a spontaneous philosophy of life. Whereas Rosa maintains that "all philosophy is rooted in suffering over the passage of time" (41), Persky reasserts Stella's philosophy of the present moment in advising Rosa, "You can't live in the past" (23).[43]

If anything, the other Jews in *The Shawl* outdo Persky in their ability to live in the present moment. Ignoring the aging process and the decay of their flesh (the "rolls of wide fat" on their necks, the dentures, the "blue-marbled sinews" on their calves), these "flirts of seventy" continue to believe in "the seamless continuity of the body" (28). So triumphant is the present moment for these old people that the past becomes wholly subsumed in it, converted into another version of time present: "Little by little they were forgetting their grandchildren, their aging children. More and more they were growing significant to themselves. . . . Every table surface a mirror. In these mirrors the guests appeared to themselves as they used to be, powerful women of thirty, striving fathers of thirty-five" (29).

Rosa of course cannot share this splendid reversion to the prime of their lives. Her mirror of the past yields not powerful women and striving fathers but a rabid skeleton compelled to watch her infant flung upon the hot wires. Her revulsion against the past is the deepest reason she smashed up her antique store in New York—"Antiques. Old furniture. . . . I had a specialty in antique mirrors. Whatever I had there, I smashed it" (26). Neither the present moment, normally sanctified by the L'Chaim! principle, nor the past, normally sanctified by the Jewish reverence for history, avails as a mode of life-meaning for Rosa, and with their loss she is no longer a Jew.

Any doubts on that score are settled by Persky's brief survey of her apartment: "I don't see no books neither. You want me to drive you to the
library?" (57). A Jew with no interest in books is an oxymoron explainable
only by the dead soul syndrome, a condition that Rosa openly lays claim to
on several occasions:

> Rosa said, "I was looking for something I lost."
> "Poor Lublin, what did you lose?"
> "My life." (55)

Eventually this discourse between Persky and Rosa produces the culminating impasse in the book, a final confrontation of Memory versus
L'Chaim!:

> "But it's over," Persky said. "You went through it, now you owe yourself
> something."
> "This is how Stella talks. . . . She wants to wipe out memory." [ellipsis mine]
> "Sometimes a little forgetting is necessary," Persky said, "if you want to get
> something out of life."
> "Get something! Get *what?*"
> "You ain't in a camp. It's finished. Long ago it's finished. Look around,
> you'll see human beings."
> "What I see," Rosa said, "is bloodsuckers." (58)

Conveniently appearing at this moment, by way of his letter to Rosa, is
"[Dr.] Tree the bloodsucker!" (61), with his slander against tribal loyalty
implicit in his chapter title, "Defensive Group Formation: The Way of the
Baboons" (60). Dr. Tree—whose name suggests an anglicization of the
German-Jewish "Baum"—undermines Persky's principle of forgetting by
extending it into a form of Buddhism that is an inhuman monstrosity of
nonattachment. In a further affront, Tree derives this philosophy from his
studies in the psychology of Holocaust survivors:

> It begins to be evident that prisoners gradually came to Buddhist positions.
> They gave up craving and began to function in terms of non-functioning, i.e.,
> non-attachment. . . . "Pain" in this view is defined as ugliness, age, sorrow,
> sickness, despair, and, finally, [a special insult to Rosa as mother] birth. Non-
> attachment is attained through the Eightfold Path, the highest stage of which
> is . . . consummated indifference. (37–38)

But if Persky's argument for forgetting is travestied by Tree's letters,
Rosa's argument for Memory is also undercut by her deepening reliance on
fantasy to bring back her lost Magda. Her brightest fantasy in the whole

book lights up these closing pages: "The whole room was full of Magda. . . . Magda's hair was still as yellow as buttercups. . . . Magda's sky-filled eyes . . . were like two obeisant satellites. Magda could be seen with great clarity" (64–65). The book ends thus in ambiguity. In a terminal confrontation, Rosa conjures up Magda's presence by means of her memory-based magic, but Rosa also invites Persky to come upstairs with his L'Chaim!-based realism. Who will prevail is an unanswered question.

Judgment

The Critical Reckoning

Cynthia Ozick, thirty-eight years old when *Trust* launched her career, was fifty-five when William Scheick and Catherine Rainwater produced the first sustained effort of Ozick scholarship, a seventy-five-page segment of the summer 1983 *Texas Studies in Literature and Language* that included an introduction, an interview, a bibliography, and my own long essay. The first book of criticism on Ozick was Harold Bloom's *Cynthia Ozick* (1986), a collection of essays intended to represent "the best criticism so far available" on Ozick's fiction. It is an accurate reflection of her career, and not a reproach to Bloom's book, that twenty years after publishing *Trust,* such a collection would consist of thirteen book reviews (eight in the *NYTBR*) with an average length of three pages, along with six essays averaging (not counting my own) nine pages. Bloom includes a bibliography with another twenty-five items, twenty of which are reviews of two or less pages. The book thus furnishes a good starting point for a quick scan of the Ozick critical spectrum as of the mid-1980s.

In Bloom's book two reviews of *Trust* establish the opposite polarities of early Ozick criticism. David L. Stevenson praises *Trust* for its originality, calling it "that extraordinary literary entity, a first novel that is produced by a rich, creative imagination, not an imitation of someone else's work or thinly disguised autobiography." Eugene Goodheart, however, faults the book for its "discontinuity between language and reality or between expression and feeling," a failure that he ascribes to the unaccountably embittered mood of the narrator. The "fog of chronic dyspepsia" emanating from "the barren ground of the heroine's sullennesses" notably envelops Allegra Vand, who thus becomes "more like an hallucinated projection of the heroine's resentment than a credible mother or wife or woman."

Taken together, these two reviews point beyond text to subtext. Stevenson's remark that *Trust* is not thinly disguised autobiography does not preclude its being well-disguised autobiography, and Goodheart's focus on the narrator's sullennesses points to the connection between the book and Ozick's own buried narrative. For Ozick, the living subtext beneath the text of *Trust* was the bitterness of her fourfold deprivation: as a victim of academic/literary misogyny; as an artist condemned to see tripe like Allegra's *Marianna Harlow* lionized while her own work languished in oblivion; as a woman prohibited by Judaic sexual taboo from participating in the Laurentian consummation of Tilbeck's apotheosis; and as a Jew whose culture has been marginalized and threatened with extinction in the era after the Holocaust. Goodheart was right to note the radical extreme in the mood of *Trust*, but he was less perceptive than Stevenson in failing to observe the high achievement of *Trust* despite the flaws caused by the narrator's sullenness.

In its coverage of *The Pagan Rabbi* (1971) Bloom's book discloses two signs of better days for Ozick criticism: the addition of a full-blown essay by Josephine Z. Knopp to its two brief reviews (the first real essay in Ozick criticism); and a consensus among the three concerning the extraordinary degree of originality in her stories—"her unique vision of the truth," as Knopp puts it. For Paul Theroux, Ozick's "imaginative daring" in conceiving "people and situations who [*sic*] are rarely if ever seen in American novels" makes her laudably different from "Malamud, Bellow, Roth and Co." Concerning "Envy; or, Yiddish in America," Johanna Kaplan risks an outright encomium: "I found myself overwhelmed by the story and . . . amazed at its effect on me. I read it, reread it and lent it to friends, all as in a fever."

Gone now are complaints of Ozick's overblown style, which has become—Kaplan says—"sharpened, clarified, controlled" so as to make her "a kind of narrative hypnotist." The argument now moves to questions of theme and credibility. Ozick's ground theme, Kaplan says, which "runs through all the stories and all the characters," is "a variant of the question: what is holy?" Is holiness a feature of "the extraordinary" (dryads or sea nymphs), or is it found in "what is . . . unthinkingly discounted" (daily life)? Theroux, though agreeing with Kaplan that "Envy" is "excellent in all ways," finds Ozick's excursions into fantasy "insufficiently dramatized and unpersuasive," in part because the narrators of these stories (such as "The Pagan Rabbi" and "The Dock-Witch") are in a crazed condition.

In these reviews of *The Pagan Rabbi*, feminist criticism makes its first response to Ozick's fiction, to the effect of illustrating the denseness of the male commentator. Though Paul Theroux calls "Virility" a "superb story" for its treatment of plagiarism, he fails to see Ozick's blatantly rendered feminist purpose. Josephine Knopp, however, observes that here Ozick "demolishes the male supremacists with the same hilarious derision that she employs against the anti-Semites in 'Envy.'" Extending Knopp's insight, we may say that the seven stories in *The Pagan Rabbi* embody a recurrence of the fourfold deprivations that demoralized the narrator of *Trust:* literary misogyny ("Virility"), Jewish sexual/religious taboos ("The Pagan Rabbi," "The Dock-Witch"), dismal failure of artistic ambitions ("Envy," "The Suitcase"), and Jewish/Gentile cultural incompatibilities ("The Butterfly and the Traffic Light" and, to some extent, all the stories). The difference since *Trust* is Ozick's more consistent grasp of narrative voice, mood, and style, which sometimes attains tour-de-force effectiveness in *The Pagan Rabbi.*

Thomas R. Edwards, in his review of *Bloodshed* (1976), brings to expression a hitherto unspoken problem in Ozick's readership, the bewilderment of the goy. "Bloodshed," he admits, "is hard for a goy to make out," and "Usurpation" is confusing enough to create his generalized "doubts about her work." Nonetheless, Edwards argues that even a Gentile cannot help but respond to "the best thing" in *Bloodshed,* "the marvelous novella 'A Mercenary.'" In addition, Ozick's preface, Edwards says, alleviates the confusion about "Usurpation"—"Certainly her gloss on 'Usurpation' is more coherent and moving than the story itself."

That opinion, however, is strongly contested by Ruth Wisse in her essay "Ozick as American Jewish Writer." Calling Ozick "a selfish and somewhat nasty finagler" for defending her plagiarism in "Usurpation," Wisse condemns the "self-justification and special pleading" of the preface, which "betrays the insecurities of both the artist and the Jew." The harshness of this attack may have influenced Ozick's later decision to say, "The Preface to *Bloodshed* is a piece of fiction like any other" (Scheick 258)—perhaps the least credible statement in all her writing. By far the most substantial essay on Ozick up to that time (the June 1976 *Commentary*), Wisse's critique places her against the larger backdrop of contemporary and earlier Jewish-American writing. As against Bellow-Malamud-Roth's "twin themes of marginality and victimization," Wisse says, Ozick is the "spokesman and most audacious writer" among a new generation of writers who are culturally secure enough to return without anxiety to "the 'tribal' and particularistic aspects of Judaism." Yet, she argues, Ozick's preface, by allowing the author to become "her own translator," reveals her contradictory craving to be understood among the Gentiles despite her claim that a Christian civilization is innately incapable of understanding indigenous Jewish literature.

By 1982, the year of *Levitation: Five Fictions,* the fifty-four-year-old author was beginning to establish a reputation. But though Leslie Epstein begins her review by calling Ozick's earlier books, *The Pagan Rabbi* and *Blood-*

shed, "perhaps the finest work in short fiction by a contemporary writer," she finds *Levitation* disappointing because *"each* of these works . . . [shies] crucially from the kind of resolution we rightly demand from imaginative fiction." Characterization turns out to be Ozick's weak suit, in Epstein's view, as exemplified by the Puttermesser-Xanthippe saga. The most humanly engaging character in the Puttermesser stories, she says, is neither Puttermesser nor Xanthippe but Uncle Zindel, who teaches the heroine Hebrew lessons until the narrator intervenes to declare him nonexistent—disheartening proof, for Epstein, of how the text "quails before the demands of, the powers of, imagination." And the title story, "Levitation," is perhaps most damaged of all by this disengagement from real characters, which occurs not only in Ozick's portrayal of Jews who supernaturally levitate "into the glory of their martyrdom" but most crucially in the portrait of Feingold's wife, Lucy. Because she is a Christian, Epstein says, "the dice are loaded against this character, the deck [is] patently stacked." Lucy's lapse from her Christian heritage into a wild vision of its pagan roots means that "the game is no longer being played by the rules of fiction. Probability, necessity, recognizable human feeling are replaced by laws of what can only be called mystical vision."

In this critique of Lucy's character, Epstein was one of the first to touch upon a serious long-term problem. Like Toni Morrison, Cynthia Ozick combines a superb ability to render her own cultural heritage with a plainly limited comprehension of the majority culture that encompasses/oppresses it. Although there is no mystery about a black or Jewish writer's lack of empathy for things white or Christian, art requires emotional discipline to avoid turning into propaganda. Such discipline may be too weak when Ozick's hatred of "the whole—the whole!—of Western Civilization" (a claim resembling Morrison's statement that "my hatred of white people is justified") produces the hypocritical William of *Trust,* the cartoonlike evangelist at the end of "Envy," and the more serious but inadequate effort to characterize Lucy as a Christian in "Levitation."[1] It is nonetheless appropriate to ask, regarding this failure of imagination, how many Gentile writers have rendered the figure of the Jew to better effect than Ozick has rendered her Christian (Lucy)? Chaucer, Marlowe, Dickens, Hemingway—as we glance back through the centuries, the portraiture of the Jew by Gentiles has not presented much solid ground from which to attack Cynthia Ozick's portrayals of Christian characters, particularly as viewed after the Holocaust.

Katha Pollitt's essay on *Art & Ardor* (1983), Ozick's first volume of essays, is an unusually penetrating and graceful exercise in Ozick criticism. Calling the book "a unified and magisterial continuation of Miss Ozick's short stories by other means," Pollitt divides these essays among three

Ozicks—"the rabbi, the feminist, and a disciple of Henry James"—who sometimes work against each other (e.g., feminist versus Jew), sometimes in symbiosis. It was the Jamesian Ozick who ripped into *Other Voices, Other Rooms* "like someone going after a hummingbird with a chainsaw," and the rabbi whose subliminal motive for doing so could have been Capote's complaint about a "Jewish mafia" in American letters. It was the rabbi and feminist who ascribed the invention of "homosexual manners" to Lytton Strachey, thereby "eliminating Oscar Wilde and a century of dandyism with a stroke of the pen." Among the inspired conjectures of Pollitt's critique is her linkup between Ozick's essay on Maurice Samuel and Yankel Ostrover in "Envy." So too she links Ozick's essay on Harold Bloom with Isaac Kornfeld in "The Pagan Rabbi."

The schism between Ozick the rabbi and the Jamesian Ozick underlies Sanford Pinsker's judgment that "the ardor of her Jewishness takes a fearsome toll on her discussions of Art." For him, however, the affirmation of her Jewish heritage in *Art and Ardor* means that "Ozick has recovered from her long Jamesian night of the soul." Something similar occurs in "Puttermesser and Xanthippe," according to Elaine Kauvar's learned analysis of that novella. Bringing a Socratic dialogue, *Theaetetus,* to bear, along with the Kabbalistic *Book of Creation* by Gershom Scholem and James's "The Lesson of the Master," Kauvar sees Puttermesser and the golem as initially reflecting two parts of a split personality—the mature and rational Jewish intellect versus "Puttermesser's primitive self" whose "cries for love and life" have been "sacrificed for dedication to the intellect." Although Xanthippe returns to earth in the end, after her sexual fire becomes too rampant for a civilized community, Puttermesser learns from the golem the need to recover "the experience of the ordinary and vital passions of humanity." To judge from this essay, Kauvar's forthcoming (as of this writing) book on Ozick will be a landmark contribution to Ozick studies—greatly learned in Jewish lore and otherwise illuminating.[2]

The timing of Bloom's book enabled it to encompass, at its far end, Ozick's second novel, *The Cannibal Galaxy* (1983). Of the four reviews that are here reprinted, Edmund White's best illustrates her status among other artists. White praises Ozick for her moral intensity—for "always submitting experience to an ethical inquiry"—and finds "the very secret of Miss Ozick's art" in her juxtaposition of "vivid hard circumstance and things that were only imagined." But as a much-admired stylist himself, he reserves his main laurels for her handling of language: "Precisely on account of her style, Miss Ozick strikes me as the best American writer to have emerged in recent years." What best illustrates her "astonishingly flexible and vital language" is her handling of metaphor, which "animates every page of the novel."

A. Alvarez, however, chooses exactly the same feature as his point of attack. Although he credits the Jamesian subtlety of the work, calling it "'The Beast in the Jungle' replayed," he faults its "startling overinflation" of style, which makes it "far less convincing than Ozick's shorter fiction." As compared with the stories, he says *The Cannibal Galaxy* has "degenerated into mannerism. The rhetoric and imagery proliferate like tropical undergrowth . . . until the narrative chokes and expires."

If this disagreement over style represents critical subjectivity—each to his own taste—the religious response is more objective and more collegial. Max Apple's biblical stance toward *The Cannibal Galaxy* relates the title metaphor to the second sentence of Genesis (which Ozick cites in the novel): "And the earth was astonishingly empty." Calling the phrase "empty and desolate" the "center of this wonderful novel," Apple ramifies its cosmic, social, and personal meanings: "Empty and desolate is . . . the uncreated universe, . . . post-Holocaust Europe, . . . suburban American life and education, . . . [and] an aging man who has no offspring." But against it all, in Apple's view, the L'Chaim! principle prevails: "From the destruction of the European Jews, from the emptiness of Brill's life, from the failures of the dual curriculum a wonder emerges: an artist." Not *an* artist (Beulah Hilt) only, but two artists, as Apple renders his closing tribute to the real-life artist and her biblical sources: "*Tohu vavohu,* emptiness and desolation. From the void the cosmos. From the Fleg School Beulah Hilt. From the mummified prose surrounding us these glorious words of Cynthia Ozick."

Margaret Wimsatt, also in the Bloom collection, sees not the Hebrew Bible but a Christological construct at the center of *The Cannibal Galaxy,* namely, the main character's role as "perhaps a prototype of the Wandering Jew." In various ways that is of course true, geographically in Brill's wanderings from France to the Great Lakes, culturally in his movement away from his Jewish heritage. But Joseph Brill is not the true subject of Ozick's novel, in Wimsatt's judgment; "her real interest is in problems, in philosophy, in mortality, in monotheism"—which is to say, religion. Ozick's final objective, Wimsatt says, is to call the Jew back from his wanderings, reminding him that "these [Western/pagan] arts were forbidden by Jahweh to his people; they were left to the Canaanites and the Greeks. For monotheists the path to wisdom is marked only by Midrash and commentary."

Finally, there is Harold Bloom's own contribution to his collection, featuring his characteristic blend of uncommon learnedness, intelligence, and willingness to promote his own obsessions. Predictably, Bloom discovers the anxiety of influence in Ozick's self-confessed usurpation of other people's stories—another instance of "agonistic strivings between writers." For Bloom, Ozick's most crucial struggle, however, is not with Jewish forebears like

Singer or Malamud but with the Gnostic heresy that has preoccupied Bloom himself for much of his academic lifetime, for did she not say that she "lusts after forbidden or Jewish magic"? (Although the Ozick-Bloom relationship is too tangled to unravel here, I recommend Erella Brown's "The Ozick-Bloom Controversy," in the *Studies in American Jewish Literature* of spring 1992, as an excellent study of their mutual misjudgment.) Because of Bloom's magisterial stature in contemporary criticism, his designation of "Envy" and "Usurpation" as "novellas unequalled in [Ozick's] own generation" comprises a milestone of appreciation.

In sum, Bloom's book, representing the best criticism available when the author was in her mid-fifties, projects a cacophony of contradictory voices. The Ozick of Harold Bloom purveys Gnostic heresy under the anxiety of pagan influence; for many Jewish critics—Kauvar, Knopp, Pinsker, Rosenberg, Wisse, et al.—Ozick the rabbi emerges triumphant; for Edwards the bewildered goy and White the fellow artist, the Jewish Ozick commands less interest than the storyteller and stylist. Though the voices sometimes contradict each other—for example, praising and damning the same story for its handling of metaphor (White and Alvarez on *The Cannibal Galaxy*)—their variety keeps the field of critical discourse free and open.

Turning from Bloom's book to the wider field of Ozick criticism, we find the Zeitgeist bringing postmodern ideology increasingly into play. Concerning feminism, Ozick quarreled early on with those separatist feminists who insisted on absolute gender difference of the intellect and imagination. One such feminist is Barbara Koenig Quart, whose review of *Art and Ardor* (1983) finds Ozick's rejection of female separatism "particularly odd in view of her enormous concern for Jewish identity, and her scorn for 'universalists' (mainly Jews who insist they are just like everyone else)." Because of Ozick's distance from "the fertility and vitality of contemporary feminism" and its "liberating effect of acknowledging that women have a different . . . experience," her essays on Edith Wharton and Virginia Woolf are seriously defective in Quart's judgment. By refusing "any degree of sympathetic identification" with these fellow women artists, Ozick herself commits sexism—observing the childless, nonresponsible state of Wharton and Woolf, for example, without realizing that by those standards "the equally childless and duty-free Henry James should be open to similar criticism."[3]

Levitation (1982) provided the occasion for E. M. Broner to transfer such doubts about Ozick's feminist loyalties from her essays to her fiction. "The Sewing Harems," according to Broner's review in the *Ms.* of April 1982, "is an attack on women bonding, on womanly gods, and on the concept of utopian society that informs much of today's feminist fiction." Worse yet, during our present period of "the rebonding of mothers and daughters in fiction, in literary studies and oral histories of our foremothers," Ozick produces "no natural births, rather miraculous ones [like Puttermesser creating Xanthippe], and the offspring turn upon their mothers." Or mothers turn upon offspring, like Puttermesser decreating Xanthippe, leaving a set of disturbing questions in the wake of this "dazzling and worrisome" book:

> What is the lesson to women here? . . . Are we the devouring vagina that Freud . . . would dream of? . . . One wonders: Why did the mothers have to kill the daughters? Why does one of our best writers, a woman, join the chorus of male voices?

Yet another mode of feminist protest came in reply to "Notes toward Finding the Right Question," Ozick's attempt to address the troubling question of woman's inferior place within Orthodox Judaism. Even her beloved Maimonides, she admits, "frequently uses the phrase 'women and the ignorant'" to denote female inferiority, and he also "recommends wife-beating."[4] Ozick's answer to the dilemma is to deny any connection between this sort of sexism and "the Voice of the Lord of History." Through lack of theological understanding, she maintains, Jewish males have emulated the worldwide pattern of their sex in elevating mere sociological bias to a divine status. The fall of man through Eve's lapse, for example, Ozick defines as a Christian and not Judaic convention. The answer to the problem of Jewish religious sexism, she concludes, requires amending the silence of Torah, which, though not justifying female inferiority, admittedly failed to specify a Mosaic Commandment: *"Thou shalt not lessen the humanity of women."* By reason of its "single missing Commandment," Ozick says, "Torah—one's heart stops in one's mouth as one dares to say these words—Torah is in this respect frayed." It is the historic task of our age to institute the missing Commandment—"not . . . for the sake of women; [nor] . . . for the sake of the Jewish people. It is necessary for the sake of Torah; to preserve and strengthen Torah itself" (151, 152).

In a rebuttal of Ozick's essay entitled "The Right Question Is Theological," Judith Plaskow insists that Ozick has evaded the theological basis of patriarchy. Comparing "the situation of the Jewish woman . . . to the situation of the Jew in non-Jewish culture,"[5] Plaskow says that real feminism thus "demands a new understanding of Torah, God, and Israel: an understanding of Torah that begins with acknowledgment of the profound injustice of Torah itself" (231). In 1984, five years after her "Notes toward Finding the Right Question" was published, Ozick put out a biblical exegesis to bear out her title, "Torah as Feminism, Feminism as Torah." Here she insists that the basic precepts of Judaism—man being made in the image of his Creator, for example—give no occasion nor example to validate male supremacy, because the image of the Creator has no face or gender. And so the quarrel between feminism and Torah springs from a false reading of Torah, with feminism, not Holy Writ, thereby falling into danger: "if Jewish feminism does not emerge from Torah, it will disintegrate."[6]

It seems reasonable to suppose that this sort of deference to Orthodoxy gives proof enough of Ozick's Jewish identity. Coincident with her emergence as a "Jewish writer," however, Ozick's fictions have provoked sharp controversy among Jewish-American intellectuals, among whom some have gone so far as to publicly declare her an anti-Semite. Ironically, the worst such storm of bitterness arose in response to one of her earliest, finest, and most "Jewish" stories, "Envy; or, Yiddish in America":

> There was a vast brouhaha over this story. A meeting was called by the Yiddish writers, I learned later. The question was whether or not to condemn me publicly. Privately, they all furiously condemned me. Simon Weber . . . compared me to the "commissars of Warsaw and Moscow," anti-Semites of the first order. I was astonished and unbelievably hurt. . . . What I had intended was a great lamentation for the murder of Yiddish, the mother-tongue of a thousand years, by the Nazis. Instead, here were all these writers angry at me. (Teicholz 179)

Bloodshed, Ozick's most purely "Jewish" book, merely extended the controversy. On one hand, Rosellen Brown thinks the title story "fails" because of Ozick's commitment to Orthodoxy: "the inhibition against tale-telling has taken its toll." Though she goes on to say that "Ozick's failures are infinitely more interesting than most writers' successes," Brown continues to fault the specifically Jewish character of Ozick's craft, which makes the stories "move like Talmudic argument, not like stories on their way to a destination." On the other hand, Pearl K. Bell, alarmed over "the apostasy of assimilation" among modern Jewish intellectuals, praises Ozick for her "most uncompromising indictment of the Jewish surrender to Gentile America."[7] But then again, from the point of view of other Jewish writers Ozick's uncompromising indictment seems nothing more than an instance of arrogant fanaticism. Deborah Heiligman Weiner writes:

> This contempt of Ozick's is overpowering. She doesn't offer a viable alternative with which to replace Jewish literature as it is today, yet she feels free to level criticism at those who make the effort. For example, she doubts whether Isaac Bashevis Singer . . . is a writer of "Jewish stories" at all, since no other writer departs so thoroughly and so deliberately from the mainstream of Mosaic vision.

> We have arrived back at that texture Ozick imposes on the world, that false
> dichotomy: the Pagan versus the Mosaic.[8]

Compounding the confusion is Ozick's own sense of weakness concerning her Jewish identity. The Second Commandment forbids not only her storytelling, she confesses, but also her passion for Jewish history, which has become another idol that she has raised "instead of" God: "I am in thrall to the history of the Jews. It is the history of the Jews that seizes me ultimately. . . . History is my master and I its servant."[9] Nor is being stiff-necked before God Ozick's only transgression against her Jewish heritage. She has also succumbed, she admits, to that very process of assimilation that she has loudly decried in de-Judaized writers like Philip Roth and Norman Mailer. R. Barbara Gitenstein reports Ozick's act of confession:

> Last Sunday night, I saw a 1938 Polish-made Yiddish film called *Teyve*. I was amazed to learn about all the layers and layers of forgetfulness and assimilation I—who am dedicated to *not* forgetting, who despise assimilation . . . discovered in myself. . . . *Mamaloshen* [Yiddish] is the language of my emotions, but I don't possess it.[10]

In case this sort of self-criticism proved insufficient, help was never very far away. Eugene S. Mornell, for example, attacked Ozick for holding a view of Judaism so narrow as to consider Harold Bloom "anti-Judaic. And not only Bloom but the Kabbalists, the Hasidim, Gershom Scholem. (What a long list she must have.)"[11] Earl Rovit, reviewing *Levitation*, also deplores Ozick's tendency "to issue exclusionary decrees," by which she divides the world between "the fold of an Orthodox sensibility and those who deviate, a category capable of expanding to include everyone except some death-camp survivors.'"[12] And Burt Jacobson too accuses Ozick of maintaining a "view of Judaism [that] is extremely narrow and historically inaccurate." Because her "rigid puritanical stance reifies the tradition into an idol," he says, she replicates "the idol-making she imputes to Bloom," cutting herself off meanwhile from those deep springs of creativity evidenced by the "mystical flights . . . [of] so great a luminary as Rabbi Akiva himself."[13]

But yet, it was the flights of mysticism in "Levitation"—the scene of levitation—that brought on Joseph Epstein's cry of protest: "Madam, I implore you, get those Jews down, please!" The "atmosphere up there, in that living room aloft, . . . finally seems extremely thin," Epstein explains. "I prefer my Jews grounded."[14] Because her stories are so fanciful—Epstein names "Levitation," "The Pagan Rabbi," and "Bloodshed" to make the point—Epstein pronounces them "willed and schematic," "a muddle." Saying, "I admire almost everything about her . . . but her stories," Epstein considers her probably "a better essayist than novelist"—mainly because the essays manifest a more credible realism.

Although Ozick renounced "the heavy mantle of 'Jewish writer'" in 1984,[15] commentary about her Jewishness continued to dominate the criticism of the later 1980s. To a large extent, this tendency reflected her readers' enhanced understanding of the theme of idolatry in her writings, but several critics moved beyond that insight to make new observations. Haim Chertok, in "Ozick's Hoofprints," makes an excellent point about Ozick's use of the concept of "waiting" in the Jewish ethos:

> Waiting entails both self-control and a sense of the purposes of history. It is for Ozick a heroic Jewish occupation and profession. . . . As she notes in "The Fourth Sparrow," [Gershom] Scholem's masterwork details the cataclysmic upheaval of the Jewish world when it surrendered to the pretensions of Sabbatai Sevi, *when it grew tired of waiting for the end of days.* Messianism run amok is likewise the very center of fictions like "Puttermesser and Xanthippe" and "The Sewing Harems." Murder itself ensues. (emphasis Chertok's)[16]

Janet Handler Burstein's contribution to the "Jewishness" discourse is to take Ozick's argument against idolatry into new ground. Citing Ozick's definition of imagination as "the power to penetrate evil, to take on evil, to become evil," Burstein identifies a peculiarly Jewish notion of evil that Ozick's fiction often propagates, most notably in "The Pagan Rabbi":

> the sense of fluid or amorphous identity . . . which is a given for the artist, is anathema to Jewish thought; the root preoccupation of Leviticus . . . is precisely to classify, to fix phenomena within their categories, and to forbid the mixing of categories that would cloud the boundaries between one form or kind of life and another.[17]

Exemplifying this mixing of categories is the tree nymph in "The Pagan Rabbi," at once "commandingly human in aspect" and "unmistakably flowerlike" and therefore illustrative of "both the seductive delights and the moral dangers that Ozick associates with art" (89–90).

Ellen Pifer's superb analysis of the Puttermesser stories adds a new complexity to this larger view of the "Jewishness" of Ozick's fiction. The narrative reflexivity and fantasy in these stories, says Pifer, do more than signify Ozick's place within postmodern or antirealist literature. More important, by refusing to "bestow apparently godlike authority on an author or biographer," they counteract the risk of idolatry that storytelling engenders by competing with God's creation.[18] In contrast to Puttermesser's ruinous lapse into the power of magic and fantasy, Ozick's artistic creativity thus "testifies to [her] profoundly moral commitment as an artist. Like most of her other fiction, both the Puttermesser stories [in *Levitation*] employ post-modernist techniques to convey a deeply orthodox vision of reality."

In 1987, the publication of *The Messiah of Stockholm* set the stage for our final chorus of cacophonous critical voices. Dismissed by Paul Stuewe as "a surprisingly lightweight and undistinctive novel," it was hailed by Harold Bloom as a "brilliant new novel" which portrays, in Lars, "the most persuasive and poignant figure" in all Ozick's fiction, while also displaying (in the "Messiah" manuscript) "certainly the most vivid and revelatory prose she has published so far."[19] Because this book reflects Ozick's "awareness that her earlier view of art as idolatry was too severe," *The Messiah of Stockholm* "marks the central point in Ozick's writing to date," Bloom says, enabling her "to reconcile her need to create tales, idols of a sort, and her desire to continue as a truster in the covenant, a moral follower of Jewish tradition." As a result, she is "helping to mature an American Jewish literature that may aid in the larger venture of seeking continuity in an authentic American Jewish culture."

Bloom's delight in seeing Ozick become "a true daughter of [Bruno] Schulz, whose Jewishness . . . is fascinatingly implicit in his writing," was not universally infectious. Janet Malcolm, for one, found the "Messiah" manuscript within the novel—which Bloom called her "most vivid and revelatory prose" yet published—both badly written and un-Schulzian: "it could not possibly have been written by Schulz. His delicate, poetic stories are about as far as you can get from the stiff, cerebral, didactic piece of surrealism that Ozick has concocted."[20] Calling the world of this novel "completely artificial," Malcolm attributes its "strange failure" to the total incompatibility between Ozick's "stern Sinaitic art" and Schulz's concept of fiction as pure escapist playfulness. For Robert Alter, likewise, the novel failed stylistically, its "wild hyperbole" betraying "an attempt to substitute rhetorical intensity for experiential depth."[21] Worse yet, in flat contradiction to Bloom, Alter declares this novel not only un-Schulzian but disastrously un-Jewish. "The location of *The Messiah of Stockholm* makes it her first pervasively 'Gentile' fiction," Alter observes, and the result of that choice is to make the book un-Ozickian as well:

> I would not for a moment suggest that a Jewish writer needs to write about Jewish subjects, but it is peculiar that so much of what Cynthia Ozick cares about most deeply . . . is excluded from this book: the Jewish people as the bearer of a distinctive history; Judaism with its uncompromising monotheistic

imperatives; Israel as a radical new possibility in the Jewish relation to history. . . . In Cynthia Ozick's new novel . . ., the absence of either Israel or of a persuasive sense of real history is a symptom of the narrow limits of the merely literary notions within which her fiction is enacted. (54, 55)

In the fall 1987 *Studies in American Jewish Literature,* Daniel Walden not only disagreed with this judgment, calling *The Messiah of Stockholm* "Ozick's most profound and well-crafted work to date" (173), but devoted the entire issue to a book-length collection of essays called "The World of Cynthia Ozick." The giant thrust given Ozick scholarship by this volume extends beyond the journal itself into the books undertaken by several of its authors: Sanford Pinsker (see below), Sarah Blacher Cohen (in progress), and Elaine Kauvar (see p. 205, note 2). The gem of the collection is Cynthia Ozick's own essay, "The Young Self and the Old Writer," which adds importantly to our conception of the artist. Calling the Old Writer "dangerous, slippery, however overtly responsible and conscientious," Ozick impersonates a postmodern sensibility ("undoubtedly Yale-derived" is her sly phrase) by raising fundamental questions about her identity:

> Isn't autobiographical writing, selective and therefore skewed—isn't *all* writing—essentially fiction? . . . The Old Writer is aware of what a trickster she has been. Is she, for instance, a "Jewish writer" at all? . . . In fiction, is there such a thing as "Jewish subject-matter," or is there only subject-matter? Who will definitively settle for the notion that a tale is about its subject-matter anyhow? (165)

Walden's introduction to the collection augments this portrait of the artist by relating Ozick's conflicted identity—as a modernist who reveres tradition, an Orthodox Jew who wants women rabbis, a rationalist skeptic who veers off into mysticism—to the inner springs of her creativity: "The point is that the tension she lives with is the energy that drives her" (2). And Diane Cole adds some new brush strokes by tracking down Ozick's random essays in "The Uncollected Autobiography of Cynthia Ozick." One of Cole's discoveries is a memoir by Ozick's mother, Shifra Regelson Ozick, about the family's difficult passage in 1906 from Russia to New York. In an *Esquire* essay about a schoolmate of Ozick's, Cole found a prototype of the parasitic Chimeses in "An Education." And in two *New York Times* essays, one written under a pseudonym ("Trudi Vosce"), Cole found good reason for Ozick's Zionist militance. In one she decried the murder of her teenaged cousin by a Palestinian terrorist, and in the other—a prelude to *The Shawl,* Cole says—she interviewed a Jewish woman imprisoned for ten years in a

Siberian labor camp and prevented for fourteen more years from emigrating to Israel.[22]

The major critical achievement in this volume belongs to Elaine M. Kauvar for her two essays "The Dread of Moloch: Idolatry as Metaphor in Cynthia Ozick's Fiction" and "Courier for the Past: Cynthia Ozick and Photography." In the first of these, Kauvar sifts through Talmudic lore, Greek legend, and aesthetic theory to construe "The Doctor's Wife," "Rosa," and *The Cannibal Galaxy* as "a midrash of the Second Commandment"—a major phase of Ozick's cultural warfare against postmodern unseriousness: "In an age devoid of values, depersonalized by autonomous technique, dehumanized by solipsism, disrupted by cultural anomie, diminished by opaque language, and deadended by ahistoricism, Cynthia Ozick's fiction replenishes, familiarizes, universalizes, connects, enlightens, and redeems" (127). The other essay, arguing that photography is Ozick's "summarizing metaphor for art," brings a powerful sense of history to bear on "Shots" and other writings: "The enduring importance of memory to the Jewish people originates in the Hebrew Bible where remembrance is pivotal, where the command to remember is absolute, and where the various declensions of the verb *zakhar* ('to remember') appear at least one hundred and sixty-nine times" (130). In both essays Kauvar makes crucial use of Ozick's "Judaic" preference for the caterpillar (in a state of "becoming") over the butterfly (the perfected thing).

Bonnie Lyons' essay, "Cynthia Ozick as a Jewish Writer" (an appropriate title for the whole collection), makes some astute observations about Ozick's cultural inconsistencies: "sometimes she defines Judaism as a unique and distinct religious vision, at other times she treats it as something like a synonym for moral seriousness" (14). So, too, Lyons observes, in rejecting feminism as biologically deterministic Ozick forgets that Jewishness also has a biological component, except for the few proselytes. Lyons' analysis of "The Pagan Rabbi" and the Puttermesser-Xanthippe stories ranks with the best criticism of those stories.

S. Lillian Kremer's "The Splendor Spreads Wide: *Trust* and Cynthia Ozick's Aggadic Voice" likewise ranks with the best criticism of *Trust*. By focusing on Enoch's conversion from Communist to observant Jew, Kremer shows how "Jewish history . . . and Jewish values function as the novel's enduring touchstone" (27). In the end, the force of the Holocaust is so harrowing as to overwhelm the Hellenic paganism associated with Tilbeck, Kremer argues persuasively, and that is why a "Hebraic coda" terminates the book with Tilbeck the nature god dead, and Vand the Holocaust scholar immersed in Orthodox worship. Kremer astutely notes how Ozick's scale of Jewish history reaches back in *Trust* to Hitler's Roman prototype, Titus (TR 152)—

two leaders of vast superpowers, separated by two millennia, whose efforts to exterminate Judaism ended in lost empires while Judaism lives on.

Of the other essays in "The World of Cynthia Ozick," space permits only a mention. Jeffrey Rush's "Talking to Trees: Address as Metaphor in 'The Pagan Rabbi'" uses Paul Ricoeur's and Tzvetan Todorov's theories to distinguish Jewish from Gentile ideas of metaphor. Ellen Serlen Uffen's "The Levity of Cynthia Ozick" extends the idea of the golem from "Puttermesser" to "Virility," "A Mercenary," "Envy," and "The Pagan Rabbi." Amy J. Elias' "Puttermesser and Pygmalion" sees pagan versus Jewish views of art— "creation-as-Galatea and creation-as-golem"—as posing "the central conflict in 'Puttermesser and Xanthippe'" (67). Sanford Pinsker's "Astrophysics, Assimilation, and Cynthia Ozick's *The Cannibal Galaxy*" applies the cannibalism metaphor culturally to the main characters. Cecilia Konchar Farr's "Lust for a Story: Cynthia Ozick's 'Usurpation' as Fabulation" cogently illuminates that greatly convoluted story with help from Robert Scholes's *Fabulation and Metafiction*. Joseph Cohen's "'Shots': A Case History of the Conflict between Relativity Theory and the Newtonian Absolutes" relates Ozick's parable about photography to the great battle of modern physics, "between relativity as promulgated by Einstein, Bohr, Heisenberg, and their associates and the principles which have come down to us from Sir Isaac Newton" (98). Sarah Blacher Cohen's "Cynthia Ozick and Her New Yiddish Golem" compares Xanthippe to earlier golem prototypes, both Jewish and Gentile (e.g., Frankenstein), as well as to the Freudian id. And finally, Mary J. Chenoweth's indispensible bibliographical essay is a comprehensive reference work for writings by and about Cynthia Ozick through June of 1986.

To complete the critical *Wunderjahr* 1987, the University of Missouri Press brought out Sanford Pinsker's brief but usefully intelligent book, *The Uncompromising Fictions of Cynthia Ozick*. Beginning with mention of Ozick's earlier American forebears, chiefly Hawthorne and Melville for their theme of "Original Sin," Pinsker also sees the lineaments of Anne Bradstreet and Emily Dickinson in the aged poetess of "Virility." Pinsker's review of Ozick's Jewish-American predecessors—Abraham Cahan, Henry Roth, Philip Roth, Delmore Schwartz, and Saul Bellow—also yields good insights, including the argument that her "uncompromising attacks on such 'pagans' as Harold Bloom, Norman Mailer, Allen Ginsberg, and Philip Roth are thinly disguised attacks against aspects of herself" (40).

Pinsker's analyses of the fiction can also be illuminating. He explains the inferiority of "The Dock-Witch" to "The Pagan Rabbi," for example, by arguing that the secular character of "The Dock-Witch" deprives it of dramatic tension, making it a portrait of Pan with no Moses for counterpoint.

He writes well about Ozick's version of the "secret sharer" theme that connects Bleilip and the rebbe in "Bloodshed," Morris and Lushinski in "A Mercenary." (He is ingenious in seeing Morris as a black version of the Jewish "hapless, and comic, *schlemiel*"—a man at ease in the African jungle but victimized by the far worse "jungle out there" in New York City.) The finest segment of Pinsker's book, I would say, is his discussion of one of Ozick's most complex, problematic stories, "Usurpation" (80–85).

In 1988 Joseph Lowin's *Cynthia Ozick* accomplished a giant stride in Ozick criticism.[23] As the director of the Midrasha Institute of Jewish Studies, Lowin brought to bear an uncommon mastery of the Judaic lore relevant to Ozick's writings. As a Ph.D. in French literature, Lowin also made good use of his direct access to European literati without lapsing into the Derrida/Foucault/Lacan style of guru jargon. And as a correspondent of Cynthia Ozick's, Lowin assembled information of crucial value concerning the personal and literary development of the author.

Tracing her career in roughly chronological order, Lowin begins with a succinct but informative chronology of the artist's life, followed by two chapters that explain her early career, including several ventures in poetry. The idea of Midrash strongly affects Lowin's commentary, coming into play in the "Teaching and Preaching" function that he finds prevalent in Ozick's work—in her essays, in such stories as "An Education" and "Bloodshed," and in such novels as *Trust* and *The Cannibal Galaxy* (52). Another of Lowin's ideas is to organize chapters that pair off Ozick's writings in dialectical fashion: "A Jewish Fantastic: 'The Pagan Rabbi' and 'Levitation'" (chapter 5) versus "A Jewish Realism: *The Cannibal Galaxy*" (chapter 6); and "Rewriting Others: 'Usurpation (Other People's Stories)'" (chapter 7) versus "Rewriting Herself: 'The Shawl' and 'Rosa'" (chapter 8). Although the whole book is a commendable achievement in criticism, I judge its finest segments to be its discussion of "Usurpation" (90–105), its analysis of the Puttermesser stories (chapter 9), and its penultimate chapter on *The Messiah of Stockholm*—a book that he considers "a culmination of Ozick's rewriting activity and the logical conclusion of much she has written to date" (145). A misfortunate lapse in Lowin's judgment, as in Pinsker's before him, arises in the book's concluding paragraph: "Of one last thing we may above all be certain: We have not yet seen Ozick's masterpiece" (165). That seems a harsh burden to impose on a highly accomplished sixty-year-old writer.

In 1989, Vera Emuma Kielsky's *Inevitable Exiles* applied an even stronger Jewish consciousness to Ozick's fiction than did Pinsker and Lowin.[24] As her subtitle indicates—*Cynthia Ozick's View of the Precariousness of Jewish Existence in a Gentile Society*—Kielsky sees Ozick's fiction as a weapon of cultural warfare: "Her fiction . . . is an undisguised assault on Jewish vulnerability to the Gentile standards, and are [sic], in effect, Jewish attacks on spheres of Gentile predominance" (11). By limiting her coverage to selected stories from Ozick's three collections, Kielsky scants a considerable range of material germane to her topic, but she gains enough space to make an in-depth analysis of these ten stories. In many of these stories Kielsky sees the Jewish characters as schizoid, torn between conscious pride in being one of God's chosen people and subconscious desire to be rid of the stigma of being Jewish (20). Her treatment of this schism in the Morris-Lushinski relationship of "A Mercenary" is especially astute (52–53), but she also writes well about Ozick's wide-ranging analogies: of "The Pagan Rabbi" and Goethe's Faust; of "The Dock-Witch," the Circe episode in The Odyssey, and Heine's "Die Lorelei"; of "Puttermesser and Xanthippe" and the Book of Genesis. Her correlation of the Undine myth ("The Dock-Witch") with the Undine of the Kabbala (132n) is another useful bit of learning.

Unlike Lowin, who sees Ozick's vision as redemptive (e.g., The Messiah of Stockholm "brings redemption both to the creation of God and the creations of man," 161), Kielsky brings her analysis of the fiction to a terminus of extreme pessimism. Puttermesser, Una Meyer, Edmund Gate, and Edelshtein—in her analysis—appear unredeemable: "In all four stories, . . . her protagonists . . . finally lose control over their destinies. . . . Her stress lies on . . . the pathology rather than the remedy, for she seems not to believe that there is a solution to the protagonists' problems" (195). Before leaving Kielsky's book, we should note with gratitude its excellent bibliography.

There remains Lawrence S. Friedman's Understanding Cynthia Ozick.[25] In his preface, Matthew J. Bruccoli (the general editor of the Understanding Contemporary American Literature series) declares modest intentions— these books "are planned as a series of guides or companions for students or good nonacademic readers." But in fact Friedman's book, like Lowin's, is exemplary criticism—astute, learned, and cogently written. Like Lowin and Pinsker, he is at his best when discussing "Usurpation" (24–25 and 107–13), but he is also good at making illuminating conjectures. The closing sentence of "Bloodshed," for example ("Then you are as bloody as anyone"), evokes for Friedman Stephen Crane's classic novella: "in this case the blood shed by Jews throughout a tragic history . . . becomes the red badge of Jewish identity" (106). So, too, Friedman sees the shadow of Philip Roth's Amy Bellette (the girl who thought she was Anne Frank) behind Lars Andemening's supposition that he was the son of Bruno Schulz (160). He expatiates in new ways on the connections between Ozick's Adela in The Messiah of Stockholm and the Adela of Bruno Schulz's two published books (164–65), and he detects the presence of Jerzy Kosinski not only in "A Mercenary" but in *The Shawl* (118). His discussion of the golem-making tradition likewise offers new insights (135–36), as does his analogy between Freudian psychology (in "Freud's Room") and idolatry (3).

In the late 1980s and early 1990s, the teachings of "Critical Theory" inevitably made inroads into Ozick criticism. Earl Rovit's "The Two Languages of Cynthia Ozick," while happily eschewing the Derridean penchant for opacity, in effect deconstructs Ozick's writings so as to find "a manner similar to that of an animated comic strip" in which "the whole enterprise seethes in a steady turbulence of rage."[26] Characters such as Bleilip, Edelshtein, and Isaac Kornfeld are offered in evidence of this thesis: "As in cartoons, motives are reduced to single adrenal urgencies, personality is equated with blunt obsession, and the fluidity of normal human intercourse is grotesquely rendered in a series of collisions when a caricatured dread or desire comes into thudding impact against its immutable or immovable limit" (37). Because this "cartoonlike style," which is "blunt, didactic, comic, judgmental, often cruel, and severely moralistic," is often juxtaposed with Ozick's "second language, the style of 'the nimbus' or . . . the *corona*-style [as seen in Beulah Hilt's paintings]," Rovit believes "the central problem of Ozick's art is the existence of two languages whose generic structures incarnate different purposes which impel them in contrary directions" (40–42). Observing that "her typical tale travels from rage to grief," Rovit considers her cartoon style "energized by the rage, her corona-style by the grief" (47). Despite his admiration for *The Messiah of Stockholm* as "a nearly sustained and breathless stylistic tour de force," Rovit considers Ozick's work badly damaged by its harsh didacticism: "even an unsentimental reader may feel that the comic mechanisms designed to expose and punish vice have themselves become vicious in their instrumentality" (44).

In Michael Greenstein's "The Muse and the Messiah: Cynthia Ozick's Aesthetics," Ozick's work gets placed (or should I say sited?) within a flowering garden of Theoretical Phrases: "self-consuming artifacts on the borderline between modernism and postmodernism," "floating signifiers that inhibit frozen signification," "an infinity of heretical hermeneutics." Fortunately, among his clumps of jargon Greenstein includes a number of useful insights, especially by way of interpreting Ozick's imagery. For example, he links the zebras at the end of *The Messiah of Stockholm* to the striped uniforms worn by death-camp inmates, and he relates Joseph Brill's name (meaning "spectacles" in Hebrew) to a pattern of sight images in *The Cannibal Galaxy*. Readers who find the dichotomy/continuity between modernism and postmodernism interesting may consult another Greenstein essay, "Ozick, Roth, and Postmodernism," for a discussion of "Ozick's alignment with some, not all, aspects of postmodernism" in *The Messiah of Stock-*

holm.[27] They may need to watch out for "the undertow of metonymic reality" (58), however, in numerous constructions like the following: "realistic novels are predominantly metonymic both in their horizontal connections and in a vessel's relationship between container and its contents" (59). Or: "In this realm of uncertainty, through a crack in the wall, and during a translucent dusk, 'no one knew' about barbaric epistemology in Sweden's no-man's-land" (57).

Since its publication in 1987, controversy over *The Messiah of Stockholm* has become a (perhaps the) major feature of Ozick criticism. Anne Redmon regrets the burning of the *Messiah* manuscript, an irresponsible act that "liberates" Lars to become "a slab of insensitivity" in the conclusion. Sylvia Barack Fishman, however, while agreeing that Lars is "wrong in capitulating to the world of easy popularity at the end of the novel," holds that Lars also was wrong to idolize Schulz and his manuscript, which got him "involved in a pagan, inhuman enterprise."[28] Elizabeth Rose differs from Redmon and Fishman in thinking that in the end the novel affirms Ozick's Jewish values, by "celebrating the end of Lars's alienation" and returning him to "an ordinary life within a community."[29] Sanford Pinsker, however, seeing nothing ordinary about it, believes that "one will have to look deeper than the work of Bruno Schulz" or even than "contemporary Jewish theology" to understand Ozick's novel: "My own hunch is that the Kabbalah explains much of the energy in *The Messiah of Stockholm*."[30] Pinsker's fine essay compares Roth's resurrection of Anne Frank in *The Ghost Writer* with Ozick's recovery of Schulz in *The Messiah of Stockholm*.

To conclude, the last decade has been a good one for Ozick criticism, ending in a plethora of awards and honors. Inasmuch as they, too, comprise a form of literary criticism, I shall end this section on The Critical Reckoning with a brief checklist of these honors (with thanks to Bloom, Lowin, Friedman, and others for their compilations): 1968—Fellow, National Endowment for the Arts; 1971—Jewish Book Council Award and B'nai B'rith Heritage Award for *The Pagan Rabbi*; 1973—American Academy of Arts and Letters Award for Literature; 1975—First Prize in *O. Henry Prize Stories* competition for "Usurpation"; 1977—Jewish Book Council Award for *Bloodshed*; 1982—Guggenheim Fellowship; 1983—Strauss Living Award from the American Academy and Institute of Arts and Letters; 1984—Honorary Doctorates from Yeshiva University and Hebrew Union College and Distinguished Alumnus Award from New York University, First Prize of *O. Henry Prize Stories* competition for "Rosa"; 1985—Presenter of Phi Beta Kappa Oration at Harvard University; 1987—Honorary Doctorate from Hunter College; 1988—Elected to American Academy and Institute of Arts and Letters.

On 28 December 1992, Cynthia Ozick gave a reading at the Modern

Language Association convention in New York City. To an overflow crowd of many hundreds who packed the large assembly hall, she recited passages from "Alfred Chester's Wig" and "Puttermesser Paired." (The two segments she read described, respectively, her fruitful rivalry with Chester in their Freshman English class, and the failed Venetian honeymoon of George Eliot and her much younger bridegroom, John Cross.) What made the occasion even more triumphant than it seemed was the coincidental scheduling of her reading at the same hour as that of Ralph Ellison, a few doors away. Probably most people in the room, including Ozick herself (so she told me), would have helped honor the grand master of African-American fiction had the schedule permitted. As it was, this large throng of admirers, in making their painful choice, confirmed how high a place she holds in the estimate of her contemporary readers.

Judeo-Christian

As the foregoing Critical Reckoning illustrates, the essential "Jewishness" of Cynthia Ozick's writing has been the primary focus of virtually every commentator. That Jewishness, in turn, rests largely on a sense of history which, for our present purpose of judgment, requires emendation. The Holocaust and, before that, the murderous pogroms that drove millions of Jews to America were European, not American, phenomena. Admittedly, immigrants from the Old World frequently brought their biases with them so that, even when diluted within the next generation of New York schoolchildren, they could inflict some "old school hurts" on a tender-age child. The American Protestant tradition at large, however, spoke in decidedly friendlier tones. If the most popular poet of nineteenth-century America may be considered a trustworthy guide, "The Jewish Cemetery at Newport" implies a powerful public empathy:

> How came they here? What burst of Christian hate,
>   What persecution, merciless and blind,
> Drove o'er the sea—that desert desolate—
>   These Ishmaels and Hagars of mankind?

If Longfellow is arguably unrepresentative—in 1854 a dubious proposition—there remains undeniable evidence of public opinion in the newspapers. At about the same time as Longfellow's poem, Emily Dickinson's local newspaper ran the following piece from the widely distributed *Congregational Journal* (of New England's foremost church), as the lead article on the newspaper's front page:

POSITION AND INFLUENCE OF THE JEWS

The existence of the Jews is the living miracle of the world. They are scattered and down-trodden, and yet, according to the most accurate statistics, are as numerous as they were when they left the land of Egypt, the return made to Bonaparte giving about three million. . . . They may be banished, but cannot be expelled; be trodden down, yet cannot be crushed. Only in the United States, France, Holland, and Prussia are they fully citizens; but in spite of British statutes, the Russian ukase and Turkish curse, they prosper still. The great nations of antiquity, the Egyptians and Assyrians, the Romans and Saracens, as well as the modern Turks and Christians, have attempted to destroy them, but in vain: while penal laws and cruel tortures have only served to increase their indomitable obstinacy.

This Christian empathy with Jewish history, told in surprising detail, is prelude to an equally fraternal assessment of time present, again told in surprising detail:

But Jews exist not only as a monument and a miracle: Jewish mind has exerted a powerful influence on the world. . . . In politics we have Metternich in Austria, D'Israeli in England. . . . In money power the Jews hold in their hands the destinies of kingdoms and empires. . . . The Rothschilds, the Barings, and Sir John Montefiero are all Jews, and with their banking establishments scattered over Europe and Asia, wield a sceptre more powerful than monarchs hold. Coming to the literary profession . . . we find the Jews prominent here as in active life. The most renowned in Astronomy have been Jews, as the Herschels in England and Arago in France. . . . Spinoza, the famous infidel, was a Jew. . . .

Such have been and are the Jews. Mysterious nation! Inexplicable enigma! A living, perpetually omnipresent miracle! A race so indomitable, so imperishable, must have been raised up and preserved for some grand purpose.[31]

A year later, on 11 May 1854, the lead article on page one again featured the drama of Jewish history—this time without borrowing its substance from a church-related journal. Theodor Herzl himself could scarcely exceed this measure of Christian exultation over the fulfillment of the promise of the Covenant for God's Chosen People:

ROTHSCHILD AND PALESTINE

It is rumored in Paris that M. de Rothschild offered the Turkish Sultan a huge loan to fight the Crimean War in return for a mortgage on Palestine. . . . Palestine is the Lord's inheritance for the seed of Abraham. The Turkish power holds it. That power must give way before the plans of Divine Providence. Its downfall is imminent; and who shall next own Palestine? Evidently the Jews. Why has Providence raised them up and placed in their hands an

amount of wealth equal to that of many an entire kingdom? May it not be for
such a time as this? . . .

. . . New forms of government arise all over Europe, and the Jews return
to their fatherland under the deed of Rothschild. These are the thoughts
which quickly spring up in our mind upon reading of Rothschild's Turkish
bargain.

Whether, outside of America, a big-city non-Jewish newspaper would
display this level of front-page zeal is a significant question. Nonetheless, in
correspondence with me, Cynthia Ozick has turned a cold eye on these
expressions of Christian empathy. Longfellow's poem, which I sent her to
illustrate how I introduced her segment of my Modern American Fiction
course, became the occasion of an MLA talk and later turned up in an essay
about Christian "supersession" of Jewish culture.[32] Beneath his superficial
sympathy, Ozick argued, Longfellow revealed "no notion that Jewish history is anything other than the history of victimization by Gentiles; no
understanding that Jewish history is above all intellectual history, the history of a continuing people, a continuing land, and a continuing literature."
Longfellow's general ignorance of the Judaic tradition in turn reflected
America's refusal to reciprocate the willingness of its Jews to learn about
Christian culture. And those friendly voices in Emily Dickinson's local newspaper, in Ozick's view, are belied by that invidious reference to Rothschild
wealth—a long-standing danger signal to anyone versed in Jewish history.

The issue at last comes down to a difference of opinion. In my reply to
Cynthia Ozick, I insisted that I know these people, having grown up among
their descendents in a New England township. According to my observation
and experience, the sentiments I have cited had no trace of envy, anti-
Semitic or otherwise. Rather, they were typical of American Christian culture in the time of Longfellow and Dickinson: in a few years similar beliefs
were to lead these Christian folk in all innocence toward enormous sacrifice
in the vineyards where the Grapes of Wrath are stored. And despite the
presence of anti-Semitism in American life, evangelical Protestantism is still
broadly philo-Semitic as typified, for example, by the popular singer Pat
Boone, who on national television declared himself a Jew inasmuch as he
defined Christianity as the fourth branch of Judaism. Back in the 1950s, the
famously Christian voice of T. S. Eliot said something similar by way of
rebuking his old friend Ezra Pound. He could accept ridicule on other
grounds, Eliot said, but he would not tolerate any further attacks on his
religion, which included the Jewish religion.[33]

Because T. S. Eliot effectively reoriented modern literature toward Christianity, his place in Ozick's canon of criticism has special significance. As

recently as 1976, in her preface to *Bloodshed,* she called *The Waste Land* "the greatest modern poem" (BL 9). In the *New Yorker* of 20 November 1989, however, she published a very long essay in which she decries her own former enlistment in the "nearly universal obeisance to an autocratic, inhibited, narrow-minded, and considerably bigoted fake Englishman" (121). Not only is his poetic oeuvre "amazingly small in the light of Eliot's towering repute," she says, but the mind behind those celebrated poems turned out to be, one might say, a dried tuber: "His reach, once broad enough to incorporate the Upanishads, shrank to extend no farther than the neighborhood sacristy, and to a still smaller space: the closet of the self" (150, 151). And one sure sign of Eliot's intellectual bankruptcy, if not outright corruption, was his post-Holocaust assertion that "if Christianity goes, the whole of our culture goes"—"as if [Ozick goes on to say] the best of European civilization (including the merciful tenets of Christianity) had not already been pulverized to ash throughout the previous decade" (126).

Revulsion against Christian culture is an understandable response to Jewish history within Ozick's post-Holocaust generation, but a proper evaluation of her achievement cannot allow this sort of grand judgment to go unquestioned. Did the best of European civilization, including Christian virtue on the Continent, really turn totally and permanently to ash during the Nazi epoch? If so, wasn't that fact as obvious in 1976 as in 1989? In which case didn't the leading apologist for a Christian society deserve condemnation rather than, or along with, praise for *The Waste Land* in the preface to *Bloodshed*? It appears that a missing middle term muddles the argument. Along with Eliot's anti-Semitic streak and other character defects (which Rossell Hope Robbins delineated back in 1951 in *The T. S. Eliot Myth*), I infer that the missing term is Ozick's long-standing resentment of supersessionism—Eliot's breezy assumption of Christian hegemony in works like *The Idea of a Christian Society* and *Notes towards the Definition of Culture*.[34] (Incidentally, I am convinced that Harold Bloom's *Kabbalah and Criticism* was written expressly from the same resentment of the Christianized graduate study of his youth.)

In part, the Zeitgeist probably explains the radical difference in tone and stance between 1976 and 1989. Postmodern theory has encouraged wholesale disdain toward the authority figures of modernism, coupled with valorization of previously marginalized cultures. But at times this zeal for revision leads to conclusions one would not expect from a writer immersed in millennia of history. In "Bialik's Hint," Ozick argues that "the Enlightenment 'Judaized' Europe" by bringing to fruition the Hebraic ideal of "moral seriousness," which she claims is "a wholly Enlightenment idea" (MM 229, 240n). The obvious question that she raises here is whether her time scale is off by fifteen centuries—whether, that is, we should really ascribe the Judaization of Europe (and subsequently America) more largely to the philosophes of the Enlightenment than to the Christian missionaries of the later Roman Empire. If we postulate that those Hebraic ideals came to the Enlightenment via its Christian heritage—a more likely influence, I think, than (as Ozick argues) that of the Jews whom the Enlightenment emancipated—then perhaps the difference between Christian and Jew is less profound and their affinities more deeply rooted than Ozick usually predicates.

Not even the Holocaust, which for many Jews stretched the Judeo-Christian hyphen to Grand Canyon proportions, can be held to represent a total Christian-Jewish rupture. Holocaust historians, it is true, sometimes appear to argue otherwise, as when Claude Lanzmann's *Shoah* portrays Polish collaborators gladly helping their conquerors establish a *Judenrein* continent, or when Ozick herself describes the Nazi massacre at Babi Yar as occurring "with the zealous complicity of the Ukrainians."[35] Yet, history has become a suspect discipline in recent times, held culpable of masking its author's personal agenda under a pretense of objectivity. As great a historian as Raul Hilberg told me that he was interested in describing only the people who killed Jews, not their saviors, which is why he made no mention of Raoul Wallenberg's heroic rescue work in his original edition of *The Destruction of the European Jews,* even though he had heard about it. In any case, the historical record of Gentile Holocaust resisters figures to be woefully incomplete, especially as regards those who perished during the course of their frightful risk taking.

Counteracting somewhat this imbalance in perspective is the testimony of Israel Shahak, a survivor of the Warsaw Ghetto and Bergen-Belsen from 1942 to 1945 who says his opinions have been confirmed in talks with many other survivors of similar experiences. Shahak, calling Lanzmann "a prisoner of his own prejudices," pronounces *Shoah* "presumptuous and racist" for associating Holocaust guilt with nationality. Citing instances he saw of Jewish blackmailers, spies, and ghetto police victimizing other Jews, he judges these turncoats as "perfectly equal in their wickedness" with the "criminal minority" of Poles and Germans who facilitated the Holocaust. These victimizers—like their heroic contraries, the Gentiles who saved Jews—"behaved in a way which is neither Jewish nor Polish but typically human," according to Shahak's passionately stated argument.[36]

Another defender of the Poles, Norman Davies, puts Polish wartime anti-Semitism in the context of the Hitler-Stalin partition. When Stalin's police took over their half of Poland, not only were the native Poles savagely brutalized by the disproportionately Jewish Soviet police; in addition, Polish Jews in large numbers publicly welcomed the Soviet conquest. The Yad

Vashem archive in Israel confirms that "the Jews welcomed the Red Army with joy"; that Jewish youth groups "toured the countryside smashing Catholic shrines"; that in Pinsk young Jews built an Arc de Triomphe for the invaders; that, in the view of many Poles, "Jews were seen to be dancing on Poland's grave"—for their own historically understandable reasons, to be sure. Ironically, Polish Jews under Stalin's rule soon found his oppression so unbearable that "thousands of Jewish refugees swarmed westward toward the Nazi zone," by one eyewitness account, creating a scene where a Nazi commission "was greeted by crowds of Jews chanting '*Heil Hitler*' in the hope of getting permission to cross the frontier."[37]

At some point, any mature philosophy of culture must subordinate its assertion of "difference"—in this case, Christian versus Jew—to the deeper mystery of the individual human personality. Nobody in the world can say why some persons brought up as Christians turned out to be death camp torturers while others gave up their lives, and risked those of their families, to save hapless strangers. Nobody knows why some Jews became Stalin's murderous Cheka agents, as cold-blooded as Hitler's Gestapo, while others have given lavishly of themselves to alleviate the world's sufferings. In the end we can only say that all human beings receive their culture as a historic given, a fixed framework within which the individual conscience will define itself according to the unaccountable moral laws of its own being. The only culture worth valorizing is finally the one that is attested through the conscience of these superior moral beings, whether Christian, Jew, Moslem, atheist, or whatever.

In 1992, Cynthia Ozick came around to praise the Christian West in an essay titled "Of Christian Heroism."[38] As an apologia, it begins rather unpromisingly with Clare Boothe Luce's (perhaps apocryphal) complaint about being bored with hearing about the Holocaust, to which a Jewish friend of hers replies that he understands her perfectly, being fatigued to tears from hearing so often about the Crucifixion. But Ozick goes on to render a stately tribute to those truest of all saviors of Western civilization, the handful of brave and compassionate and mostly Christian people who risked their own and their families' lives to save thousands of Jews from destruction: "They are the heroes of Nazified Europe. They are Polish, Italian, Romanian, Russian, Hungarian, . . . and [*nota bene*] German. They are urban and rural; . . . sophisticated and simple; . . . nuns [as in *The Cannibal Galaxy*] and socialists." Though few, their importance is enormous, belying the "brainwashing process by philosophers who [for centuries have] emphasized man's despicable character." In the end, "It is from these undeniably heroic and principled few that we can learn the full resonance of civilization."

Despite her fears of cultural cannibalism, then, Ozick can sometimes show enthusiasm for an assimilationist perspective. In "Bialik's Hint," she credits the influx of "pagan" culture into Judaism for the famous "bookishness" of modern Jews: "It was the gradual superimposition of the Socratic primacy of intellect upon the Jewish primacy of holiness that produced the familiar, and now completely characteristic, Jewish personality we know. . . . [Thus] there is no Jew alive today who is not also resonantly Greek" (MM 236). And she regards the converse as equally valid—that there is no "Greek" (Euro-American) alive today who is not resonantly "Jewish." Ozick proves the latter theorem in her closing tribute to the language of the first, Sinaitic, "Enlightenment." Speaking of Hebrew as "the original vessel for the revolution in human conscience," she says:

> Because of the power of scriptural ideas, there is hardly a language left on the planet that does not, through the use of its own syllables and vocabulary, "speak Hebrew." All languages have this Hebrew-speaking capacity, as the literatures of the world have somewhat tentatively, yet honorably, demonstrated. If this is true, it is a proof that Hebrew does not have a unique ability, by divine right, so to say, to carry certain ideas, although the genius of Abraham and Moses and the Prophets runs like mother milk through its lips. (MM 239)

As she concludes "Bialik's Hint," Ozick predicts an accelerating "fusion of what we are as the children of the Enlightenment, [and] what we are as the children of Israel" (MM 239). According to this essay, then—in which Ozick also makes her peace with the "Jewish writer oxymoron"—the differences between Christian and Jew, however orthodox both may be, are secondary to what they hold in common, which includes both their secular public life and their Hebraic cultural roots. Despite the saturation of her work in Jewish subject matter, then, and despite the plethora of perfectly valid "Jewish" commentary about this work, Cynthia Ozick's final definition as an artist is: an American writer. For all her fears of cultural loss, she is as American as Herman Melville, as Samuel Clemens, as William and Henry James.

Amerikaner-Geboren

In her fiction, essays, and interviews, the fear of cultural loss has assumed increasing importance for Cynthia Ozick. The one great counterweight to this fear—the restoration of Israel—has elicited single-minded exultation on Ozick's part, but even this miracle of modern history has its bitter ironies, including Israeli indifference toward the death of Yiddish culture along with the rekindling of the war with the Canaanites that began four millennia ago.

In any case, the predicament of Jews in the Diaspora, not the success of those in Israel, has claimed the center stage of her writings. Concerning these Jews Ozick's most common term of anxiety is "impostor"—a phrase she uses repeatedly in interviews to describe the cultural exchanges that so threaten her characters' Hebraic heritage.

As we look back over the roll call of Ozick's protagonists, we find instance after instance of characters who abandon their actual birthright (frequently a Judaic, not merely Jewish, heritage) in vain pursuit of some apparently superior culture—which is what Ozick really means by the word "idolatry." For the Jewish-manqué narrator of *Trust,* the deadly temptation is the double appeal of WASP aristocracy and its nemesis, Tilbeck's irresponsible paganism; for the Pagan Rabbi and for Tchernikhovsky in "Usurpation," it is the allure of pantheism; for Lushinski in "A Mercenary" and Bleilip in "Bloodshed," the danger arises from that cultural pit of blackness called secularism; for Joseph Brill in *The Cannibal Galaxy* and Rosa in *The Shawl,* the Jewish soul's enemy is assimilation into America or "Europe"; for Puttermesser, the irresistible lure inheres first in golem magic and then in the high literary culture of Victorian England; for Lars Andemening in *The Messiah of Stockholm,* the adversary is Ozick's own vocation in the magic realm of art. For all these characters the idea of impersonation is bound up with exchanging one's own true culture for another.

Because this fear of cultural assimilation, expropriation, and supersession has been strongly present, criticism of Cynthia Ozick has taken so relentlessly "Jewish" a coloring as to obscure her affinities with the traditional American mainstream. But in fact, Ozick's long-term portrayal of her cultural heritage under siege places her in a long and stately American tradition. In this respect, she resembles not only other preservers of a threatened minority heritage—Toni Morrison, Maxine Hong Kingston, Louise Erdrich—but also the canonical names of the majority culture, many of whom also deplored the loss of their native heritage beneath a tidal wave of change. One thinks, for example, of Cooper's jaundice, via Leatherstocking, toward the arrival of Jacksonian democracy; of Twain treating with contempt America's migration from Edenic St. Petersburg to the citified corruptions of the Gilded Age; or of Faulkner's bitter irony—in *Sanctuary,* for example—on witnessing the Snopesist New South displacing the Old. According to Robert Penn Warren, this sense of a culture under siege is required for the highest level of imaginative writing:

> The old notion of a shock, a cultural shock, to a more or less closed society— you know, what happened in the Italian Renaissance or Elizabethan England. After 1918 the modern industrial world . . . hit the South and all sorts of

ferments began. . . . There isn't much vital imagination, it seems to me, that doesn't come from some sort of shock, imbalance, need to "relive," redefine life.[39]

Apropos of Warren's thesis, the Holocaust and Restoration of Israel produced a cultural shock that contributed to the primacy of the "Jewish novel" during the two decades after the war, the time of Ozick's own artistic incubation.

Despite the uniqueness and magnitude of those two events, however, Ozick's artistic sensibility discloses a profile made familiar by earlier writers of the American mainstream. Let us start with Ozick's obsessive theme of dualities—her way of portraying her own conflicted affinities with Tilbeck and Enoch, Pan and Moses, Puttermesser and Xanthippe, Bleilip and the rebbe, Feingold (the Jewish history fanatic) and his Gentile wife Lucy (who reads Jane Austen's *Emma* "over and over again"), and Joseph Brill's Dual Curriculum. What is this schizoid condition, after all, if not her version of Faulkner's assertion, in his Nobel Prize address, that "the problems of the human heart in conflict with itself . . . make good writing because only that is worth writing about"?

Faulkner had his own obsessive version of the theme, notably his pride and guilt regarding the South, but it did not begin with him. Tracing back, we have Mark Twain's very name implying the theme of duality (twain, twin, two-ness), and Twain too invested himself in a series of contrary characters—Huck the realist (Twain's version of Ozick's Sinaitic conscience) versus Tom the pagan-romantic; the Connecticut Yankee (Twain's rationalism triumphant) versus Joan of Arc (Twain's sentimentality personified); and those extraordinary twins in *Pudd'nhead Wilson*. In the end, Ozick's fundamental dualities extend a tradition that traces back to the American Renaissance movement, embracing both the transcendentalists and their adversaries. On the latter side we have Poe, who foreshadowed Freud by pitting his "Spirit of Perverseness" against "Conscience Grim" in "The Imp of the Perverse," "William Wilson," and other stories; we have Hawthorne, with his subtle interplay of guilt and innocence; and we have Herman Melville (selected by Ozick for membership in Puttermesser's mayoral cabinet), whose subtitle to *Pierre*—"Or, The Ambiguities"—is a key to all Melville's thought: to "The Conflict of Convictions" in his Civil War poems; to his incongruous empathies with both Ahab and Ishmael; to his arguments for and against the hanging of Billy Budd. On the transcendentalist side even those two ur-monists, Ralph Waldo Emerson and Henry David Thoreau (namesakes respectively of Sonny and Throw Purse in *Trust*), prove to be dualists with respect to the human personality. "We are conscious of an animal in us, which . . . is reptile and sensual, and perhaps cannot be wholly expelled," Thoreau writes in *Walden;* "I fear that we are such gods or demigods only as fauns and satyrs, the divine allied to beasts" (*Walden,* chapter 11, "Higher Laws"). And Emerson reminds us vividly that the true basis of duality is neither Christian nor Jewish but the condition of being human:

> Man is . . . a stupendous antagonism, a dragging together of the poles of the Universe. He betrays his relation to what is below him,—thick-skulled, small-brained, . . . hardly escaped into biped. . . . But the lightning which explodes and fashions planets and suns, is in him. . . . [Here] they are, side by side, god and devil, mind and matter, . . . riding peacefully together in the eye and brain of every man.[40]

For Ozick, as we are told again and again, the most painful version of this innate duality was the "Jewish writer oxymoron." That too has its perfect correlative in the American tradition, as for example in Melville's "Christian writer oxymoron" after finishing *Moby-Dick:* "I have written a wicked book, and feel spotless as the lamb."[41] Janet Handler Burstein put it well in "Cynthia Ozick and the Transgressions of Art":

> In asking whether art impedes the making of moral choices Ozick, of course, takes her place in a distinguished line of American artists from Hawthorne and James to Pound and Cather. All ideologies, the Calvinist as well as the Judaic, civil religion as well as aestheticism, limit choice. (85)

Going beyond mere blasphemy, Faulkner, that purveyor of the old heroic virtues and verities of the heart, pronounced the serious writer a criminal species, capable of any wickedness—Faulkner cited killing his own grandmother—if it will advance his art. This paradigm of the artist as criminal-blasphemer was heralded again by Ralph Waldo Emerson, most notably in "Uriel." In this poem, cited by Robert Frost (in *A Masque of Reason*) as "the greatest Western poem yet," Uriel speaks such blasphemous truths that heaven is shaken:

> The balance beam of Fate was bent;
> The bounds of good and ill were rent;
> . . .
> . . . out of the good of evil born,
> Came Uriel's voice of cherub scorn,
> And a blush tinged the upper sky,
> And the gods shook, they knew not why.

Far from being a Jewish peculiarity, Ozick's fear that her art flouts the divine Command is well within the mainstream of major American authors.

Even apart from questions of blasphemy and crime, there remains, prominent in Ozick's work, the chief nightmare of the writer agonistes: the impossibility of being understood. Among Ozick's haunting procession of isolatos are several who clearly represent her own crushed hopes—Beulah Lilt, incognito in Brill's school; Edelshtein, unreadable without a translator; Edmund Gate's Aunt Rivka, stripped of glory on account of her gender. These are poignant figures, to be sure, but what could really be more classically American than the portrait of the wounded artist? Bartleby the Scrivener, Melville's surrogate fugitive from the Dead Letter Office; the anathemized Walt Whitman, who (the *New York Times* declared in 1856) "roots like a pig among a rotten garbage of licentious thoughts"; the reclusive Emily Dickinson, plucker of sour grapes like "I'm Nobody! Who Are You?"; Faulkner, begging for hack work as his great novels went out of print during the war—these figures and many others form a main line of American literati among whom Ozick's wounded artists might find easy blood kinship at last. There is nothing inherently or distinctively Jewish about this syndrome.

Nor does Ozick's long flirtation with pantheism bespeak a particularly Jewish sensibility. Emily Dickinson, for example, expresses a Christian version of the Pagan Rabbi mode when she ends "My Sabbath" ("The gentian weaves her fringes") in a pantheistic parody of the Trinity—"In the name of the bee / And of the butterfly / And of the breeze, amen!" Although Ozick mentions Spinoza in "The Pagan Rabbi," that great Jewish-pantheistic philosopher had no direct influence on this story; instead she was writing from the American mainstream tradition. In answer to my query about who promoted her pantheistic leanings, she refers to the cluster of luminaries who have sustained American literature from the beginning—the Romantic and transcendentalist writers:

> In high school and college I was saturated in the Romantic poets, yes, and wrote a college honors thesis on Blake, Coleridge, Wordsworth, and Shelley. I was a zealous monist then, captivated by the fusion of soul and nature. Spinoza, however, never took my attention or allegiance—have you ever tried *reading* Spinoza? (Ltr 6/6/90, emphasis hers)

Among the transcendentalist literati after whom she named the Purse children in *Trust*—Manny (Whitman), Sonny (Emerson), Al (Alcott)—the boy named Throw (Thoreau) calls to mind a particularly impressive analogy between a passage in *Walden* and one in "The Pagan Rabbi":

It is false history, false philosophy, and false religion which declare to us that we live among Things. . . . The molecules dance inside all forms, and within the molecules dance the atoms, and within the atoms dance still profounder sources of divine vitality. There is nothing that is Dead. There is no Non-life. Holy life subsists even in the stone, even in the bones of dead dogs and dead men. (PR 20–21)

The earth is not a mere fragment of dead history, . . . not a fossil earth, but a living earth; compared with whose great central life all animal and vegetable life is merely parasitic. (*Walden,* chap. 17, "Spring")

One could cite many other instances in which Cynthia Ozick displays ties that transcend the surface exotica of her Jewish materials. Eliot's *The Cocktail Party,* for example, has structural analogies with "Levitation," particularly in that both works center upon a cocktail party at which the true identities of the participants get sifted out: a Christian martyr in Eliot; Jewish martyrs in Ozick. Ozick's recurring motif of the impostor is likewise a familiar American theme: the fabrication of a deracinated self readily links her Lushinski ("A Mercenary") and Dr. Eklund (*The Messiah of Stockholm*) with figures ranging from Jay Gatsby to the King and the Duke to Melville's Confidence Man. And nothing is more characteristically American than the jaundiced view of class discrimination that links the creator of Allegra Vand and Rosa Lublin with writers as various as Dreiser, Fitzgerald, Joyce Carol Oates, and Toni Morrison.

The conflicted nature of Ozick's fiction also places her in the American mainstream. Although she speaks of the Judaic need for art "to judge and interpret the world," her fictional closures often turn out to be as ambiguous as the significance of Hawthorne's *A,* or Melville's whale, or Strether's decision not to live all he can with Maria Gostrey. In this respect, her essays contrast with her fiction exactly according to William Butler Yeats's formulation: rhetoric (Ozick's essay writing) is a quarrel with other people, poetry (Ozick's fiction) a quarrel with oneself. And, as the critics have engagingly demonstrated, the latter quarrel is finally unresolvable. At the end of *Trust,* will the artist-heroine go forth to forge in the smithy of her soul an oeuvre in the mold of her natural Hellenistic father, Tilbeck, or of her spiritual stepfather, Enoch Vand? We must look to her next book for an answer, where "The Pagan Rabbi" merely repeats the question: how much of Ozick goes into the rabbi's exultant apotheosis, and how much lingers with its nemesis, the constraining strictures of the Law?

And the conflicts continue to the end of the Ozick oeuvre. In "Bloodshed," who really gets the last word, Bleilip the despairing skeptic or the orthodox rebbe? In *The Cannibal Galaxy,* should we consider America the

Jewish Eden to be also a cannibal galaxy? In *The Messiah of Stockholm,* is Lars better off in possession of Schulz's Eye or as a companion of the stewpot? And what should we make, in either case, of the book's closure—a man in a long cloak carrying a box toward the chimneys? Which is better for Rosa to choose as *The Shawl* closes—Magda filling the room or Persky on his way upstairs? Magic or reality? Imagination or L'Chaim? Despite its Judaic call to judgment, Ozick's artistic sensibility proves as protean in these dilemmas as Melville's regarding Captain Vere, Robert Penn Warren's regarding Willie Stark, or Updike's regarding Rabbit Angstrom. In being fraught with dualities, Ozick's Jewish art is quintessentially American.

Even Ozick's most distinctively Jewish feature, her fidelity to "ethical monotheism" (as she defines the essence of Judaism), is centrally within the American grain. In calculating our debt to the Jewish heritage, Upton Sinclair traced the modern crusade for social justice directly to the ethical enlightenment of Hebrew antiquity, almost as though he had been reading "Bialik's Hint":

> No, there is one thing and one thing only which distinguishes the Hebrew sacred writings from all others, and that is their insistent note of proletarian revolt, their furious denunciation of exploiters, and of luxury and wantonness, the vices of the rich. Of that note the Assyrian and Chaldean and Babylonian writing contain not a trace. . . . [The] true, natural-born rebels of all time were the Hebrews. They were rebels against oppression in ancient Judea, as they are today in Petrograd and New York; the spirit of equality and brotherhood which spoke through Ezekiel and Amos and Isaiah . . . speaks today through . . . the Socialist and Anarchist agitators, following the same tradition, possessed by the same dream as the ancient Hebrew prophets.[42]

Culminating Ozick's "Americanness" are her numerous affinities with those two models of ur-WASP high culture, the brothers James. In her early work, Henry James's "international theme" was evidently an example that Ozick would have followed if the Holocaust had not redefined the European half of that Jamesian compound. Throughout her career, we may ascribe to James more than any other mentor Ozick's central obsession with the theme of the impostor—the trusted and crucially influential friend who is not what he/she seems. Whether we look at the narrator's phony father figures in *Trust* or the faithless tutors of Joseph Brill and Lars Andemening, the ancestral figures of Milly Theale and Isabel Archer come to mind, stalked by trust-breaking predators. But the James-Ozick connection is not simply a matter of the lesson of the master. If Allegra Vand expressed the Jamesian lure of Europe for the young Ozick, a reversal of sorts occurred for the older Henry James, drawing him into belated embrace of the L'Chaim!

principle via his dread of the wasted life in *The Beast in the Jungle* and other stories. Broadly considered, what better defines the L'Chaim! concept than Lambert Strether's much-touted summation in *The Ambassadors,* "Live all you can. It's a mistake not to"?

In the *New Criterion* of January 1993, Ozick presents perhaps her final major revision of the Ozick-James connection in her essay "What Henry James Knew." Whereas she began her career in fiction trying to emulate the success of James, what intrigues her now is James's deepest experience of failure. When James was booed off the London stage on 5 January 1895, this lapse into (as he put it) "the most horrible hours of my life" compounded other recent tragedies—the untimely death in 1892 of his sister Alice and the suicide in 1894 of Constance Fenimore Woolman. To some degree, Ozick remarks, James had reason to feel complicity in both deaths, if—as it seemed— Alice's talent had been fatally suffocated by the brilliance of her older siblings and if Woolman's hunger for intimacy with James had remained coldly unreciprocated. Suffusing this whole wretched period, moreover, was James's deepening sense of *"the essential loneliness of my life"* (James's emphasis, as Ozick notes)—a predicament worsened by his hopeless infatuation with several younger men of his acquaintance. James's homoerotic isolation comprises a reasonable fascimile, we might say, of Ozick's recurring sexual misfit—the narrator of *Trust,* Una in "An Education," the doctor in "The Doctor's Wife," Edelshtein in "Envy," Joseph Brill and Lars Andemening in the later novels. Increasingly, the later Henry James came to approximate an Ozick character.

Ostensibly, Ozick's interest in James's dark night of the soul focused on the way it affected his late fiction. "James is one of that handful of literary proto-inventors—ingenious intuiters—of the unconscious," she says of this period; "it is the chief reason we count him among the imperial moderns" (18). Particularly in *The Awkward Age,* she argues, his "descent into an interior chaos" made him, "finally and incontrovertibly, a modernist" (22). But the unconscious works on the critic as well, most pointedly in affecting her choice of a subject. If the triumphant youthful James now yields in her esteem to the older James who was tormented by grief, guilt, and failure, perhaps her new empathy touches on something deeper than his rebirth in the modernist canon. Their deepest affinity, one may surmise, is that James has become more like Ozick herself as a result of his sufferings, having drunk deeply from the bitter cup of artistic rejection, wounded self-confidence, and outsider status—a condition made all the worse by his easy early victories (in contrast to her career). Withal, this most WASPish of American writers has become more Judaized, being touched to the quick by a tragic knowledge (recalling her title "What Henry James Knew") that makes his later affirmation of the

L'Chaim! attitude—"Live all you can"—all the more resonant. In this late essay of Ozick's, it may be said, these two writers, one quintessentially WASP and the other quintessentially Jewish-American, display a newly deepened, because painfully earned, cultural intercourse.

Sustaining that cultural intercourse, I would say, is a bedrock of affinity between Ozick's ethical monotheism and the religious thought of the greatest and most quintessentially American philosopher, William James. Ozick's Pan-versus-Moses formulation translates readily into James's monism versus pluralism, which he considered, in "Pragmatism and Religion," not only "the final question of philosophy" but "the deepest and most pregnant question that our minds can frame."[43] Like Ozick, James eschewed the God-in-Nature heresy—"Now I am myself anything but a pantheist of the monistic pattern"[44]—while favoring a religious sensibility committed to ethical action. For Enoch Vand in *Trust*, ethical action is the immovable anchor to which his Jewish sensibility holds fast despite even the Holocaust and its enticement toward atheism. "Dedication to one's work in the world is the only possible sanctification," he says (TR 560), a view that he earlier upheld against his wife's incomprehension:

> [Allegra] "You're always making things sound as if the universe depended on . . . every single private act."
> [Enoch] "Maybe it does." (TR 141)

Ozick's fidelity to that idea is echoed everywhere in William James. "Today," James says in *The Varieties of Religious Experience*, "helpfulness in general human affairs is . . . reckoned as a species of divine service."[45] And again, in "Pragmatism and Religion," James declared, "I believe that each man is responsible for making the universe better, and that if he does not do this it will be in so far left undone."[46] In "The Dilemma of Determinism" he claims that "the final purpose of our creation seems most plausibly to be the greatest possible enrichment of our ethical consciousness."[47] At the bottom of these imperatives is James's Torah-like evocation of the design set forth by the Creator:

> Suppose that the world's author put the case to you before creation, saying: "I am going to make a world not certain to be saved, a world the perfection of which shall be conditional merely, the condition being that each several agent does its own 'level best.' I offer you the chance of taking part in such a world." (*Pragmatism* 187)

Such echoes of the Judaic ethos remind us why Cynthia Ozick is as American as William James. Although Gentile America may not be as "Jewish" as Cynthia Ozick with regard to Yiddish speech and kosher laws, its Christian past brings with it a profoundly Jewish soul. The theological grounds for argument—whether, on one side, God degrades himself via Incarnation; or whether, on the other, God elects a Chosen People on a biologically determined (tribal) basis—can perhaps be bypassed in favor of the common culture. That broadly Judeo-Christian heritage, promulgating the "moral seriousness" that made William James the kind of thinker he was, is a final reason why the Jewish fiction of Cynthia Ozick is essentially, not marginally, American.

Major/Minor

In her 1986 oral interview with Kay Bonetti, Cynthia Ozick defined her place in the literary pantheon as "minor, minor, minor." Not until 1992, however, in "Alfred Chester's Wig" (in the *New Yorker* of 30 March), did Cynthia Ozick define the term and its implications. Initially, the designation reads like a death certificate for the small-fry stranded below the heights of Olympus:

> The economy of writing always operates according to a feudal logic: the aristocracy blots out all the rest. There is no middle class. The heights belong to, at most, four or five writers, a princely crew: the remainder are invisible, or else have the partial, now-and-then visibility that attaches to minor status. (84)

Even more chillingly, she asserts, apropos of Alfred Chester, that "minor writers are mainly dead writers who do not rise again." The word "mainly," however, opens a loophole of hope that expands into a larger sense of usefulness:

> To be able to say what a minor writer is—if it could be done at all—would bring us a little nearer to defining a culture. The tone of a culture cannot depend only on the occasional genius, or the illusion of one; the prevailing temper of a society and a time is situated in its minor voices. . . . There can be no major work, in fact, without the screen, or ground, of lesser artists against whom the major figure is illuminated. (96)

Concerning the criteria separating major from minor, she observes that "quantity is not irrelevant." Among those who demonstrate that "abundance counts" she cites Balzac and James, though she allows for the possibility of "blazing exceptions" like *Wuthering Heights*. Another defining term is "sectarianism," a monomaniac narrowness of interest always indicative of minor status: "Nothing displays minorness so much as the 'genre' novel, however brilliantly turned out, whether it is a Western or a detective story . . ., even when it is being deliberately parodied as a postmodernist conceit" (97). "Parochialism," by contrast, bespeaks a universal applicability present in major fiction: "All 'parochialisms' are inclusive. Sholem Aleichem's, Jane Austen's, Faulkner's, Garcia Marquez's villages have a census of millions" (97). So, too, the minorness of monomania plays off against the major character of "obsessiveness": "Geniuses are obsessive: Kafka is obsessive, Melville is obsessive. Obsessiveness belongs to ultimate meanings; it is a category of metaphysics" (97). Lastly, the category of minor can result, as in Alfred Chester's case, from the practice of "ventriloquism," which Ozick defines as a flight from reality related to an "excessive love of literature." "What ventriloquist writers want is to live inside *other literatures*," Ozick explains; "[Chester] saw landscapes and cities through a veil of bookish imaginings" (97, emphasis hers).

Clearly, by her own definition of the term, Ozick is not a major author, one of the four or five Titans bestriding the stage of her lifetime—a Joyce, Mann, or Faulkner. She lacks both their vast abundance of pages and their huge, ongoing impact on the world of letters both during their own time and later. But at the same time, her own self-designation as triply minor is unreliable. Like Hawthorne rendering his Puritan heritage, Ozick breathes life into a parochial, not sectarian, vision of Jewish-American life, and she does so with obsessive, not monomaniac, urgency. Where Hawthorne journeyed across two centuries of time to reach his subject, burying himself for years in ancestral lore to do so, Ozick crosses a quarter-globe of space, immersing herself in *her* ancestral lore so as to situate herself in the European-American ground of twentieth-century Jewish identity. Her "village," a site that includes the imagined Auschwitz and Warsaw of *The Shawl* as well the observed Jewish enclaves of Miami and New York, has its census of millions.

For Cynthia Ozick, the designation "minor" relates substantially to her choice of a form. Although she has written several novellas that rank with the best in the language—with Conrad's "Youth," Melville's "Bartleby the Scrivener," Faulkner's "The Bear"—she has nothing to match up with the great novels by those writers. In effect, she is a strong contender for the championship of something less than the heavyweight division. Yet, in her own words, "minor status is not always the same as oblivion." Her list of minor immortals, which includes Edward Lear, W. S. Gilbert, and Max Beerbohm, ends modestly in a parenthesis: "(There are a handful more among the living)" (97). But all writers, major or minor, have the same end in mind:

"what they really *work* for is that transient little daily illusion—phrase by phrase, comma after comma—of the stay against erasure." A major poet, Robert Frost, defined that last phrase memorably: "The utmost of ambition is to lodge a few poems where they will be hard to get rid of, to lodge a few irreducible bits where [Edwin Arlington] Robinson lodged more than his share."[48]

I would judge that Ozick's finest work—including "Envy," "A Mercenary," "Usurpation," "Bloodshed," "The Pagan Rabbi," many scenes in *Trust* and the other novels—is so stunningly original and brilliantly rendered as to fit Frost's measure. She is a minor writer, that is to say, in the classic fashion of Stephen Crane, Katherine Anne Porter, and Flannery O'Connor, whose best work, though limited in abundance, figures to retain literary immortality. By way of suggesting what characteristics make her "irreducible bits" most "hard to get rid of," my final section on Judgment will be a brief postscript of personal evaluation.

Postscript: An Appreciation

Ten years ago, I ended my long essay "The Art of Cynthia Ozick" with a brief personal assessment of her career. Although the intervening decade has seen a wide expansion of both Ozick's own oeuvre and criticism about her, nothing has happened to substantially alter my original opinion. I am therefore reprinting my comments largely, though not completely, as they were.

My greatest regret in ending this work is that even a book-length study cannot do justice to Ozick's style, which she rightly described—speaking of *Trust*—as "mandarin" and "lapidary," making "every paragraph a poem" (BL 4). Of her writing at large, she says, "nothing matters to me so much as a comely and muscular sentence. . . . I miter every pair of abutting sentences as scrupulously as [my] Uncle Jake fitted one strip of rosewood against another" (MM 109–10). Of her prose rhythms she says, "Cadence is the fingerprint, isn't it?" (Teicholz 170). Her favorite metrical device is to put the main statement up front and then attach to it a long string of modifiers to form a rising curve of feeling. Here, for example, that curve of mounting excitement rests upon a fantasy of reversing the Holocaust in the name of the "To Life!" ethos:

> As if the reel of history . . . could be run backward: these mounds of ash, shoes, teeth, bones, all lifted up, healed, flown speck after speck toward connection, toward flowering, grain on grain, bone on bone, every skull blooming into the quickness of a human face, every twisted shoe renewed on a vivid

foot, every dry bone given again to greening. Ezekial's vision in the valley of bones. (AA 230)

As she warms to her subject, the style of this passage illustrates Ozick verging into prose poetry, especially evident in the incantatory rhythm resulting from her use of repetition: "every" repeated three times, "bone" and "grain" and "toward" and "speck" repeated twice in quick succession. Special rhetorical power is gained from verbal nouns and adjectives that give the sense of immediate action happening now: "lifted," "healed," "flown," "flowering," "blooming," "renewed," "greening," and "twisted." The four-part repetition of bone/bones, the last time being "dry bone," plays off against the imagery of fertility—"flowering," "blooming," "renewed," "greening." And the short final line about Ezekiel's vision, thumping in anapestic tetrameter, gives a rhythmically emphatic close to this apocalyptic paragraph.

Ozick did not require a sublime subject like this one, however, to summon up her powers of cadence. From "Alfred Chester's Wig," in the *New Yorker* of 30 March 1992, we cull a sentence about the pleasure of visiting Manhattan's musty used-book stores: "Gradually, the cellar smells would be converted, or consecrated, into a sort of blissful incense; nostrils that flinched in retreat opened to the tremulous savor of books waiting to be aroused, and to arouse" (84). Here, with Hawthornesque precision, delicacy, and wit, Ozick moves within the scope of one sentence from metaphors of church worship ("converted," "consecrated," "incense") to those of sexual seduction ("tremulous," "to be aroused, and to arouse"). Given her propensity to view literature as a violation of her religion, that metaphorical progression from sacred to profane seems particularly appropriate.

As these examples imply, I was first attracted to Ozick's stories by the continous execution of her art—the line by line, scene by scene, page by page vivacity of imagination and vigor of style. If we postulate that the scene in fiction corresponds to the image in poetry, we may say that Cynthia Ozick's interplay of fictional devices consistently develops scenes answering to Ezra Pound's Imagist Manifesto of 1913: they "transmit an intellectual and emotional complex in an instant of time." The pagan motifs converging into the night of Tilbeck's apotheosis; the Pagan Rabbi's breathtaking consummation of love with the dryad; Puttermesser chanting her beloved golem back to a pile of mud; Tchernikhovsky insolently at ease in Zion; Lushinski in Africa contemplating his buried self in Warsaw; the living idols turning cannibalistic in *The Messiah of Stockholm;* the total immersion of the senses in Auschwitz to begin *The Shawl*—such scenes bespeak a gift of the first order of talent. Likewise, the irreducible bits that Robert Frost spoke of must include the many dramatic verbal battles that Ozick renders with a perfect ear for speech patterns: Edelshtein versus the evangelist in "Envy," Bleilip versus the rebbe in "Bloodshed," German versus Jew in "The Suitcase," Brill versus Hester Lilt in *The Cannibal Galaxy,* Rosa's letters versus her niece's letters in *The Shawl.* Though not prolific in the fashion of Joyce Carol Oates or Saul Bellow, her stream of creativity has been outstandingly pure.

The confrontations at the center of her art emanate in turn from a profoundly conflicted mind. She hates the whole of Western civilization but takes pride in the Jewish groundwork of that civilization. She protests the reduction of "Jewish history" to what has been done to Jews but saturates her writings with just that version of Jewish history. She calls America a Jewish Eden but thinks its cannibal's eye is fixed on her four-thousand-year heritage. Her fiction exemplifies the Jewish writer oxymoron, every page a blasphemy against the Second Commandment, every book a revelry of pagan enticement. Her life propounds another oxymoron, that of an Orthodox Jewish feminist, who reveres the ancient Sinaitic Law but demands an Equal Rights Amendment to Torah. Happily married since age twenty-five, she invariably portrays marital estrangement or self-willed singlehood in her characters. She embodies, that is to say, the modern precepts announced by Yeats, that poetry is a quarrel with oneself; by Joyce Carol Oates, that "the spirit of contrariety lies at the heart of all passionate commitment"; by John Updike, that "to be a person is to be in a situation of tension, is to be in a dialectical situation. A truly adjusted person is not a person at all—just an animal with clothes on."[49]

But in the end her work is unified, all the same, by the admonitory temper that turns her tales into parables of failure. Ethical monotheism does have its final say in the ruin of Lushinski, who fails to keep his Jewish self in its Polish grave; of Puttermesser, whose cultural apostasies fail to save her city or her marriage; of Brill, whose neglect of Jewish history turns his Dual Curriculum into mush and his student-genius into a pagan; of Rosa, whose class-based anti-Semitic feelings block access to the healings of the L'Chaim! principle. Under the fault lines of Ozick's schizoid creativity lies the granite core of her Judaic heritage, which finds expression in an unrelenting consistency of ethical judgment.

Although her ensconcement within a minority culture may initially seem to limit her appeal to a larger audience, I have found, despite my Gentile upbringing, that the obstacles to understanding her work have little to do with her Jewish materials. They result, rather, from her willful adherence to basic aesthetic principles. A holdover (aesthetically) from the modern period— the Age of Eliot, Faulkner, Joyce—she is no more inclined to simplify her complex art, so as to ease her reader's task, than she is to falsify her view of reality, so as to thrive in the marketplace. Her Jewish heritage, for the most part, is no more exclusionary than Hawthorne's or Faulkner's regionalism.

What matters in the end is the imaginative power to elevate local materials toward universal and timeless significance. By that standard, I judge Ms. Ozick's work to be memorably successful. Her variety and consistent mastery of style; her lengthening caravan of original and unforgettably individualized characters; her vivid dramatization through these characters of significant themes and issues; her absorbing command of narrative structure; her penetrating and independent intellect undergirding all she writes—these characteristics of her art perform a unique service for her subject matter, extracting from her Jewish heritage a vital significance unlike that transmitted by any other writer. In the American tradition, Cynthia Ozick significantly enhances our national literature by so rendering her Jewish culture into a fine, if irremediably conflicted, art.

Notes

Index

Notes

Chapter 1. The Matrix of Art

1. Because my Chapter 1 delineates the writer's intellect rather than her biography as such, I provide the following biographical outline, with special thanks to Joseph Lowin for the chronology in his Twayne Series book, *Cynthia Ozick* (Boston: G. K. Hall, 1988).

Cynthia Ozick was born on 17 April 1928 in New York City, the second child of William and Shifra Regelson Ozick and the niece of the writer Abraham Regelson. From 1933 to 1941 she attended the local school, P.S. 71 in the Pelham Bay region of the Bronx; from 1942 to 1946, Hunter College High School in Manhattan; from 1946 to 1949, New York University, graduating Phi Beta Kappa with English Honors. In 1950 she earned her master's degree in English at Ohio State University with a thesis on Henry James, after which she spent a dozen years working on two huge novels, *Mercy, Pity, Peace, and Love* (unpublished) and *Trust*. In 1952 she married Bernard Hallotte, a lawyer; on 24 September 1965 she gave birth to their only child, Rachel. Additional biographica are included as relevance dictates within my main text.

2. Wallace Fowlie, *Memory: A Fourth Memoir* (Durham and London: Duke University Press, 1990), 3; Joan Didion, "On Morality," in *Slouching toward Bethlehem* (New York: Delta Books, 1968), 158; and Cynthia Ozick, "Spells, Wishes, Goldfish, Old School Hurts," *New York Times Book Review* (NYTBR) for "The Making of a Writer" column, 31 January 1982, 24. In *Art & Ardor* this essay is reprinted under the title "A Drugstore in Winter," and my citation appears on page 304.

3. Ltr 6/6/90. The comment on childhood reading is cited from *Conversations with Reynolds Price*, ed. Jefferson Humphreys (Jackson and London: University Press of Mississippi, 1991), 195.

4. Arthur Hertzberg, *The Jews in America* (New York: Simon and Schuster, 1989), 13. Although the historian Lucy Dawidowicz condemned this book for its condescending snobbery—"not so much a history as a sermonizing put-down"—she does not dispute the reality of immigrant Jewish poverty (*Commentary* 89, no. 1 [January 1990]: 49). Along with poverty, Hertzberg identifies one other chief characteristic shared by Jewish immigrants: "a conscious anti-European streak." This resentment, Hertzberg says, targeted not only Gentile persecutors but also rich European Jews and their rabbis whose failure to help their poor relations contributed to the exodus of the latter to America.

Among Ozick's characters, Edelshtein in "Envy" well illustrates Hertzberg's points. A Europe hater who decries "Western Civilization, that pod of muck" (PR 42), he says "Our [Jewish] reputation as ... scholars is mostly empty. In actuality we are a mob of working people, laborers, hewers of wood. . . . [But] tickle the lawyer and you'll see his grandfather sawed wood for a living" (85)

5. In reviewing Richard Lingeman's biography of Dreiser in the *New York Times Book Review* of 9 November 1986 (29–31), Ozick declared *Sister Carrie* "the first recognizably 'American' novel—American in the way we feel it now." Superseding Howells, Wharton, and James in this respect, Dreiser's book enables us "to experience the unfolding of literary history—to see how the English novel, itself an immigrant, finally pocketed its 'papers' and became naturalized."

6. I am much obliged to my colleague Kalman Bland, of the Duke Religion Department, for these translations. He also suggested that perhaps Cynthia Ozick profoundly relates to the word *Oz* that she cites from Psalm 138.3, a Hebrew word meaning "strength."

7. NYTBR, 2 December 1979, 59.

8. Apropos of Chester's unappealing appearance, Ozick cites Gore Vidal's remark, in his introduction to a posthumous collection of Chester's writings, that "I did have the great good luck never to have so much as glimpsed Alfred Chester." But clearly his appearance did not offend Truman Capote, who wrote his private telephone number in Chester's address book while Chester was still Ozick's college classmate.

9. "We Are the Crazy Lady and Other Feisty Feminist Fables." First published in *Ms.* magazine (Spring 1973); republished in *The Dolphin Reader,* 2d ed., ed. Douglas Hunt (Boston: Houghton Mifflin, 1990), 673–74. Hereafter cited in my main text as "CL."

10. Ltr 10/26/82. In "Toward a New Yiddish," she remarks of *Trust* that "my work did not speak to the Gentiles, for whom it had been begun, nor to the Jews, for whom it had been finished" (AA 158).

11. Vera Emuna Kielsky, in *Inevitable Exiles* (New York: Peter Lang, 1989), cites Ozick's denial that she is an Orthodox Jew: "I don't even like the phrase 'Orthodox.' . . . It's a Christian word . . . meaning right belief. And how are those words—right belief—Jewish? They just aren't" (25). Because "Orthodox Jew" is a widely used designation among Jews of all persuasions, I do not regard Ozick's disclaimer as a binding prohibition.

12. In her interview with Elaine Kauvar, Ozick said, "I don't find a contradiction between Judaism and feminism," mainly because these problematic traditions are late-blooming effects of assimilation. For example: "In the Orthodox Synagogue, that *mehitzah* (partition in the synagogue separating men from women during prayer), that line of division. . . . Ironically, its origin is very late, and it comes out of an assimilatory impulse. It came about in the tenth century under the influence of Moslem culture" (Kauvar 387).

13. Linda Zatlin, "Cynthia Ozick's *Levitation: Five Fictions,*" *Studies in American Jewish Literature* 4 (1985): 121.

14. Miriam Cooke, "War and Gender," *Newsletter of the Center for International Studies* (Duke University) 3, no. 2 (Spring 1991): 3.

15. Barbara Gitenstein lectured on Ozick at the American Literature Association Convention in Washington, D.C., on 24 May 1991.

16. Ozick, "The Seam of the Snail" (MM 109).

17. In "A Mercenary," the African tribesman Morris becomes the spokesman of

this Jewish idea (along with many others): "'At bottom,' Morris said, "there is no contradiction between the tribal and the universal. Remember William Blake, sir: 'To see a world in a grain of sand'" (BL 33).

18. Because the King James translation of the Bible is generally considered excellent, I am quoting it here. The Hertz edition of the Hebrew Bible (1973) gives translations that are very close to the King James.

19. Rabbi Leo Baeck, who strongly influenced Ozick, reads the Jacob-Esau and Isaac-Ishmael stories in this fashion in *This People Israel* (Philadelphia: Jewish Publication Society of America, 1964), 250–60.

20. Leo Baeck, *Judaism and Christianity* (New York, 1958), 189–92, 212.

21. *Faulkner in the University*, ed. Frederick L. Gwynn and Joseph Blotner (New York: Vintage, 1965), 161.

22. Ltr 8/11/90. Apropos of the Jewish avoidance of an image of God, Camille Paglia, in her magnum opus *Sexual Personae* (New York: Vintage, 1991) observes that "Judaism's campaign to make divinity invisible has never fully succeeded" (139).

23. According to the British ambassador to Germany, the idolatry of Hitler worship was compounded by the führer's own instance of Ozick's idolatry-of-art thesis. In 1939 the Nazi leader stated: "All my life I have wanted to be a great painter in oils. . . . As soon as I have carried out my program for Germany, I shall take up my painting. I feel that I have it in my soul to become one of the great artists of the age and that future historians will remember me not for what I have done for Germany, but for my art." *Sewanee Review* 77 (Autumn 1969): 701.

24. Leo Baeck, *This People Israel: The Meaning of Jewish Existence* (Philadelphia, 1964), 124.

25. NYTBR, 4 December 1977, 66.

26. Among the transcriptions I have seen of this widely quoted passage, I consider Leni Yahl's the most plausible. See her *The Holocaust: The Fate of European Jewry, 1932–1945* (New York: Oxford, 1990), 115.

27. George Bernard Shaw, chapter 7 of "The Revolutionist's Handbook," in *Man and Superman* (Baltimore: Penguin Books, 1966), 240.

28. In "Idolatry in Miami," Francine Prose's piece about "The Shawl," Ozick is quoted as saying, "Like everyone else, . . . I required a dawning. I was having the life that Anne Frank would have had simultaneously. I can never think of my high school years without realizing how normal they were, and how, at that very moment, the chimneys were roaring away" (NYTBR, 10 September 1989, 39).

29. Ozick, "A Liberal's Auschwitz," in *The Pushcart Prize: First Edition* (New York, 1976–77), 152.

30. Ibid. 151.

31. Ozick, "Jews and Gentiles," *Commentary*, June 1971, 106.

32. Ozick, "A Liberal's Auschwitz" 152.

33. All the comments by Ozick in this paragraph are cited from the Symposium "The Changing Culture of the University," *Partisan Review* 58, no. 2 (1991): 400.

34. Ozick, "The Holidays: Reply to Anne Roiphe," *New York Times*, Section C, 28 December 1978, 1 and 6. Subsequent citations in this paragraph come from this same source.

35. In the *New Republic* of 20 May 1991, Robert Alter argues in a long essay, "From Myth to Murder," that Martin Luther, "who had no French or English counterpart," was a crucial reason "why anti-Semitism turned genocidal in Germany, and not in France or England" (38). Luther's "scurrilous pamphlet, *The Jews and Their Lies,* [was] reissued in a popular edition by the Nazis in 1935," Alter observes. In it, Luther denounced the Jews for usury, for poisoning wells, for drinking the blood of Christian children, and, not least, for killing Christ. In revenge, he famously called for genocide: "So we are even at fault for not avenging all this innocent blood of our Lord and of the Christians which they shed. . . . We are at fault for not slaying them" (37). On the other hand, Heinrich Graetz—a favorite source for Ozick—in his *History of the Jews* (Philadelphia: Jewish Publication Society of America, 1891–98) cites Luther's pamphlet "Jesus Was Born a Jew" as calling for "Christian love" toward Jews, who "are blood-relations of our Lord; therefore, . . . the Jews belong to Christ more than we. . . . Therefore, it is my advice . . . that we treat them kindly" (4:470).

36. "The Intermarrying Kind," *Newsweek,* 22 July 1991, 48–49.

37. Cited from Howard M. Sachar's *A History of the Jews in America* (New York: Knopf, 1992) in NYTBR, 28 June 1992, 29. Sachar describes how the revelations of the death camps transformed both Jewish and Gentile attitudes in America, changing public opinion from 72 percent against any U.S. involvement in Palestine in 1945 to 76 percent in favor of a Jewish homeland in Palestine in 1946.

38. Ozick, "Jews and Gentiles" 106.

39. In addition to scanning Graetz's enormous work, I also drew information about Jewish history in Europe from Martin Gilbert's succinct but richly informative *Atlas of Jewish History* (n.p.: Dorset Press, 1976).

40. According to Heinrich Graetz, the Puritan Commonwealth assumed so philo-Semitic an attitude that "the only thing wanting to make one think himself in Judaea was for the orators in Parliament to speak Hebrew" (*History of the Jews* 5: 27–28).

41. These two stories about Ozick's parents appear in her essay "All the World Wants the Jews Dead," *Esquire* 82, no. 5 (November 1974): 104, 207. The ubiquity of "Jewish history" in her fiction is seen in the reappearance of this dreadful episode in the otherwise farcical satire "Virility," in which the protagonist's whole family was murdered: "—his mother, raped and slaughtered; . . . his father, tied to the tail of a Cossack horse and sent to have his head broken on cobblestones" (PR 224).

42. Wesley A. Kort, *Shriven Selves: Religious Problems in Recent American Fiction* (Philadelphia: Fortress Press, 1972), 111–12. "Very little is said in the Bible about this period of darkness. Where was God between the death of Joseph and the call of Moses? . . . No use or meaning can be seen . . . in the darkness and pain of Egypt, and Egypt remains the great black hole of the Bible."

43. Ozick, "A Contraband Life," *Commentary* 39, no. 3 (March 1965): 92.

44. See Prose, "Idolatry in Miami" 39: "I worry very much that [the Holocaust] is corrupted by fiction and that fiction in general corrupts history."

45. John Toland, *Hitler: The Pictorial Documentary of His Life* (Garden City, NY: Doubleday, 1978), 1.

46. *Newsweek* (8 April 1991, 50) reported that the Law of Return "offers auto-

matic Israeli citizenship to any Jew (which it defines as anybody having a Jewish grandparent)"—a definition that would apparently embrace Adolf Hitler. For a learned discussion that traces the "Who Is a Jew?" controversy back a millennium to Maimonides and Halevi, see Baruch Frydman-Kohl's essay in *Judaism* 41, no. 1 (Winter 1992): 64–80.

A vastly influential opinion, because it was laid before tens of millions of newspaper readers, was Ann Landers' effort to resolve the biology-versus-culture question. To the question whether "a person who was born of Jewish parents [can] become a Gentile if he would rather not be Jewish," Ms. Landers replied: "One's ethnic makeup can neither be chosen nor changed. A Jew who wishes to dissociate himself from Judaism and take up Catholicism, Christian Science or Confucianism, for example, is still a Jew by heritage. No amount of disavowing will transform him into a Gentile" (*Durham Morning Herald,* 9 September 1984).

47. Ltr 6/6/90. Despite her rage over the Holocaust, Cynthia Ozick declares that "I cannot imagine finding the notion of 'collective guilt' anything but abhorrent . . . as applied to Germans or anyone else" (Ltr 5/26/90). It is worth mentioning, in this respect, that far from choosing Hitler as their leader, the German people in their last free election (March 1932) chose Paul Hindenburg as president by a margin of almost six million votes, despite the issues that played powerfully in Hitler's favor: the humiliation of Versailles, fear of Communism, and Depression-era unemployment for perhaps eight million Germans. See John Toland, *Adolf Hitler* (New York: Doubleday, 1976), 262–65.

48. Ronald Sanders, *The Shores of Refuge* (New York: Henry Holt and Company, 1988), 483. Leni Yahl, in *The Holocaust,* says that Himmler and Heydrich seriously supported the Madagascar plan, and that "Hitler appeared to favor the scheme and referred to it several times in the summer of 1940" (253–54).

49. For much of what I know about the Holocaust, I am indebted to Raul Hilberg's *The Destruction of the European Jews* (Chicago: Quadrangle, 1961; Revised and Definitive Edition, New York: Holmes and Meier, 1985).

50. Obviously playing on Solzhenitsyn's title "One Day in the Life of Ivan Denisovich," Ozick's "24 Years in the Life of Lyuba Bershadskaya" was published in the *New York Times Magazine* of 14 March 1971 under the pseudonym Trudie Vocse to protect Ozick's relatives in the Soviet Union. Among the Nazi-like brutalities that she cites is a twenty-eight-day train ride to the gulag in a tiny cage shared by six women, during which water was given only three times and food not at all. Many corpses were hauled down the aisle during the journey.

51. Hilberg, *Destruction of the European Jews* 358–59.

52. See Istvan Deak, "Who Saved Jews? An Exchange," *New York Review of Books,* 25 April 1991, 60; and Leni Yahl, *The Rescue of Danish Jewry: Test of a Democracy* (Philadelphia: Jewish Publication Society of America, 1969). Deak writes: "During the initial stages of the rescue operation, only well-to-do Danish Jews could afford the short voyage to Sweden. Private boatmen set their own price and the costs were prohibitive. . . . Afterward, when organized Danish rescue groups stepped in to coordinate the flight and to collect funds, the average price per person fell [dramatically]. . . . The rescue operation took place with the connivance of the local German

naval command." Hilberg describes the German army command in Denmark as also thwarting the Gestapo (*Destruction of the European Jews* 360).

53. Ozick, "All the World Wants the Jews Dead" 103.

54. Ernest Hemingway, *The Sun Also Rises* (New York: Scribner's, 1954), 22. Robert Cohn effects an interesting correlation between "L'Chaim!" and the pagan fertility gods in this scene, in that for him to "Choose Life!" means to possess Lady Brett sexually. But later, he reasserts the ancient Judaic anathema toward Astarte when he calls Brett "Circe," claiming that "she turns men into swine" (144).

55. Toni Morrison, *The Bluest Eye* (New York: Pocket Books, 1972), 125. My subsequent reference to "brown girls" cites pages 67–68.

56. This appalling fact was reported in *Harper's Magazine,* August 1991, 11.

57. See Scott Donaldson, *By Force of Will* (New York: Viking Press, 1977), 147, 200.

58. Ozick's sharpest juxtapostion of these values occurs in "The Suitcase." Here Genevieve relentlessly pursues the Jewish principle of truth telling, which her WASP adversary subordinates to the ideal of "class": "'Dignity,' Mr. Hencke said. 'Dignity before all. I subscribe to that'" (PR 125).

59. AA 164, 182n. The more recent critics came to Ozick's attention through an essay by Irene H. Chayes entitled "Revisionist Literary Criticism" in *Commentary* (April 1976).

60. Ozick's review of *The Wapshot Chronicle,* titled "Cheever's Yankee Heritage," appeared in the *Antioch Review,* Summer 1964, 263–67.

61. "Culture and the Present Moment," *Commentary,* December 1974, 35.

62. Although Ozick reproduced some of this discourse on Hardy in *Art & Ardor* (see "Innovation and Redemption: What Literature Means"), this quotation comes from her original version, "Query: Where Are the Serious Readers?" in *Salmagundi,* Summer-Fall 1978, 72–73.

Chapter 2. Readings

1. The general reader, unfortunately, does not have ready access to Ozick's poetry, which is scattered about in many magazines. That situation is being somewhat alleviated by a special edition of some poems presently being prepared by a publisher in Ohio, but its limited and very expensive character still rules out any wide access to Ozick's poetry.

2. Ozick was sufficiently impressed by this story to repeat it in "Envy": "The disciples of Reb Moshe of Kobryn . . . had no awe for their master when he hung in air, but when he slept—the miracle of his lung, his breath, his heartbeat!" (PR 87).

3. For a compelling argument on the other side of this polarity, see Lillian Kremer's excellent essay "The Splendor Spreads Wide: *Trust* and Cynthia Ozick's Aggadic Voice" (*Studies in American Jewish Literature* 6 [Fall 1987]: 24–44). In Part III of my book I comment briefly on this article.

4. *The Portable Wolfe,* ed. Maxwell Geismar (New York: Viking Press, 1946), 582.

5. "Gustave Nicholas Tilbeck was an unashamed borrowing from E. M. Forster's Greeky heroes" (Ltr 1/14/82). In "Toward a New Yiddish," first published in 1970, she wrote: "In my thirties I worshipped E. M. Forster for the lure of his English

paganism. Fifteen years [i.e., her first two novels] went into a silent and shadowed apprenticeship of craft and vision" (AA 157).

6. A student of mine, Andrew Ginsberg, remarked how the incongruous WASP-Jew marriage of Allegra and Enoch corresponds in many ways to the relationship between Leonard and Virginia Woolf that Ozick discusses in "Mrs. Virginia Woolf: A Madwoman and Her Nurse" (AA 27–54). Her essay on Edith Wharton (AA 3–26) likewise evokes many resemblances to Allegra Vand, especially regarding the deleterious effect of great wealth on the development of personality.

7. I discuss Leo Baeck under "Judaism" in Chapter 1. His essay on "Romantic Religion," Ozick says (in his *Judaism and Christianity*), "broke open the conceptual egg of my life" (Ltr 1/14/82).

8. NYTBR, 4 December 1977, 66.

9. Sophocles, *Antigone*, trans. E. F. Watling (Baltimore: Penguin, 1960), 148.

10. Ozick's esteem for Emerson has remained constant through the decades (unlike her stance toward T. S. Eliot). In "The Master's Mind," an essay about Henry James's ambiguous sexuality, Ozick incidentally calls Emerson "the philosopher of individualism who stands as a kind of Muse to all subsequent American culture and society" (*New York Times Magazine*, 26 October 1986, 52).

11. *Selections from Ralph Waldo Emerson,* ed. Stephen E. Whicher (Boston: Houghton Mifflin, 1960), 177.

12. Epigraph is from *Commentary* 86, no. 6 (December 1988): 48. Republished in MM as "S. Y. Agnon and the First Religion," where Ozick softened the force of the cited sentence by adding "Nevertheless" before (and omitting "even" from) "one cannot be sure."

13. Through its pattern of role reversals, "Virility" clearly argues Ozick's case for gender as a social construct. As Gate slips from virile to feminine status when his failure becomes manifest, so Margaret moves from feminine status—conventional wife and mother—to become a supersuccessful business manager when the chance offers. ("She's a very capable businesswoman—she's simply never had the opportunity," PR 250.) She also usurps the traditional male privilege of sexual freedom, taking Gate as her lover with impunity while she is still married.

14. The would-be writer's characterization as a goat has no connection with the Judaic tradition of the scapegoat. Instead, he embodies the medieval symbol of lust—not sexual desire in this instance but lust after success as an artist. "Age makes no matter," the ghost of Tchernikhovsky tells him. "Lust you can count on. I'm not speaking of the carnal sort. . . . Teetering on the edge of the coffin there's lust. After mortality there's lust, I guarantee you. In Eden there's nothing but lust." Ozick confirms the motif in her own voice in her preface to *Bloodshed*: "Why do I, who dread the cannibal touch of story-making, lust after stories more and more?" (BL 153, 12).

15. Kauvar's essay, "Courier for the Past: Cynthia Ozick and Photography," is the best discussion in print about this subject (*Studies in American Jewish Literature* 6 [Fall 1987]: 128–46).

16. The *Smithsonian* magazine of August 1990 includes a splendid set of photographs of Freud's room, with many separate shots of the figurines. The accompany-

ing text by Helen Dudar describes Freud's avid lifelong interest in the collection; his deep envy of Heinrich Schliemann, the archeologist who dug up Troy; and his deeply rooted classical education, which made "the old Greek and Roman civilizations and even-older cultures . . . familiar territories for him" (104). Ozick too spent her formative high school years imbibing a classical education.

17. The pacifist implications of Puttermesser's name were first assigned to the pseudo-Jewish African tribesman Morris in "A Mercenary": "He believed in civilizing influences; even more in civility. If he thought of knives, it was for buttering scones" (BL 51).

18. It is worth noting, however, that in contrast to Eliot, Ozick has staunchly affirmed her identity as an Orthodox Jew throughout her career; George Eliot may have earned extra approval from Ozick by turning against her evangelical Christian heritage, for example in essays like "Evangelical Teaching: Dr. Cumming."

19. Extended segments of *Daniel Deronda* read as though Eliot had turned into a nineteenth-century Cynthia Ozick. Eliot's rendering of Jewish-Christian history, for example, sounds like Feingold's discourse in "Levitation": "[near] the Rhine at the end of the eleventh century, . . . in the ears listening for the signals of the Messiah, the Hep! Hep! Hep! of the Crusaders came like the bay of bloodhounds; and in the presence of those devilish missionaries with sword and firebrand, the crouching figure of the reviled Jew turned round erect, heroic, flashing with sublime constancy in the face of torture and death. . . ."
Eliot likewise displays Ozick-like tones regarding the Hebraic heritage in this novel: "Where else is there a nation of whom it may be as truly said that their religion and law and moral life mingled as the stream of blood in the heart. . . . They struggled to keep their place among the nations like heroes,—yea, when the hand was hacked off, they clung with the teeth; but when the plough . . . passed over the last visible signs of their national covenant . . . they said, 'The spirit is alive, let us make it a lasting habitation,—lasting because movable,—so that it may be carried from generation to generation, and our sons may . . . possess a hope built on an unchangeable foundation.'" *Works of George Eliot: Daniel Deronda,* Vol. 3 (New York: Bigelow, Brown, n.d.), 150, 369.

20. In a real-life analogy, Camille Paglia, the high priestess of contemporary sexual psychology, shares the Puttermesser/George Eliot dilemma: at age forty-four, she says younger men are too immature to interest her while men her own age are too far over the hill to satisfy her physically.

21. See "Alfred Chester's Wig" in the 30 March 1992 *New Yorker.* In this long essay she cites Mann's Greek affinities: "Aschenbach noted with astonishment the lad's perfect beauty. His face recalled the noblest moment of Greek sculpture . . ." (91).

22. In her letter of 1/14/82 Ozick called *The Centaur* "a beautiful novel that moved me and killed me with envy." She spent so many years writing *Trust,* however, that by the end of that period "I had eradicated from my brain the least trace of Writer's Envy. . . . It simply came to me one day that the world is enriched and augmented by the multiplicity of gifts that adorn it."

23. Camille Paglia, in her magisterial *Sexual Personae* (Vintage: New York, 1991), roundly confirms Ozick's view of the Catholic-pagan connection: "Christian saints

are reborn pagan personae. . . . The Romanism in Catholicism is splendidly, endur-ingly pagan" (139).

24. "A Jewish soul, a Greek mind, and a Roman body" was Huston Smith's definition of the Catholic Church in an essay called "The End of Religion" (NYTBR, 25 July 1971, 6). I find the phrase equally applicable to the whole Western heritage.

25. See "We Are the Crazy Lady and Other Feisty Feminist Fables," first pub-lished in *Ms.* magazine (Spring 1973).

26. Ltr 6/6/90: "You ask whether it is 'worthwhile' for me to forego seeing ancient sacred sites, like the thousand-year-old Jewish cemetery in Worms. . . . I have to confess that I think of the whole continent of Europe as one vast Jewish graveyard."

27. Ozick's negative critique of *Maurice,* which first appeared in *Commentary* in 1971, has been reprinted in *Art & Ardor* (61–79).

28. Judging from her one year of college teaching, Ozick herself was none too sanguine about American students. In "The College Freshman" (*Confrontation,* Spring 1968, 41) she writes: "Imagination he does not recognize. . . . He scorns or suppresses talent. . . . [He] despises learning and is oafishly contemptuous of it. . . . He is a moral idiot." This sense of limitations, however, does not excuse Principal Brill, educated at the Sorbonne, from the pursuit of excellence.

29. In Chapter 1, "Beginnings," I denote Ozick's expressions of outrage toward her early schooling, especially in "We Ignoble Savages" (*Evergreen Review* 3, no. 10 [November-December 1959]).

30. *Street of Crocodiles* and *Cinnamon Shops* are interchangeable titles for the same book, drawn from two of its contrapuntal chapters. The Cinnamon Shops—so named for their dark paneling and filled with "strange and rare books, old folio volumes full of astonishing engravings and amazing stories"—signify the warm, sheltering comfort of the imaginative life in which Schulz's father escapes the dismal darkness and cold of a Polish winter: "At the time of the shortest, sleepy winter days . . . my father was already lost, sold and surrendered to the other sphere." The Street of Crocodiles represents the grubbiness of ordinary reality—the town's "industrial and commercial district, its soberly utilitarian character glaringly underlined" (trans. Celina Wieniew-ska [New York: Walker and Company, 1963], 78, 82, 94). Heidi's bookshop, Lars's entrance to a magic world, relates to the one title, and the stewpot relates to the other: "'Crocodiles!' Nilsson yelled up. 'Always after a sensation'" (ME 65).

31. Ozick's citation is from Schulz's "Treatise on Tailors' Dummies or The Sec-ond Book of Genesis" (*Street* 49–50). The occasion for the father's treatise occurs in the previous chapter, "Tailors' Dummies," after his nemesis, the maid Adela, has thrown out his collection of exotic birds: "The affair of the birds was the last colourful and splendid counter-offensive of fantasy which my father . . . had led against the trenches and defence-works of a sterile and empty winter" (40). Ozick's Adela, by contrast, helps perpetrate Lars's fantasy, and so becomes herself birdlike— "the beautiful little bird-bone of her nose! . . . the dove-colored feathers of her hair!" (ME 125).

32. Schulz originally wrote: "Reality is as thin as paper and betrays with all its cracks its imitative character" (*Street* 99).

33. Ozick's essay on Bruno Schulz decries both the man's cultural apostasy as "an

assimilated, Polish-speaking Jew, not so much a Jew as a conscious Pole" and the novel's religious intentions. "What is being invented" in *The Street of Crocodiles,* she says, "is Religion—not the taming religion of theology and morality, but the brute splendors of rite, gesture, phantasmagoric transfiguration, sacrifice, . . . repugnance, terror, cult. The religion of animism, in fact, where everything comes alive with an unpredictable and spiteful spirit-force, . . . where there is no pity" (AA 226). Her fictional rendering of this religion clearly reflects her revulsion.

34. Schulz's father in *Street* stands guilty of Lars's accusation: "We wish to be creators in our own, lower sphere; we want to have the privilege of creation, . . . we want—in one word—Demiurgy. . . . [We] wish to create man a second time" (50–52).

35. In her interview with Francine Prose, Ozick describes her great abiding fear of "making art out of the Holocaust. . . . I worry very much that this subject is corrupted by fiction and that fiction in general corrupts history." She traces the origin of "The Shawl" to William Shirer's *The Rise and Fall of the Third Reich:* "There was a line in there, just one line in a very, very fat book, that spoke about babies being thrown against electrified fences, and I guess that image stayed with me" (NYTBR, 10 September 1989, 1, 39).

36. "The Experience of Activity," in *A Pluralistic Universe* from *The Philosophy of William James,* ed. Horace M. Kallen (New York: Modern Library. 1925), 156. Jean-Paul Sartre, *Being and Nothingness* (New York: Washington Square Press, 1966), 347–54, 445.

37. This image haunted Ozick long before *The Shawl.* In "The Pagan Rabbi" she describes an infant saved by a *deus ex machina:* "they were about to throw her against the electrified fence when an army mobbed the gate; the current vanished from the wires" (PR 7).

38. The prototype of Rosa Lublin's maternal passion appears in *The Cannibal Galaxy* (a book dedicated to Cynthia Ozick's daughter Rachel) under the name of Madame de Sévigné, an eighteenth-century French noblewoman who made a living icon of her daughter: "The mother, according to one source, was 'insane'—she loved her daughter obsessively, pathologically, so much so that she spent her life penning her longing in letter after letter. 'How I should like to have a letter from you! It is nearly half an hour since I received the last!' she once wrote" (10). In the same vein, Rosa writes to her lost child: "Magda, my Soul's Blessing: Forgive me, my yellow lioness. Too long a time since the last writing. . . . And so half a day passes without my taking up my pen to speak to you" (40).

39. The names of Rosa, Stella, and Magda are Latin cognates for the images associated with the Christ child's Advent: Rose (signifying the Incarnation); Star (over Bethlehem); and Magi (three Wise Men).

40. Ronald Sanders, *The Shores of Refuge* (New York: Henry Holt, 1988), 411. The Pilsudski regime, which took power in 1926, proved very friendly to the Jews of Poland, so that by 1931, Sanders says, "56 percent of [Poland's] doctors, 33.5 percent of its lawyers, and 22 percent of its journalists, publishers, and librarians were Jews" (413).

41. "[Hitler] claimed that he got the idea for concentration camps from the British camps in the Boer War and from American Indian reservations." See John

Toland, *Hitler: The Pictorial Documentary of His Life* (Garden City, NY: Double-day, 1978), 8.

42. See Martin Gilbert, *Atlas of Jewish History* (n.p.: Dorset Press, 1984), 97; and Raul Hilberg, *The Destruction of the European Jews* (Chicago: Quadrangle Books, 1961), 137–39.

43. In terms of William James's *The Varieties of Religious Experience,* Rosa and Persky/Stella are here exhibiting the two types of innate disposition into which (James thought) the human species divides itself, the morbid-minded versus the healthy-minded. An ability to live exclusively in the present moment is precisely the defining and enabling characteristic of the latter. Persky also illustrates Henry James's famous dictum in *The Ambassadors:* "Live all you can. It's a mistake not to."

Chapter 3. Judgment

1. Toni Morrison's comment appears in her interview with Tom LeClair in the *New Republic* 21 March 1981, 29.

2. My book, which was completed in the summer of 1992 and revised to suit my editors that fall, was not affected by Elaine Kauvar's subsequent publication, in April 1993, of *Cynthia Ozick's Fiction: Tradition and Invention* (Indiana University Press). Having just now been asked to review it for *American Literature* magazine, I feel assured from scanning its contents that our approaches to Ozick's oeuvre are so different as to pose no serious problems of duplication. As I had supposed, Kauvar's fusion of a brilliant critical intelligence with a rich knowledge of Jewish and classical lore figures to render her critique permanently unsurpassed in the shelf of Ozick criticism. Because her study is so perceptive and substantial on a page by page basis, I cannot hope to summarize it here. Instead, I urge my reader to turn to it as an essential landmark of Ozick criticism. So far as my own book is concerned, I consider it to be complementary to rather than competitive with Kauvar's superb exegesis.

3. Barbara Koenig Quart, "An Esthete in Spite of Herself," *Nation,* July 23–30, 1983, 87.

4. See "Notes toward Finding the Right Question," reprinted in *On Being a Jewish Feminist* (New York: Schocken Books, 1983), 131.

5. Judith Plaskow, "The Right Question Is Theological," *On Being a Jewish Feminist* 226.

6. Ozick, "Torah as Feminism, Feminism as Torah," *Congress Monthly,* September/October 1984, 7–10.

7. Rosellen Brown, review of *Bloodshed* in the *New Republic,* 5 June 1976, 30–31; Pearl K. Bell, "New Jewish Voices," *Commentary,* June 1981, 63.

8. Deborah Heiligman Weiner, "Cynthia Ozick, Pagan vs. Jew (1966–1976)," *Studies in American Jewish Literature* 3 (1983): 186.

9. On page 183 of her essay, Ms. Weiner (see note 8 above) cites this passage from Ozick's "Four Questions of the Rabbis," *Reconstructionist,* 18 February 1972, 23.

10. R. Barbara Gitenstein, "The Temptation of Apollo and the Loss of Yiddish in Cynthia Ozick's Fiction," *Studies in American Jewish Literature* 3 (1983): 194.

Gitenstein considers Ozick's yearning for a Yiddish art to be in conflict with her status within modern American literature: "She does not feel that such self-contradiction can be overcome in Jewish literature" (200).

11. Eugene S. Mornell, letter to the editor, *Commentary,* May 1979, 8. By way of refuting Jacobson and Mornell (8), Ozick extends the definition of "literature in the service of God" to include not only Midrash and Talmud but also writings by such Gentiles as Thomas Mann, George Eliot, Jane Austen, and Tolstoy.

12. Earl Rovit, "The Bloodletting," *Nation,* 20 February 1982, 207–8.

13. Burt Jacobson, letter to the editor, *Commentary,* May 1979, 7–8.

14. Joseph Epstein, "Cynthia Ozick, Jewish Writer," *Commentary,* March 1984, 67. My other citations from this essay occur on pages 66–69.

15. Ozick, letter to the editor, *Commentary,* May, 1984, 10.

16. Haim Chertok, "Ozick's Hoofprints," *Modern Jewish Studies,* Annual 6, published by *Yiddish* magazine 6, no. 4 (1987): 11.

17. Janet Handler Burstein, "Cynthia Ozick and the Transgressions of Art," *American Literature* 59, no. 1 (March 1987): 87.

18. Ellen Pifer, "Cynthia Ozick: Invention and Orthodoxy," in *Contemporary Women Writers: Narrative Strategies,* ed. Catherine Rainwater and William J. Scheick (Lexington: UP of Kentucky, 1985), 91.

19. Review by Paul Stuewe in *Quill & Quote,* May 1987, 25. Harold Bloom, "The Book of the Father," NYTBR, 22 March 1987, 1, 36.

20. Janet Malcolm, "Graven Images," *New Yorker,* 8 June 1987, 102–4. This quote is cited from page 103.

21. Robert Alter, "Defenders of the Faith," *Commentary,* July 1987, 52–55. This quote is cited from page 53.

22. The "Trudie Vosce" essay was published in *The New York Times Magazine* on March 16, 1978 (A26); the other essay in the *Times Sunday Magazine* of 14 March 1971.

23. Joseph Lowin, *Cynthia Ozick* (Boston: G. K. Hall, 1988).

24. Vera Emuma Kielsky, *Inevitable Exiles* (New York: Peter Lang, 1989).

25. Lawrence S. Friedman, *Understanding Cynthia Ozick* (Columbia: University of South Carolina Press, 1991).

26. Earl Rovit, "The Two Languages of Cynthia Ozick," *Studies in American Jewish Literature* (SAJL) 8, no. 1 (Spring 1989): 36, 34.

27. Michael Greenstein, "The Muse and the Messiah," *SAJL* 8, no. 1 (Spring 1989): 50–65, and "Ozick, Roth, and Postmodernism," *SAJL* 10, no. 1 (Spring 1991): 54–63.

28. Anne Redmon, "Vision and Risk," *Michigan Quarterly Review* 27, no. 1 (Winter 1988): 210; Sylvia Barack Fishman, "Imagining Ourselves," *SAJL* 9, no. 1 (Spring 1990): 91.

29. Elizabeth Rose, "Cynthia Ozick's Liturgical Postmodernism," *SAJL* 9, no. 1 (Spring 1990): 99.

30. Sanford Pinsker, "How Philip Roth and Cynthia Ozick Reimagine Their Significant Dead," *Modern Fiction Studies* 35, no. 2 (Summer 1989): 234.

31. I am grateful to the American Antiquarian Society in Worcester, Massa-

chusetts, for letting me research this item from the *Springfield Republican* of 3 June 1853.

32. Ozick, "Poetry and the Parochial," *Congress Monthly* 53 (November/December 1986): 7–10.

33. I heard Pat Boone's comments on Johnny Carson's "Tonight Show." T. S. Eliot's comment appeared in a letter to Pound that is cited in Lyndall Gordon's *Eliot's New Life* (New York: Farrar, Straus and Giroux, 1988), 341n.

34. Louis D. Rubin, Jr., a distinguished Jewish-American professor of English at the University of North Carolina, wrote in a generous spirit about Eliot's anti-Semitism in "The Mencken Mystery," *Sewanee Review* 94, no. 3 (Summer 1991): 447: "In certain circles it is the fashion to label persons such as T. S. Eliot and several of the more prominent Nashville Agrarians as fascists, in part because of comments made about Jews during the 1930s. What is wrong with this attitude is that it draws upon the knowledge of what anti-Semitism led to in hate-crazed post-1918 Europe—the systematic slaughter of millions of innocent people—and attributes the emotional motivations behind that slaughter to people who had no such objective remotely in mind and, if given the choice, would doubtless have died before allowing it to happen."

35. Ozick, "All the World Wants the Jews Dead," *Esquire* 82, no. 5 (November 1974): 207.

36. Israel Shahak, "'The Life of Death': An Exchange," *New York Review of Books*, 29 January 1987, 46. Professor Shahak supports other contrarian arguments in this article, insisting that the Holocaust was not a singular, incomparable act of genocide; that some Israeli partisans are guilty of Nazi-like racism toward Palestinians; and that the sacred Torah itself decrees pseudo-Nazi exterminations: "No significant . . . discussion of the human significance of the Holocaust of the Jews can . . . take place if people more courageous than Lanzmann will also not ask questions of those Jews who believe in the 'essential' holiness and rightness of such texts as 'you shall save nothing alive that breathes' (Deuteronomy 20:16) or 'do not spare them, but kill both man and woman, infant and suckling' (I Samuel 15:3) or the Nazi-like 'selection' described as being carried out in cold blood on women and children by the orders of Moses: 'Now therefore, kill every male among the little ones, and kill every woman who has known man by lying with him. But all the young girls who have not known man by lying with him keep alive for yourselves' (Numbers 31:17–18)" (48).

37. Norman Davies, "Poles and Jews: An Exchange," *New York Review of Books*, 9 April 1987, 43. Davies does not, of course, make these statements to exculpate Poles guilty of assisting the Holocaust; his motive is to indicate, as did Israel Shakar, the common humanity of both peoples—the fact that "Jews given the chance will behave as well or badly as anyone else."

38. Cynthia Ozick, "Of Christian Heroism." *Partisan Review* 59, no. 1 (1992).

39. Floyd C. Watkins, John T. Hiers, and Mary Louise Weeks, *Talking with Robert Penn Warren* (Athens: University of Georgia Press, 1990), 29–30.

40. I have cited Emerson's "Fate" from Stephen Whicher's edition, *Selections from Ralph Waldo Emerson* (Boston: Houghton Mifflin, 1960), 340.

41. Melville made this statement in a letter to Hawthorne, dated 17 November 1851. See the Norton Critical Edition of *Moby-Dick,* ed. Harrison Hayford and Hershel Parker (New York, 1967), 566.

42. *An Upton Sinclair Anthology* (New York: Farrar & Rinehart, 1935), 218.

43. William James, *Pragmatism* (New York: New American Library, 1955), 189.

44. William James, *The Will to Believe* and *Human Immortality* (New York: Dover Publications, 1956), Preface to the Second Edition [of the latter essay], vi.

45. William James, *The Varieties of Religious Experience,* Foreword by Jacques Barzun (New York: Mentor Books, 1968), 275.

46. William James, "Pragmatism and Religion," in *Pragmatism* (New York: New American Library, 1955), 181.

47. William James, "The Dilemma of Determinism," in *The Will to Believe and Other Essays in Popular Philosophy* (New York: Dover Publications, 1956), 169.

48. The citation is from Frost's 1935 Introduction to *King Jasper.*

49. Joyce Carol Oates, *Contraries: Essays* (New York: Oxford Press, 1981), ix; and John Updike Interview, *Paris Review,* Spring 1969, 101.

Index

Asterisk marks indicate writings of Cynthia Ozick.

The Wisconsin Project on American Writers

Frank Lentricchia, General Editor